I0822986

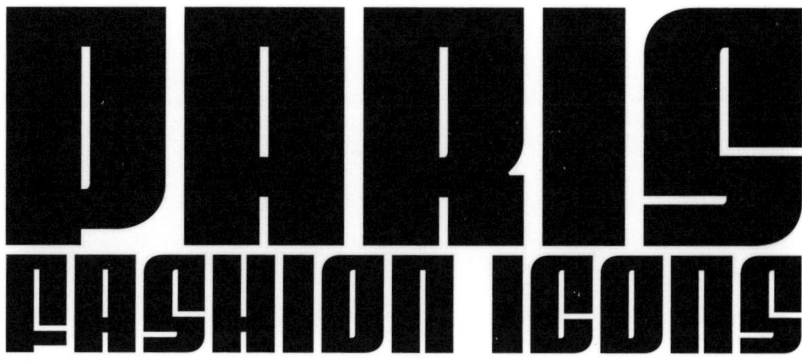
PARIS
FASHION ICONS

This edition published in 2026 by Welbeck

An Imprint of HEADLINE PUBLISHING GROUP LIMITED

1

Cataloguing in Publication Data is available from the British Library

ISBN 9781035430376

Printed and bound in China

Headline's policy is to use papers that are natural, renewable and recyclable products and made from wood grown in well-managed forests and other controlled sources. The logging and manufacturing processes are expected to conform to the environmental regulations of the country of origin.

HEADLINE PUBLISHING GROUP LIMITED

An Hachette UK Company
Carmelite House
50 Victoria Embankment
London EC4Y 0DZ

The authorised representative in the EEA is Hachette Ireland, 8 Castlecourt Centre, Dublin 15, D15 XTP3, Ireland (email: info@hbgi.ie)

www.headline.co.uk
www.hachette.co.uk

50 STYLE LEGENDS OF PARIS

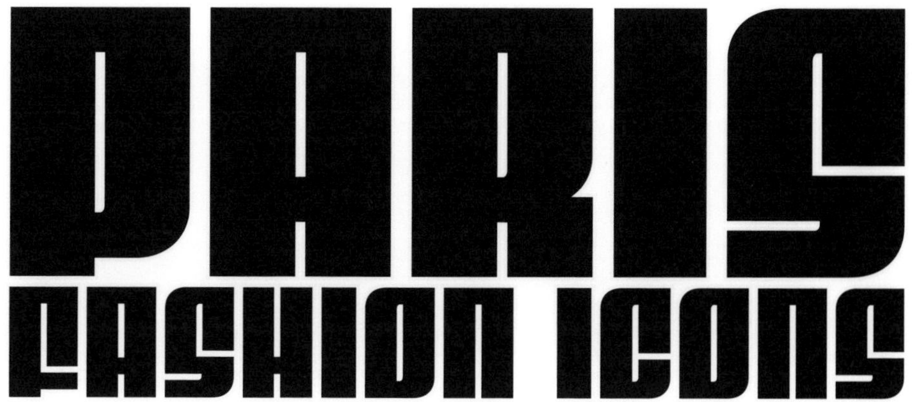

AMELIE STANESCU

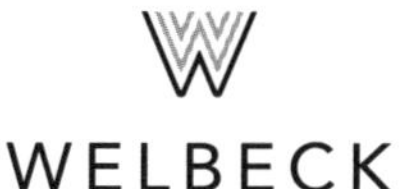

WELBECK

Contents

Introduction 6

Chapter 1:
The Architects 12

Coco Chanel 14
Christian Dior 18
Yves Saint Laurent 22
Cristóbal Balenciaga 26
Hubert de Givenchy 28
Pierre Balmain 32
Jeanne Lanvin 36
Madeleine Vionnet 40
Elsa Schiaparelli 42
André Courrèges 44
Paco Rabanne 48
Christian Lacroix 52
Kenzo Takada 56
Sonia Rykiel 60
Gaby Aghion 64

Chapter 2:
Les Enfants Terribles 68

Thierry Mugler 70
Jean Paul Gaultier 74
Rei Kawakubo 78
Yohji Yamamoto 82
Martin Margiela 86
Rick Owens 90
John Galliano 92
Raf Simons 94
Dries Van Noten 98
Nicolas Ghesquière 100
Patrick Kelly 102
Azzedine Alaïa 106

Chapter 3:
The New Guard of Designers & Creative Directors **110**

Karl Lagerfeld 112
Hedi Slimane 116
Marc Jacobs 120
Demna Gvasalia 124
Maria Grazia Chiuri 126
Anthony Vaccarello 131
Phoebe Philo 132
Isabel Marant 136
Jacquemus 140
Olivier Rousteing 144

Chapter 4:
Muses & Faces **148**

Jane Birkin 150
Loulou de la Falaise 154
Betty Catroux 158
Edwige Belmore 162
Farida Khelfa 166
Marpessa Dawn 170
Vanessa Paradis 174
Isabelle Huppert 178
Josephine Baker 183

Chapter 5:
Voices, Writers & Power Brokers **186**

Simone de Beauvoir 188
James Baldwin 192
Diane Pernet 197
Lucien Pagès 198
Afterword – Using the code 200

Index **204**

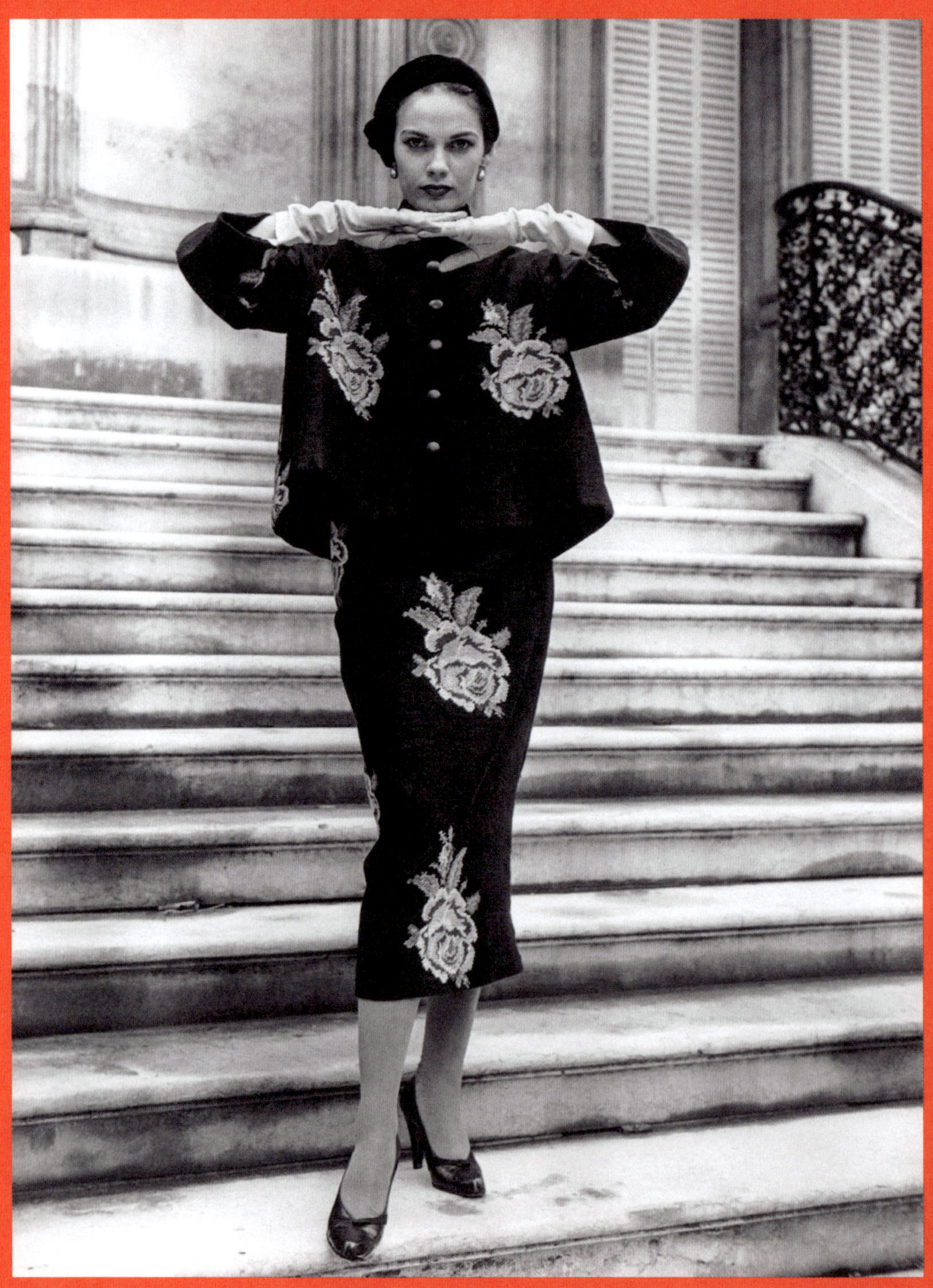

Introduction

Paris still matters because it rewards discipline and art over noise. In a decade often ruled by feeds and algorithms, the city is a place where an idea must stand up to the fitting room, the archive and the calendar. The runway is a public square, but the cut is what carries across seasons: proportion, balance and the slow refinement of a line until it feels inevitable. Here, a jacket is more than a product. It can showcase a decision about how a body meets the world – how it moves, what it says and how much room it claims. Paris tests those decisions without sentimentality. If a silhouette can survive the room, the camera and the copy, it stays. If it cannot, the city lets it go. That contract keeps talent honest, welcomes outsiders and turns experiments into the status quo. It is also why the city continues to produce creations that outlast trend cycles.

The city's infrastructure explains the rest. Ateliers translate drawings into structure; pattern tables teach proportion; model fittings police fantasy and there is an insistence on function. Museums hold memories and sharpen arguments; schools train ears as much as hands. Buyers, editors, publicists and photographers build a circulation system that either carries a good idea or lets a weak one sink. Paris is tough because it is open: the network that enforces standards is the same network that, once persuaded, can anchor a designer's place for years.

Opposite: Paris, early 1950s. A couture client pauses on the steps of an *hôtel particulier* (private mansion) in a dark wool suit embroidered with oversized climbing roses – the kind of mid-century silhouette that made the city's staircases feel like runways.

This book looks for decisions that travel well. Why does a shoulder line move a room? Why does a shoe change pace? Why does a dress feel inevitable before anyone names the reference? The answers live on in repeated choices – materials that stay honest under light, proportions that hold across bodies, rhythms that balance risk with restraint. Each chapter is a set of case studies: these are not museum labels or fan notes; these are trusted tools a reader can use.

The people within these pages made Paris a capital of fashion by building systems from moments. The most durable ideas start as structure – hems, shoulders, collars – and then travel through casting, stores, photography and the internet without losing coherence. Paris accelerates that travel because the city already knows how to read a cut. Editors and buyers share a dialogue with ateliers and archives; debates happen in fittings as much as they do in reviews. When a design enters that circuit and survives, it becomes public property. Once seen, the line is hard to *unsee*.

What follows is practical in spirit. Here, I point to repeatable choices:

- how a silhouette remains legible across lighting and decades;
- how an accessory carries code from look to look;
- how a studio rhythm becomes a brand's heartbeat.

There are dates where dates matter and names where names move the plot forward. The aim is clarity without flattening nuance. If you leave with a better sense of why a garment feels inevitable – for example, why a bag carries a certain shape – then Paris has done its work again.

Opposite: Two friends sit *en terrasse*, enjoying cups of tea over coffee and cigarettes. Can this be any more Parisian?

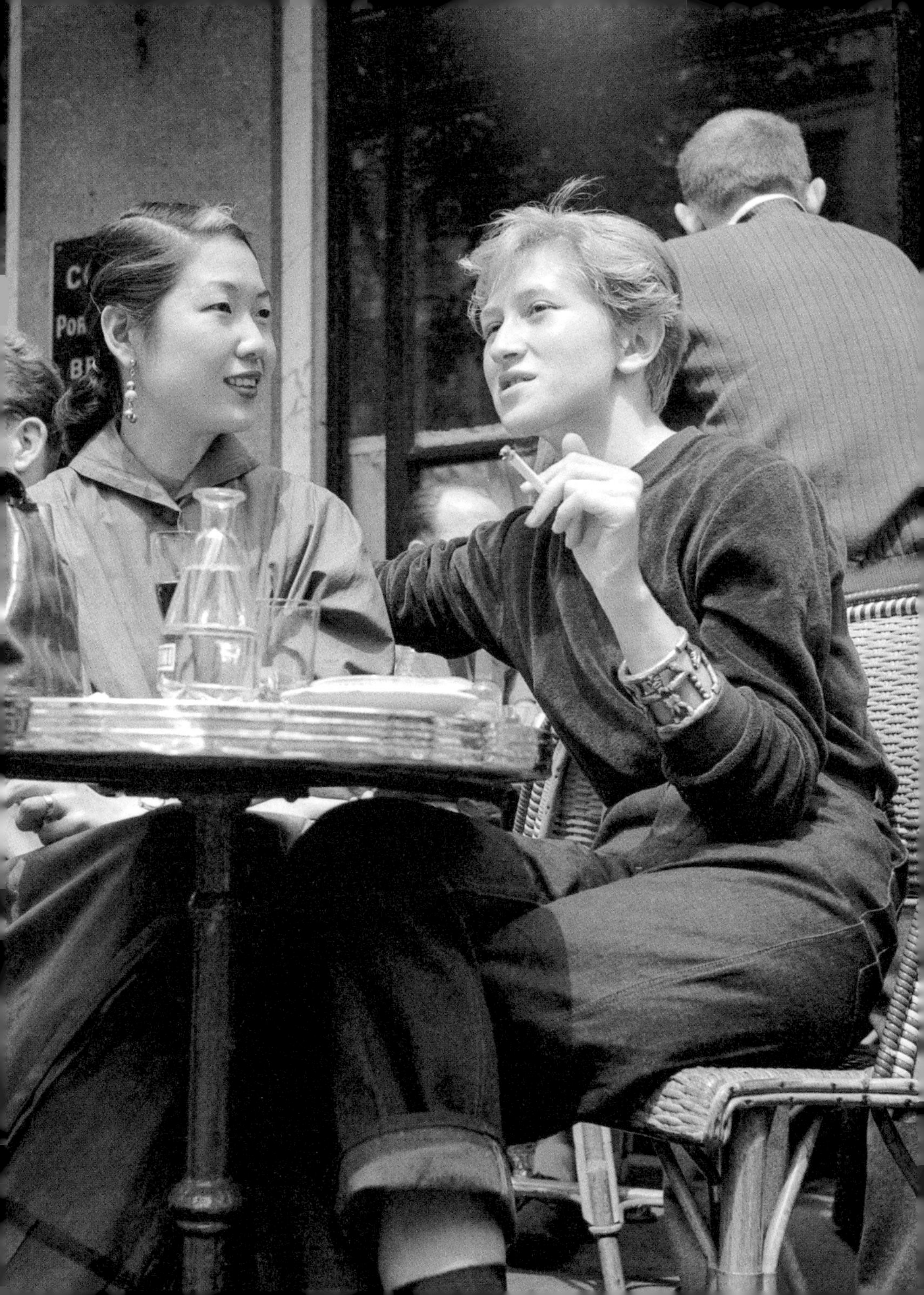

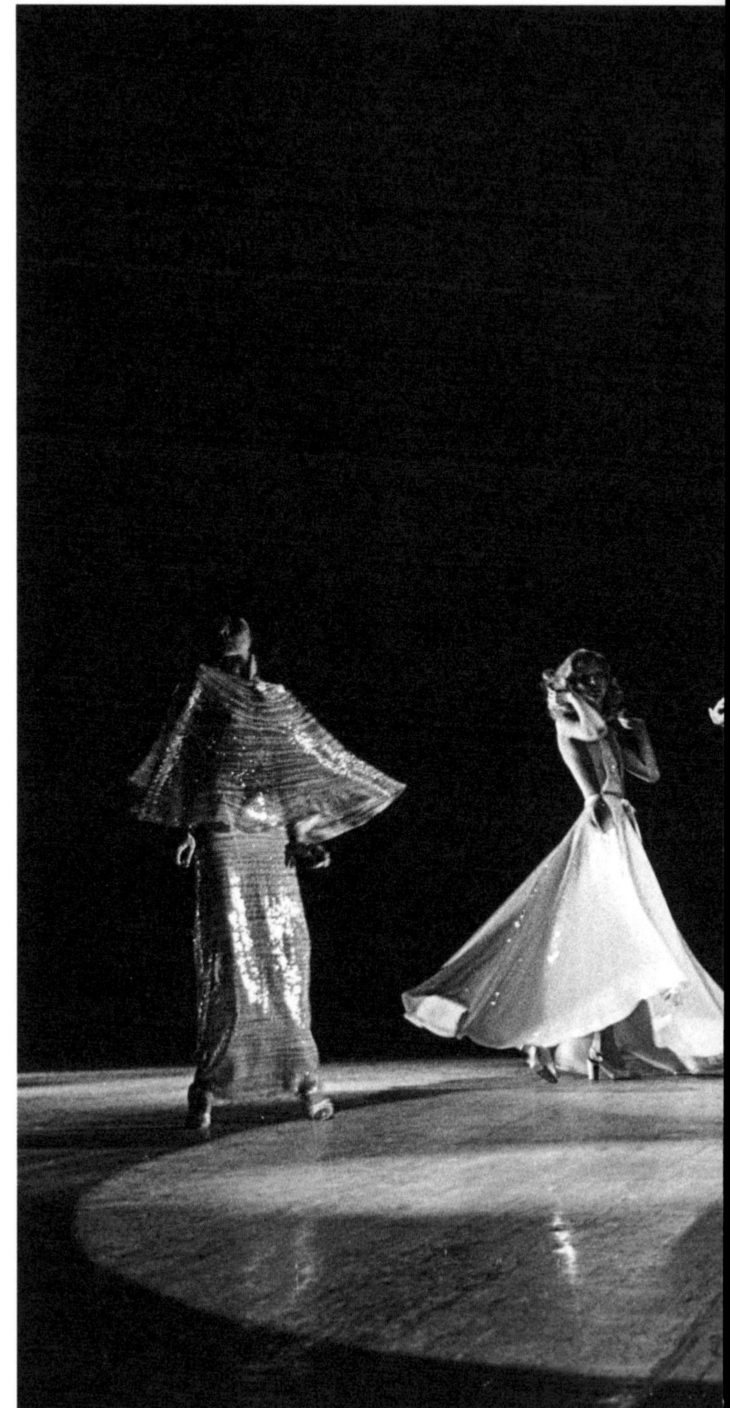

Right: The Battle of Versailles fashion show, 1973. Models in pleated gowns by Halston turn slowly on a circular stage, their dresses catching the light like moving sculpture – couture as an evening's entertainment as much as a collection of clothes.

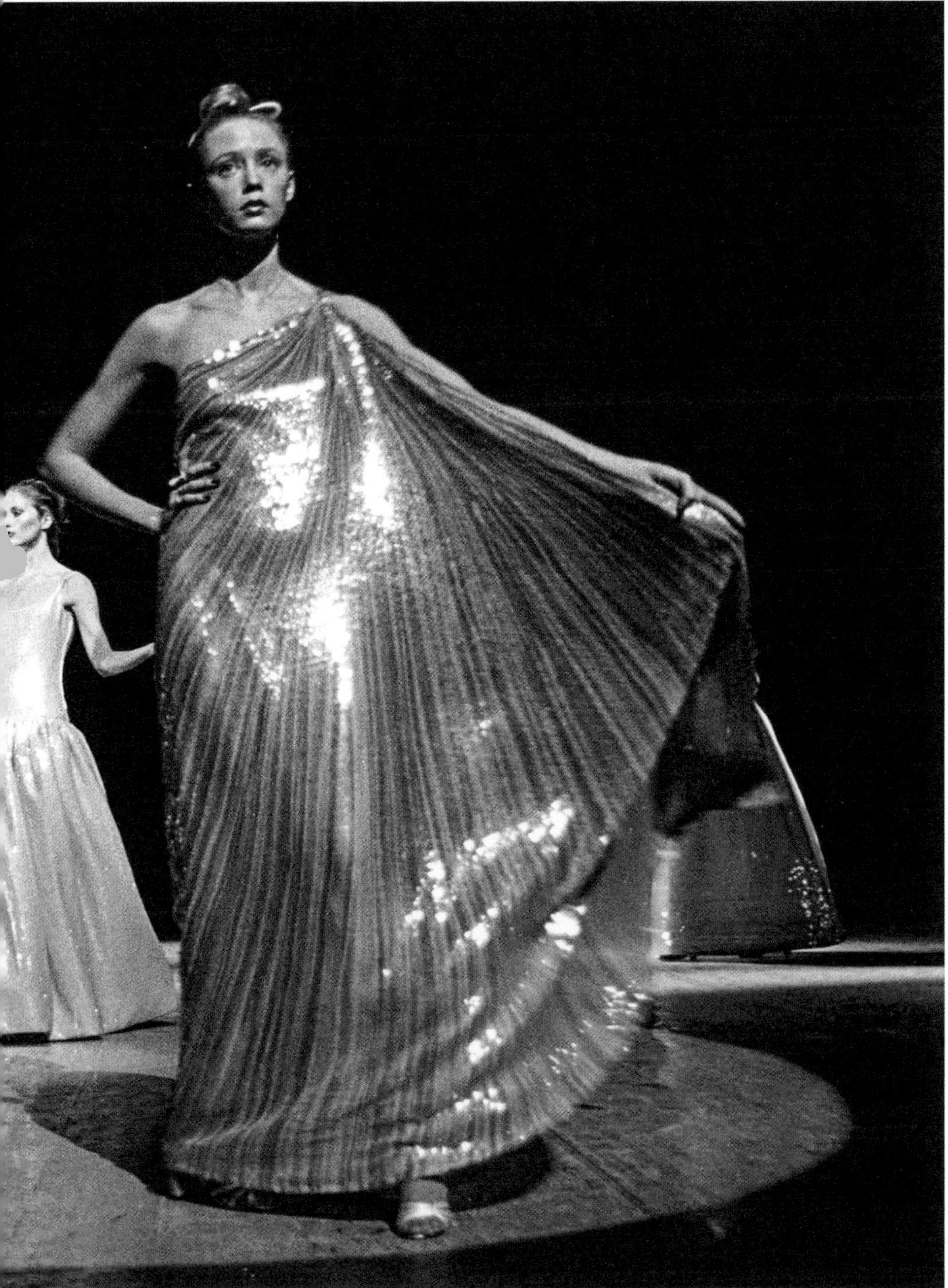

CHAPTER 1:

THE ARCHITECTS

The canon begins with fit. A shoulder that settles, a waist that knows when to disappear, a skirt that keeps pace… These rooms made Paris exact. No fuss, just precision that reads at a distance. Patterns become codes. Codes become archives. Archives feed new hands. The city's great silhouettes start here and return here when the noise fades. This chapter is a map of those origins, how each line was built and how it kept its nerve.

COCO CHANEL

Paris meets Gabrielle Chanel as a milliner, then watches her redraw daily life. Her breakthrough is not a set of items; it is a new rule about time and freedom. She looks at how a woman lives and edits everything that wastes a second or a breath. Jersey stops being underwear and becomes a fluent skin. Stripes and knit cardigans are not "borrowed from the boys". They are recoded as tools to move, to work, to be seen without effort. The little black dress is a social invention that lets you enter any room without asking for permission. The suit is not armour; it is a frame that keeps the ribcage free and the mind available.

Chanel wires the business. In 1921 she launched N°5 with Russian-French perfumer Ernest Beaux and proved a scent can carry a house further than any dress. Parfums Chanel scales distribution, while the couture atelier guards the cut, so image and revenue reinforce each other. Shops open where real life happens, from Deauville to the rue Cambon staircase that becomes a stage for fittings and photographs. She pauses in the Second World War, then returns in 1954 with the suit that will anchor wardrobes for decades – a comeback that shows Paris how a code can age and still feel current.

Coco's impact on the city is to make elegance usable. She gives Paris a grammar that moves: clean jackets, fine knits, two-tone shoes that steady proportions, a bag that assumes you have places to be. Editors learn to describe what clothes do, not only how they look. Women learn they can carry the day without changing fits. The result is a system that still runs: function first, posture next, ornament last of all.

Opposite: Gabrielle 'Coco' Chanel lounging in a chair.

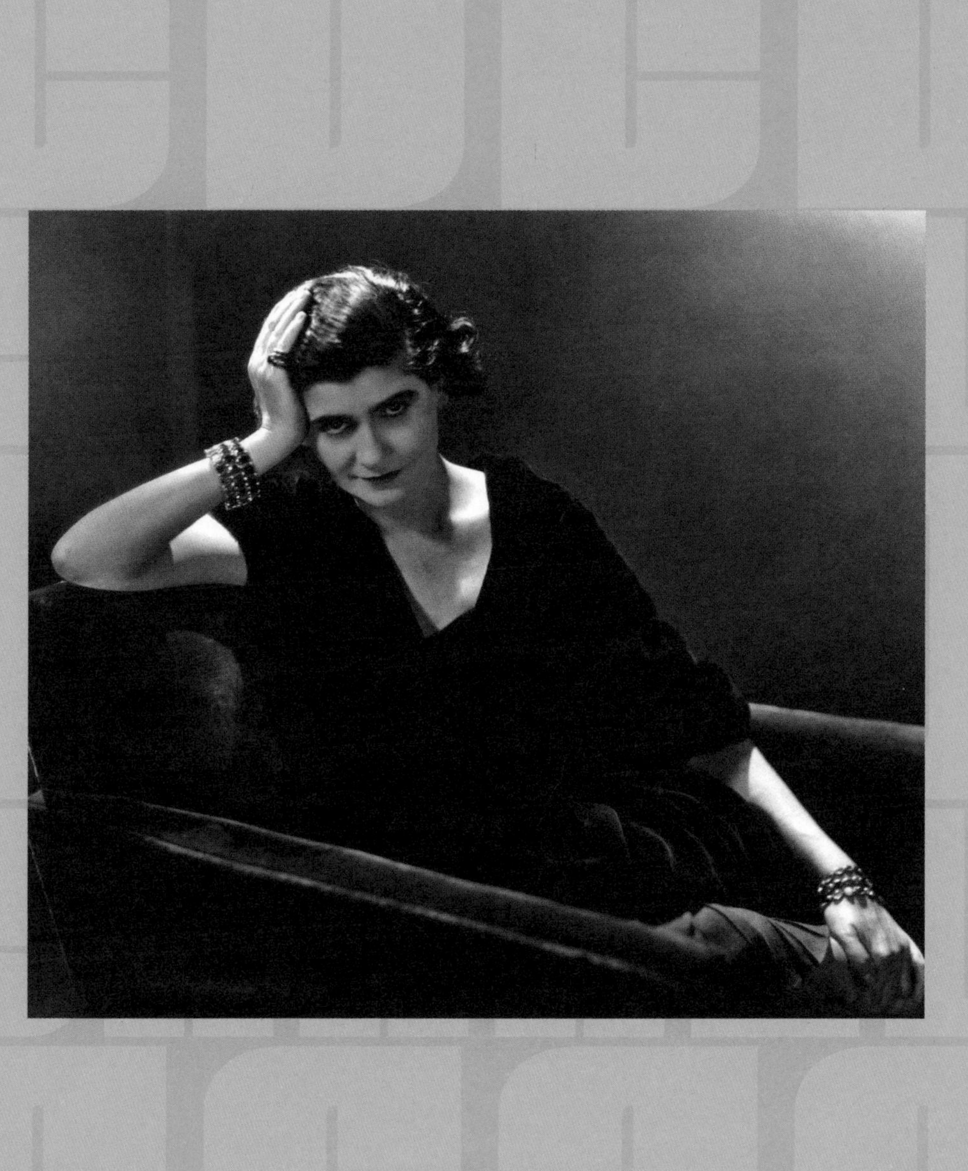

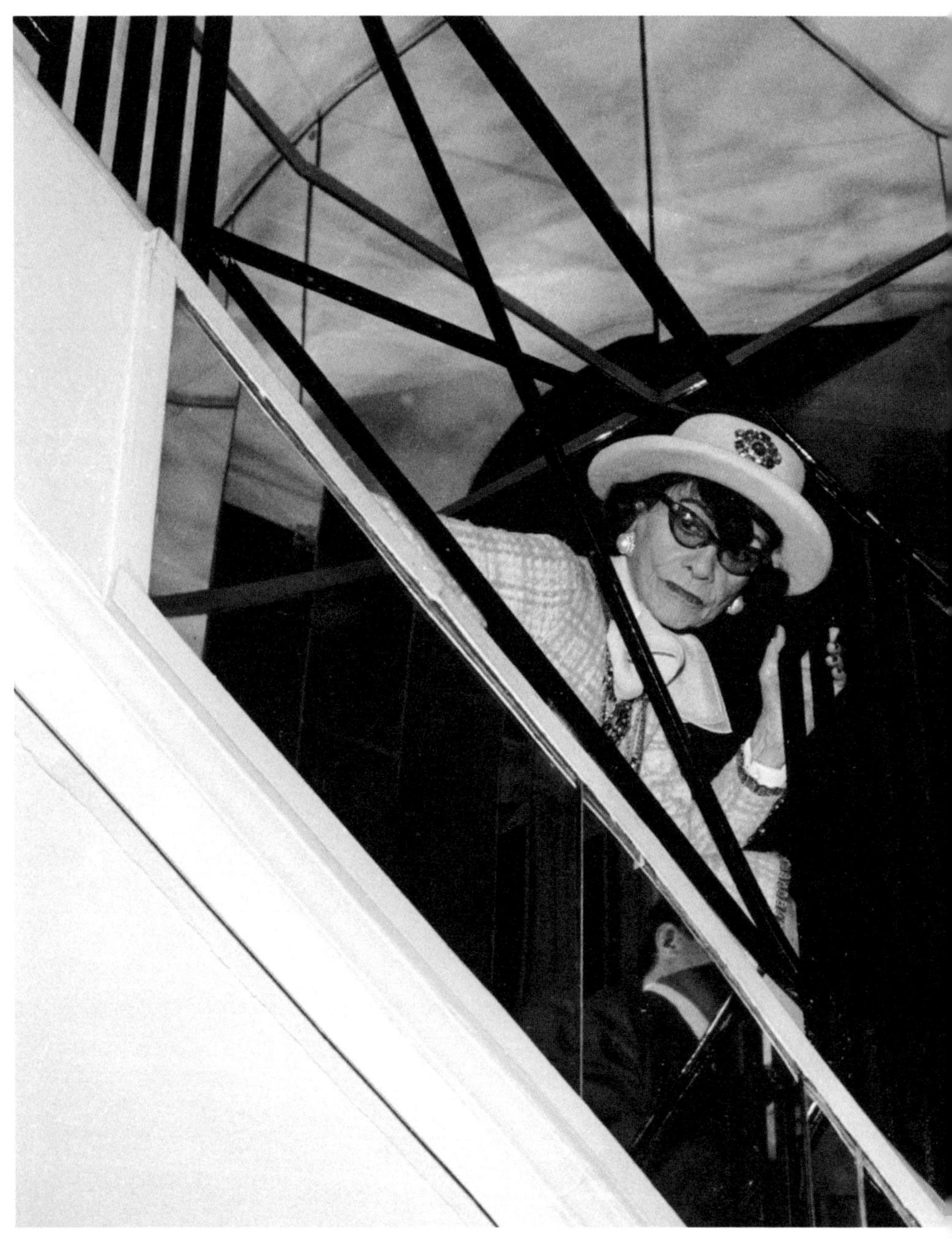

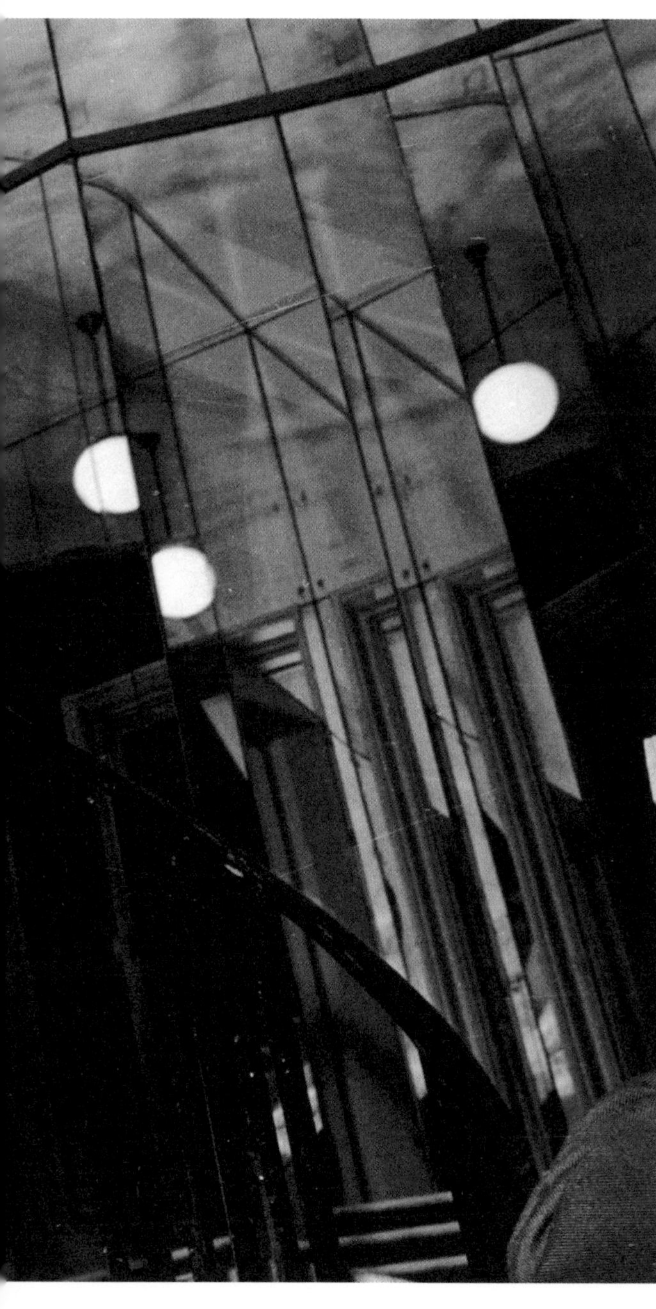

Left: Gabrielle Chanel on the mirrored staircase at 31 rue Cambon in the early 1960s.

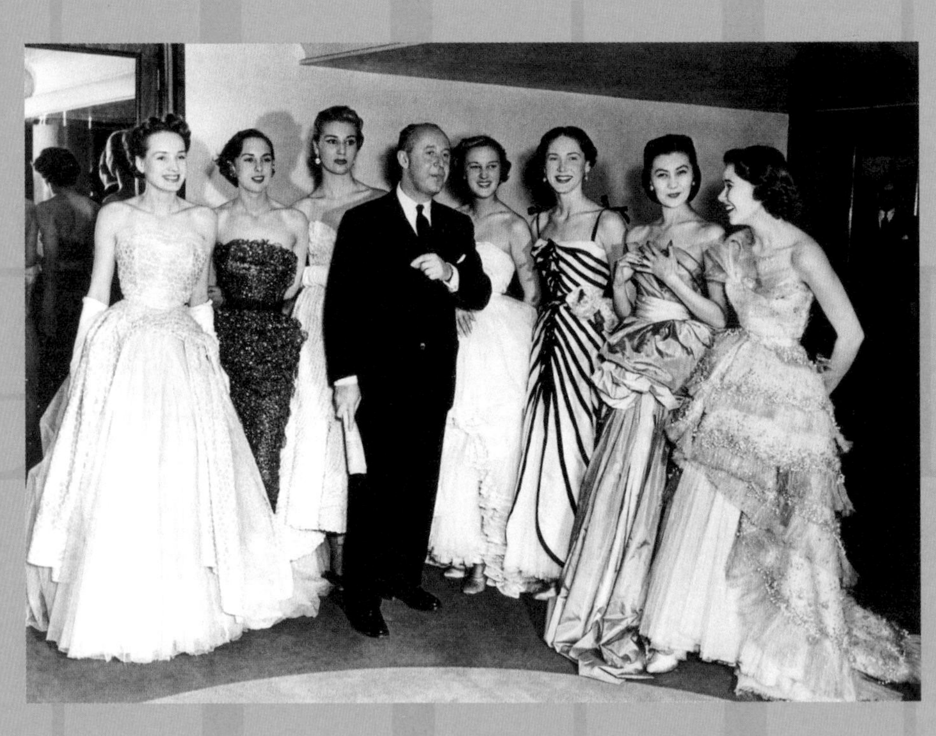

CHRISTIAN DIOR

In 1947 Christian Dior invented the New Look at 30 Avenue Montaigne. Paris was still on food rationing and the ateliers lacked fabric and hands. The Bar jacket (neat shoulder, curved hip and pulled-in waist) was the core of the "New Look" – the 1947 silhouette that resets the industry, and the city really.

Before the war, Dior worked around art. During the German Occupation (June 1940 to August 1944) he learned to save fabric: every inch mattered. After liberation, though, he returned to full skirts, which became a signature. He also set up an alphabet of silhouettes: "H" stands tall and unbroken; "A" narrows at the top and opens at the hem; "Y" builds power at the shoulders and tapers clean. The letters teach you to read the outline before the fabrics, which is why the idea travels so well. The house still communicates in that alphabet: "A"-lines, "H"-columns and "Y"-shoulders keep structuring the collections under the gaze of more contemporary creative directors, Maria Grazia Chiuri and Kim Jones, and recently Jonathan Anderson.

Among his peers the reaction to Dior's work is split. Some designers praise the cut; others worry about the fabric while Paris is still rationing post-war. The press celebrates it, but students even protest against the longer skirts. This argument sets the tone for the 1950s fashion industry in the French capital that will echo worldwide.

Opposite: Christian Dior stands with a group of models wearing his evening dresses in the mid-1950s. The line is unmistakable: narrow shoulders, defined waists and skirts engineered in tulle, silk and organza to hold their own architecture. These show moments reveal how Dior's grammar quickly became a language the whole city could read.

Christian Dior and Cristóbal Balenciaga were rivals on paper, but it's fair to say they quietly coordinated behind the scenes. They showed on the same days at different times, creating a new Paris rhythm – what was to become Fashion Week. Unheard of then – houses acted like islands. Synchronizing concentrated press and buyers helped turn the 1950s into couture's golden decade. Fashion is not only about art and creation; you have to set the room into structure to be able to take in your product. Paris was the first place to realize this and Monsieur Dior played a huge part in it.

Gabrielle Chanel, meanwhile, positioned herself as the counter-argument. She called the New Look "old-fashioned", a return to corsetry. When she reopened in 1954, she put the relaxed suit back on the map – soft jacket, no waist, less fabric. An everyday uniform was now pitched against Dior's sculpted silhouettes.

Dior's luck lies in his wonderful talent, but his real achievement is definitely method: today, Paris still runs on fashion, showcasing unique avant-garde ways to wear clothes and with a new efficient structure.

Opposite: A model wearing the Bar Suit walks along the Seine in 1947. The photograph shows the impact of the silhouette in the real world on a real woman – and look how good she looks in it!

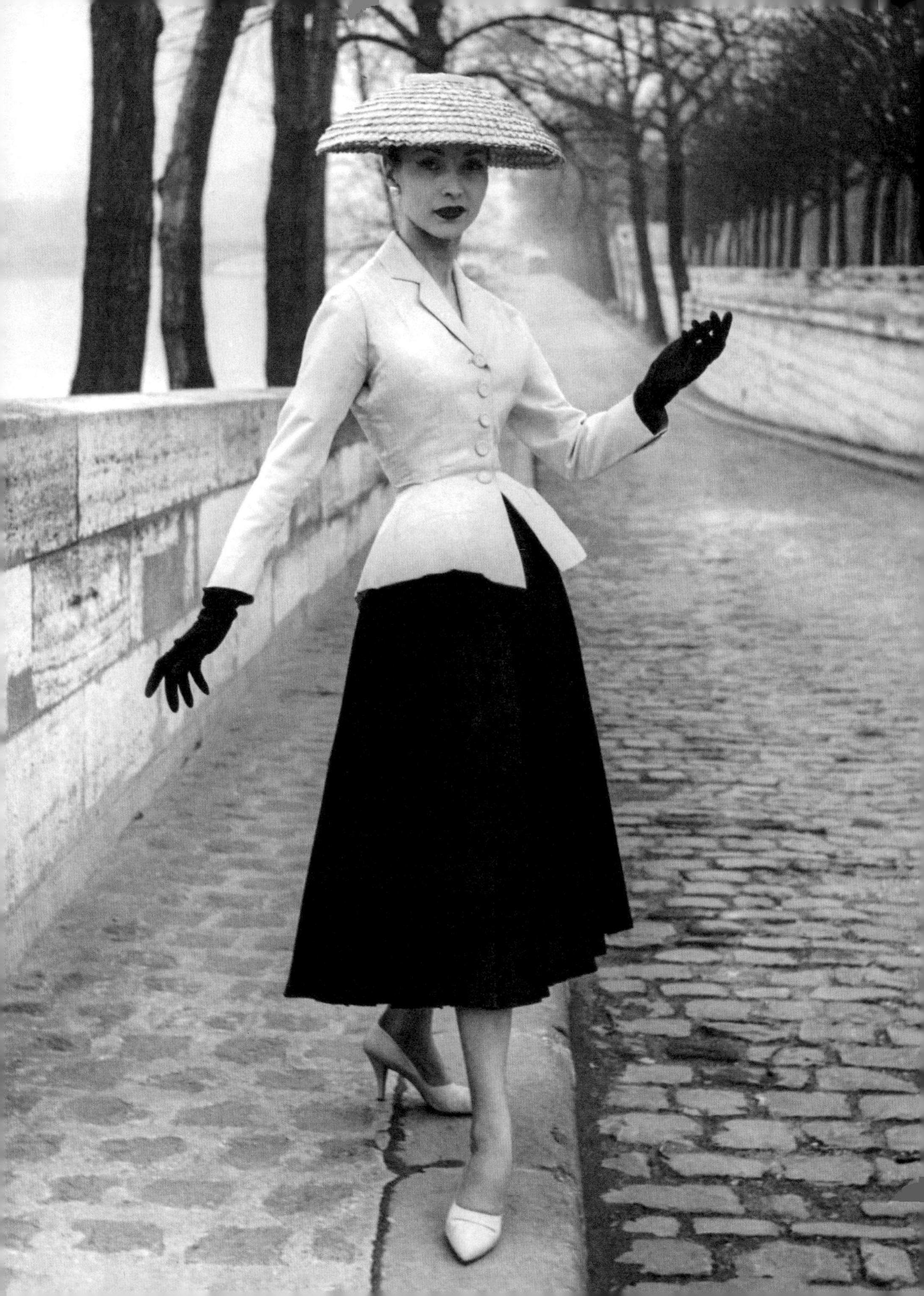

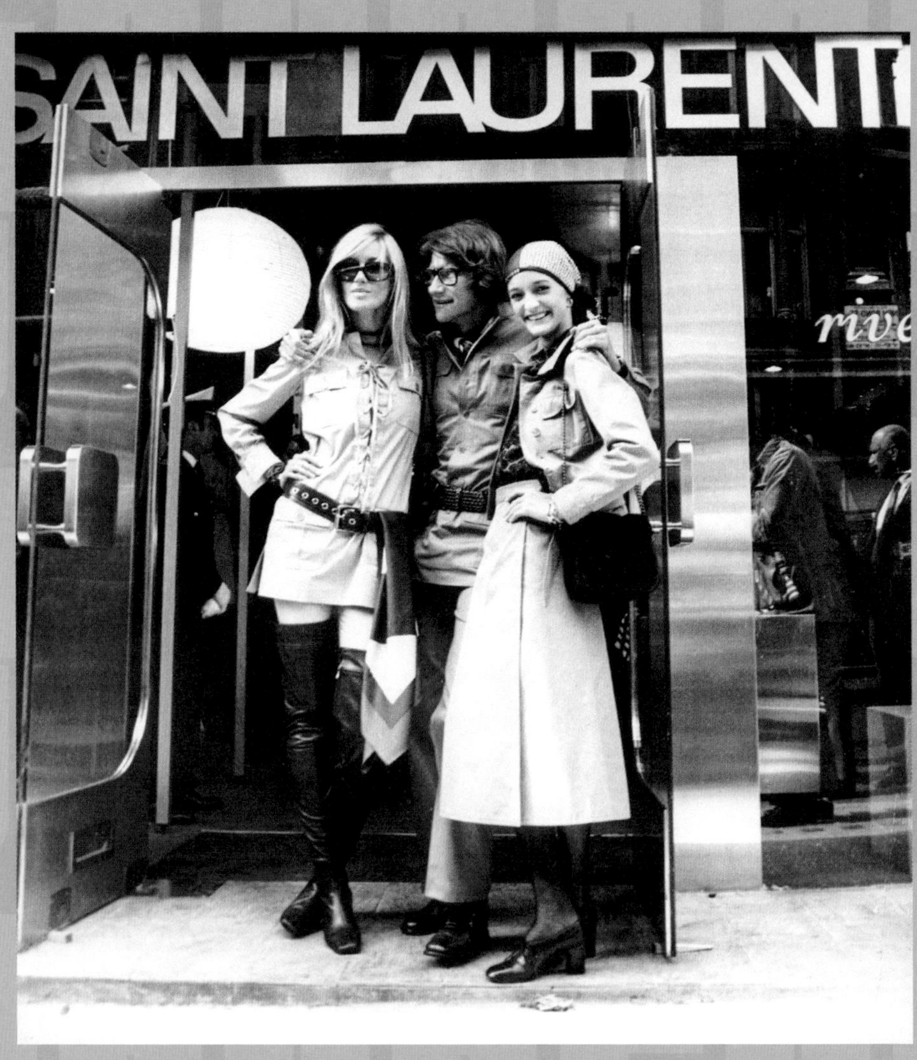
SAINT LAURENT

Yves Saint Laurent

A teenage Yves Saint Laurent arrived in Paris from Oran, Algeria, winning the International Wool Secretariat (IWS) prize and entering Christian Dior's studio. At 21 he took over the helm after Dior's death from a heart attack, aged 52. In 1958 he showed the "Trapeze" line – a dress that fell from the shoulder and widened towards the hem. This A-shaped flare released the waist and marked a clean break from the New Look. Paris read the shift immediately: there was a new visionary in town.

Saint Laurent then made another turn, "Le Smoking". This new outfit formula – stolen from the boys – cut a precise shoulder, a straight trouser and a satin lapel for women and launched the tuxedo into nightlife: restaurants, clubs, the whole circuit. His muses, Loulou de la Falaise and Betty Catroux, wore it first, proving the design on real bodies outside in the real world. They make it clear: women can feel hot and free in a tailored jacket, trousers and lapel usually reserved for men. And crucially, Saint Laurent sells it as ready-to-wear – you try it on in the afternoon and walk out in it that night. What looks like a restrictive work uniform flips into a permission slip.

That same year, Saint Laurent opened Rive Gauche, a boutique on the Left Bank – the more bohemian side of Paris across the Seine from the couture houses on Avenue Montaigne (bookshops, cafés, students instead of salons and embassies). The address matters: fashion leaves the ateliers and takes a street corner, where ready-to-wear meets real life.

Opposite: Yves Saint Laurent surrounded by his muses at the opening of his Rive Gauche boutique in 1966. Couture steps into ready-to-wear and Paris gains a new and faster way of dressing.

You can only imagine the impact at that time. Saint Laurent literally rerouted fashion from the salon to the street: tuxedoed women going out, a Left Bank address turning retail into culture. Ready-to-wear became a new way of being in a massive shift in how fashion was perceived, accessed and consumed. Paris, the capital of couture, learned a new posture – and then maintained it.

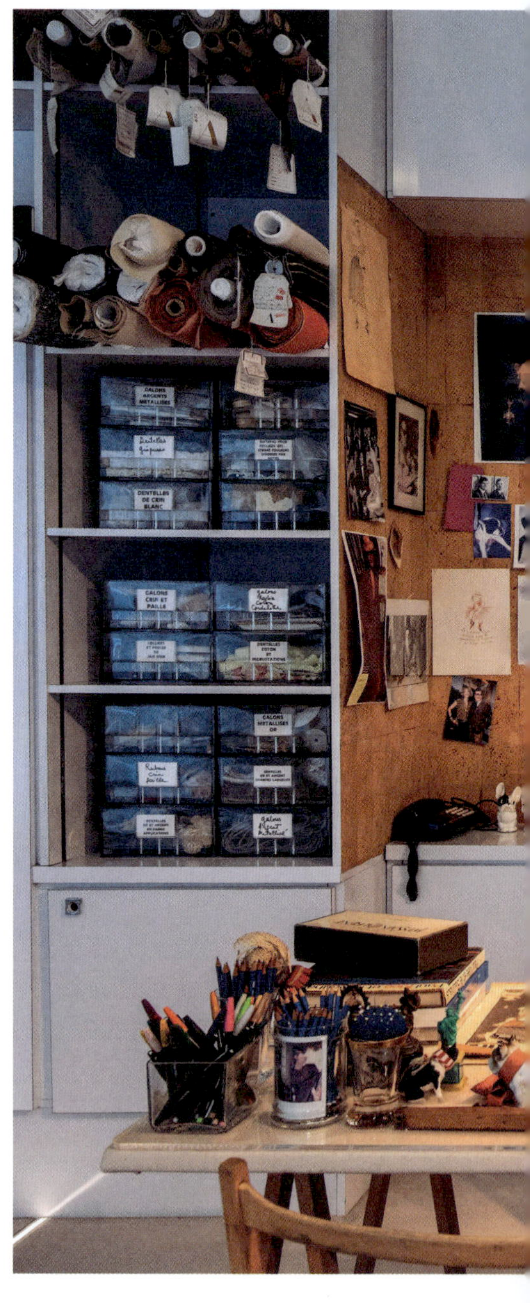

Right: YSL's office, where for decades real fashion magic kept happening.

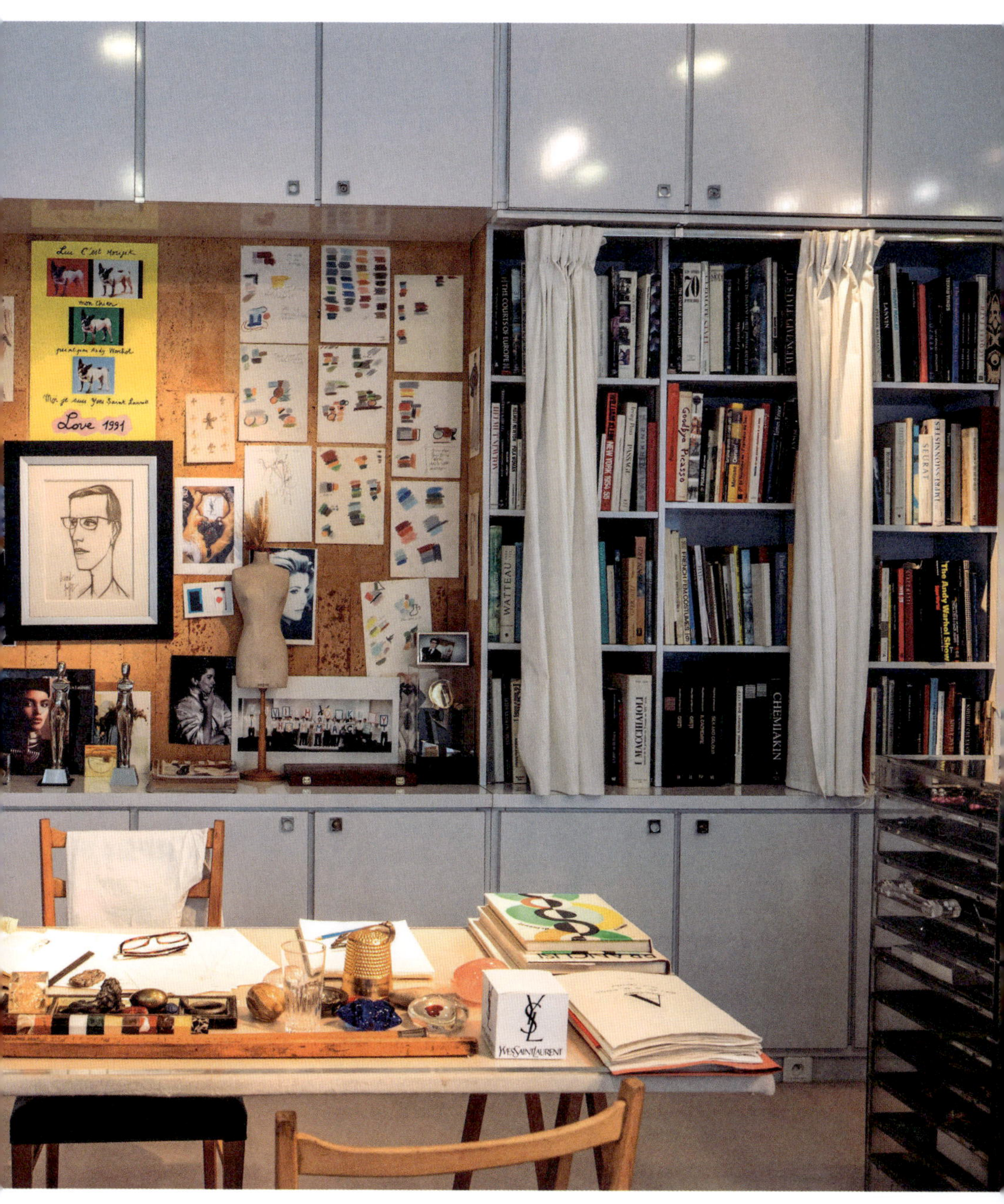

mon chien
Love 1991
WATTEAU
SEURAT
LANVIN
Picasso
The Andy Warhol Show
CHEMIAKIN
YvesSaintLaurent

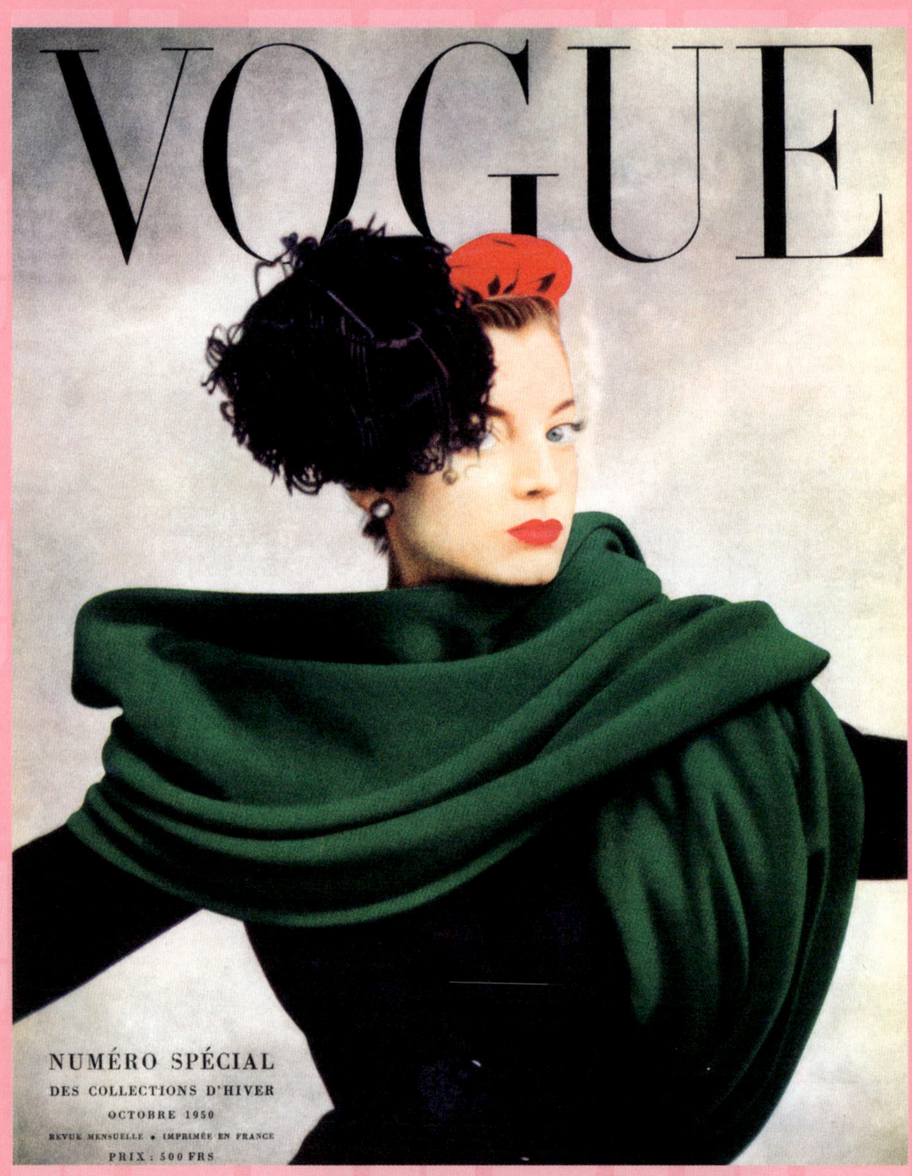
VOGUE
NUMÉRO SPÉCIAL
DES COLLECTIONS D'HIVER
OCTOBRE 1950
REVUE MENSUELLE • IMPRIMÉE EN FRANCE
PRIX : 500 FRS

CRISTÓBAL BALENCIAGA

After the Civil War forced him to close his stores, Cristóbal Balenciaga left Spain and settled in Paris, aged 42, in 1937. From a quiet address on Avenue George V, he changed how clothes behaved. Christian Dior's New Look had cinched the waist, but Balenciaga did the opposite. He sculpted the garment, so that it held its own shape and let the waist disappear. Fabric lifted off the skin, the neckline lifted the face, and when the wearer walked, the outline stayed intact. In a city still addicted to the waist (think the New Look silhouette), he moved the gaze higher and wider.

Balenciaga's private clients, such as the American socialite Mona von Bismarck and the Duchess of Windsor, wore the look in salons and to state dinners, illustrating a new take on shape and craftsmanship. Outerwear made the message even more obvious: rounded coats that carry their own weather became the new trend. With textile partner Gustav Zumsteg at Abraham Limited, Balenciaga developed gazar, a springy silk that allowed those sculpted shapes to survive movement without noise.

Balenciaga closed the couture line in 1968, but Paris kept his vocabulary: space around the body with lots of discipline underneath. The city learned a new way of dressing – structure over spectacle – and you can still spot it from a block away.

Opposite: *Vogue Paris*, October 1948. This cover is key to capturing the precision and theatricality of post-war Paris fashion.

HUBERT DE GIVENCHY

Hubert de Givenchy arrived in Paris from his hometown of Beauvais at the tender age of 17 to study at the École Nationale Supérieure des Beaux-Arts. He learned fast and opened his house in 1952. Paris was rebuilding its confidence after the end of the war and Givenchy offered a lighter hand: where others sculpted, Givenchy streamlined.

Givenchy designed a wardrobe that his clientele could rotate – pieces worn on repeat without becoming tiring, day into evening, taxi to work – so the woman arrived before the dress. His partnership with the screen legend Audrey Hepburn made that logic visible around the world.

On-screen and off, the same clarity holds: clothes that sit cleanly under light, move through and keep their line when the scene shifts. It was quiet luxury from the past century. That consistency is the point: it proves a couture house can write character rather than chase spectacle. Buyers read reliability; editors read legibility; Paris reads a calmer kind of authority.

Retail follows: everyone loves elegance you can pack and trust. It becomes an aspirational look for the modern woman of the time: simplicity earns attention because it works everywhere. This is the city's impact. Givenchy lowered the volume and tightened the cut, so Paris was able to export a new idea of glamour – understated, precise, usable. The line survived decades because it was built to rotate, not to shock. That's the lesson Givenchy left on the Right Bank and beyond: make elegance readable, keep posture steady and allow discretion to carry the room.

Opposite: Hubert de Givenchy adjusts a dress on Audrey Hepburn, while a seamstress shapes the hem. The collaboration between couturier and muse becomes visible in this working moment, a snapshot of what might be the first celebrity endorsement in the business of fashion.

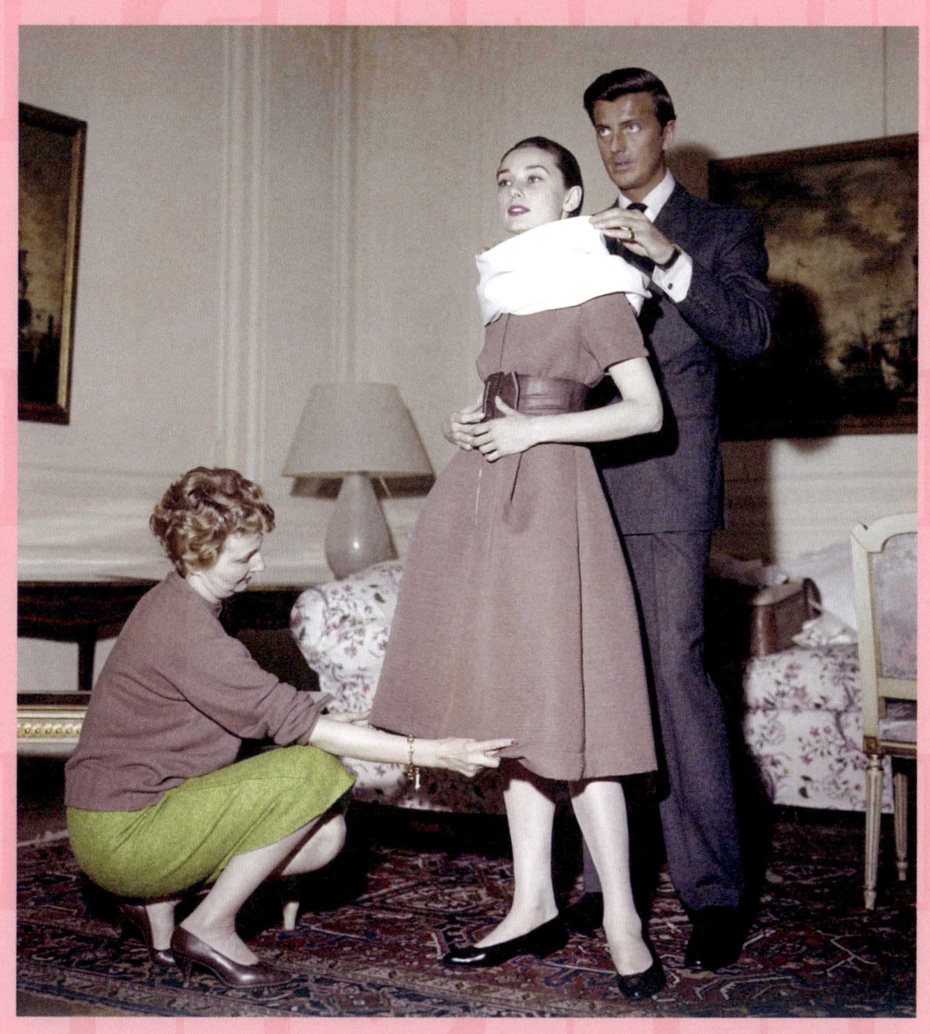

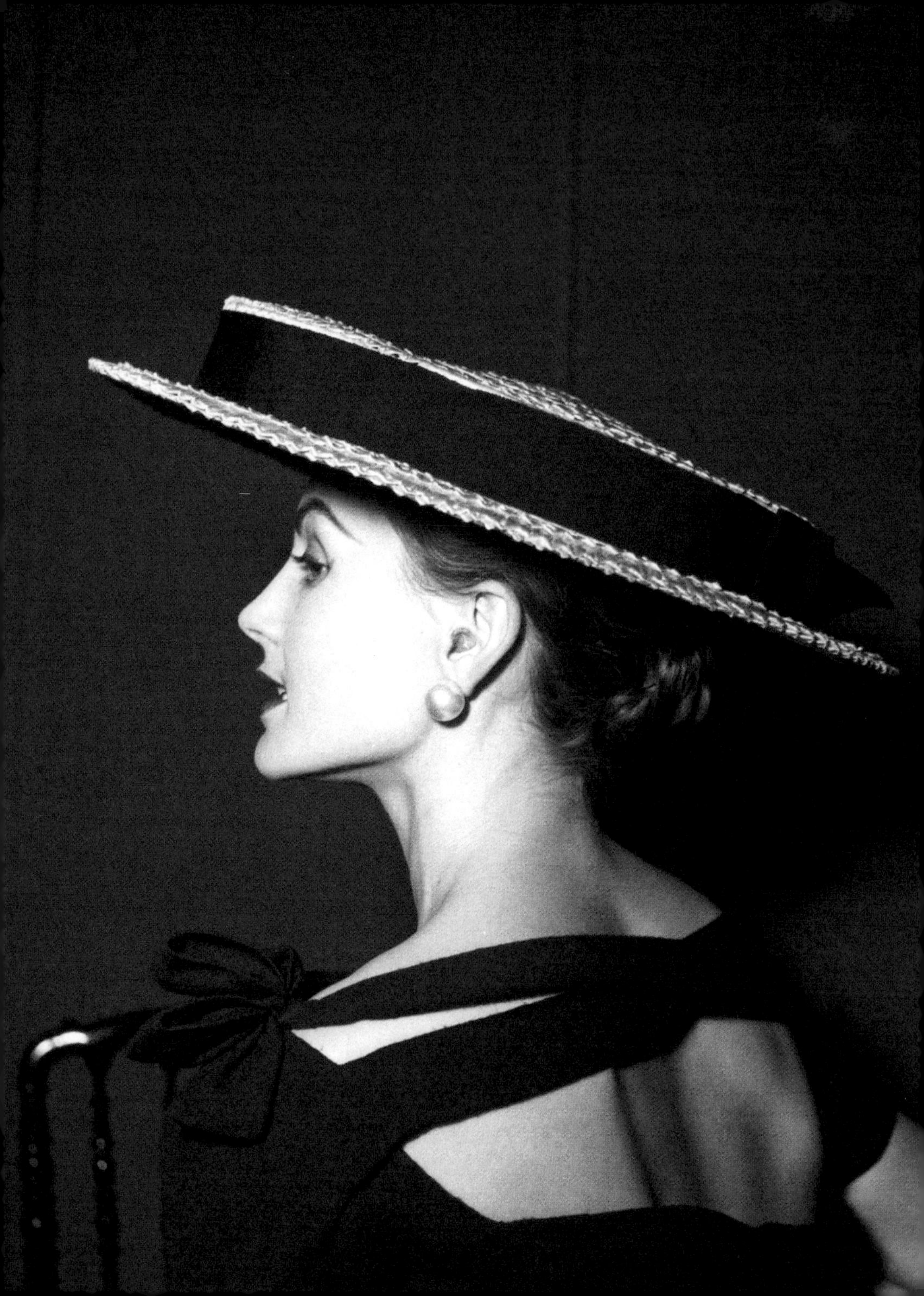

Right: A model wears a Givenchy, Shetland wool dress in grey. The collarless neckline of the long-sleeved bolero is innovatively held together with a drawstring. The bolero, which comprises the top half of the dress, provides a fullness, contrasting with the sheath dress underneath.

Opposite: A model wears one of Givenchy's 1950s boater hats.

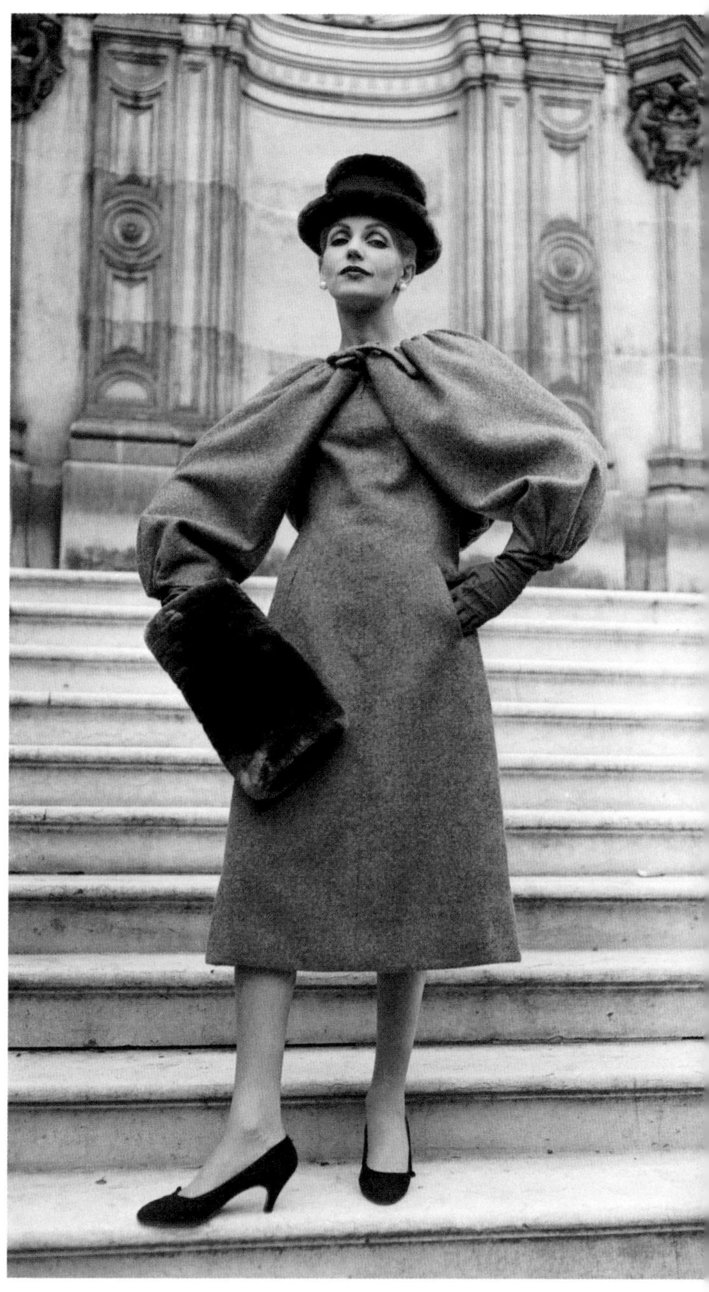

PIERRE BALMAIN

Pierre Balmain opened his house in 1945, while Paris was still rebuilding after the conflict. He became known for Jolie Madame. Let me explain: a look for real life in public. Smart, calm, put-together. Not costume couture. Clothes you could wear to a business meeting, cross a hotel lobby, get into a car, and still be ready for dinner. Shoulders that steady you, a waist that tidies the line, coats and skirts that move without resistance. The look gave women a way to step back into the city with confidence after the war.

But Balmain's biggest change was in how he ran the house. He treated it like a working network, not a private club: clear calendars, reliable deliveries, press to explain the idea and products that carried the name when the dress wasn't in the room. Meaning? He was part of the first wave of post-war couturiers (alongside Christian Dior and Hubert de Givenchy) to use perfume strategically, not as a vanity extra but as a business vehicle. A bottle of fragrance travels further than a gown; it turns the Paris message into something people can take home. Balmain chose his licences carefully for the same reason: the image spreads without necessarily thinning out the craft.

Shops follow the rhythm, so clients build a wardrobe they can rotate through a whole day – office at noon, theatre by night – without changing who they are. Airlines, embassies and cultural institutions choose Paris again because Balmain makes elegance dependable and exportable. Journalists and buyers keep returning and this is how money and attention flow between seasons.

Opposite: This photograph looks so modern – it could be on your Instagram feed! What frames this moment is the mid-century couture, unmistakably high-end and structured enough to make the whole image feel timeless.

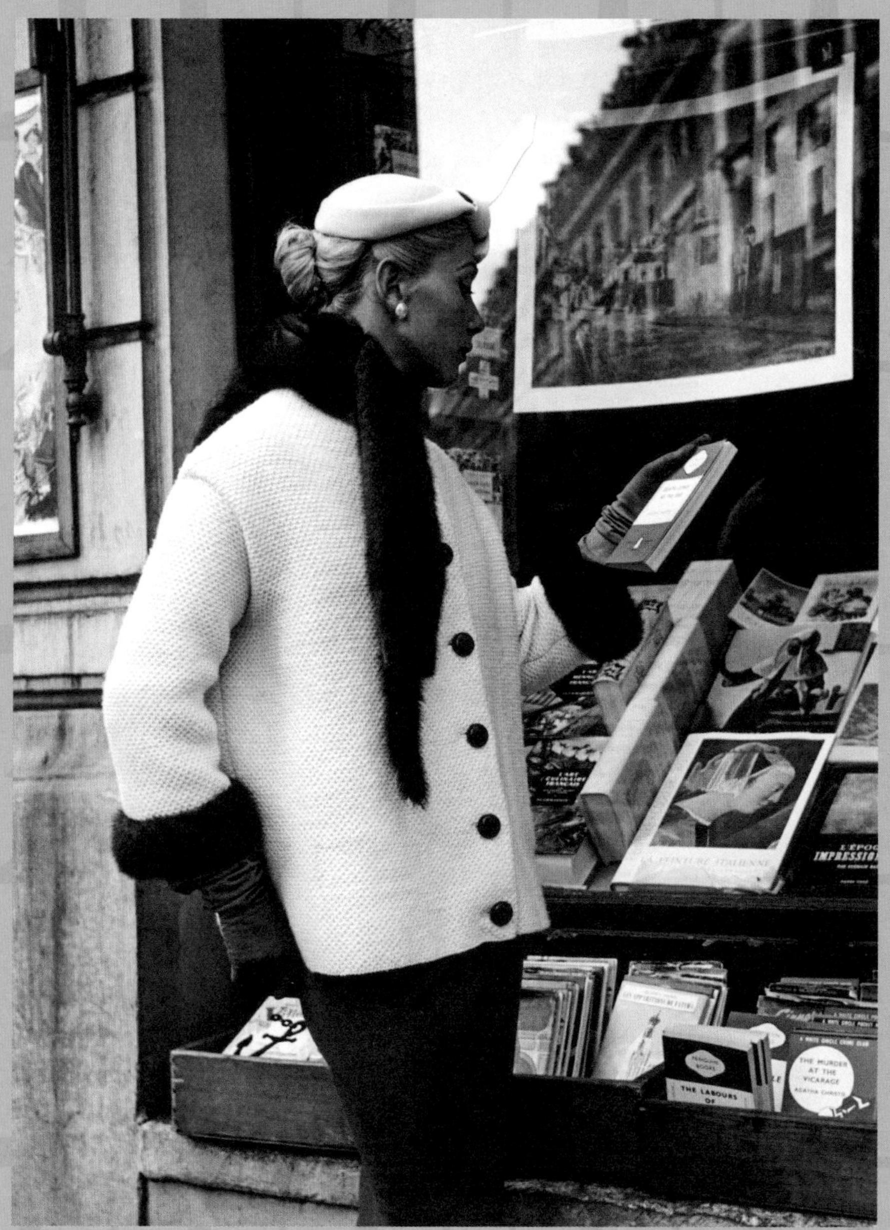
THE MURDER AT THE VICARAGE
AGATHA CHRISTIE
THE LABOURS OF

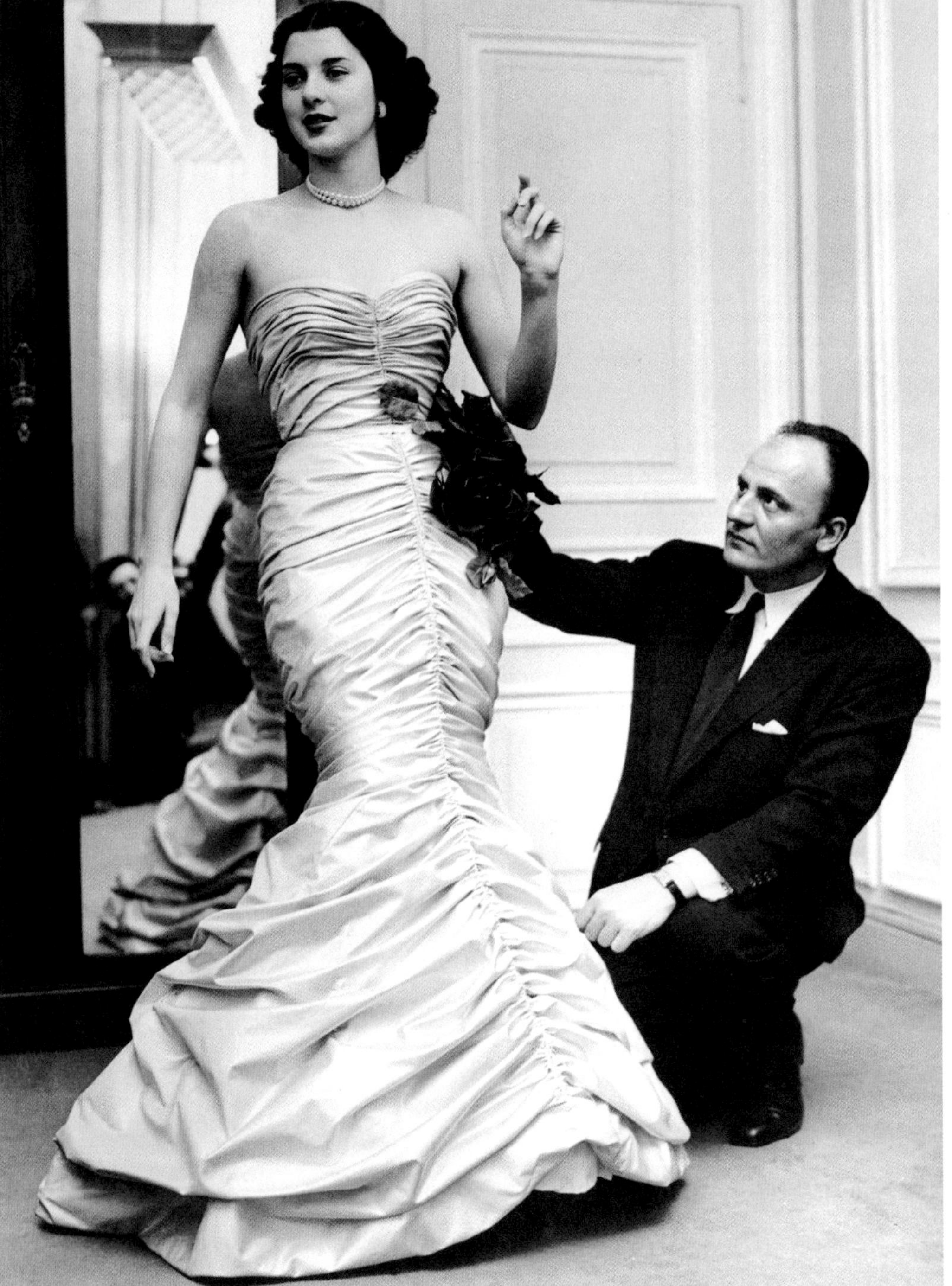

What he is known for isn't a single "It-dress" but an overall habit: structure with purpose. The designer changed the industry by proving that service, timing and clarity matter as much as a sketch. That's his legacy: making Paris look sure of itself and its business because it can still show up, hold the room and keep going. A huge step towards building the fashion empire the city remains today.

Below: Balmain in the fitting room, adjusting a breathtaking black chiffon evening gown designed in pure Balmain style.

Opposite: A ruched satin evening gown being carefully refined in the atelier.

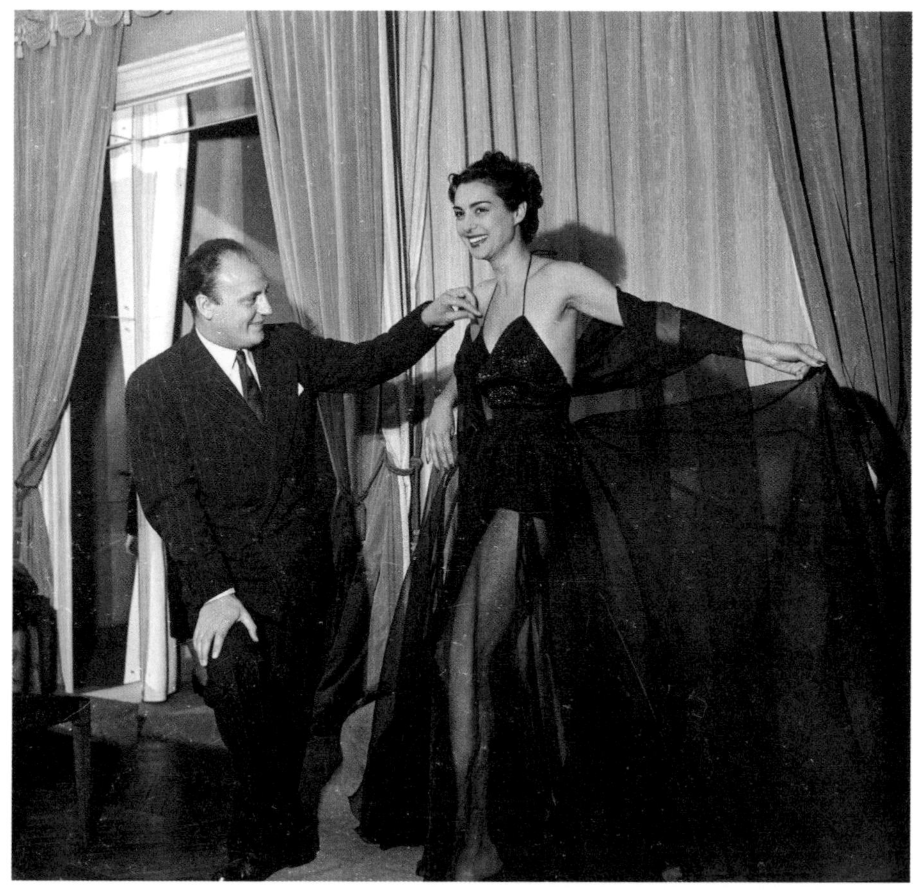

JEANNE LANVIN

The designer Jeanne Lanvin started her career in 1889 as a hat-maker in Paris. Her clientele then began to ask for dresses for their daughters; the mothers wanted the same touch, and soon she was dressing whole families. By the 1920s Lanvin's house on rue du Faubourg Saint-Honoré was being run like a small enterprise with children's wear, women's day wear and eveningwear, menswear, furs, lingerie, interiors and – by the mid-decade – perfume. Paris already had its own couturiers, but Lanvin built a departmental "house" years before the word felt modern.

Her craft had its own distinguishing signatures you could point to. For example, she kept a dye workshop, so colour was deliberate – Lanvin blue became a reference shade. She funded permanent embroidery rooms, so motifs were repeated with precision. And while the decade adored a slim line, the designer kept faith with the *robe de style*, a dropped waist over a full skirt, because her clients wanted grace combined with the ability to move through salons with freedom. The trademark emblem on her boxes showed a mother and daughter holding hands: not a marketing spin, but the customer she built from day one.

Lanvin also designed the setting. With a dedicated décor studio she created sombre, modern rooms that made shopping feel organized, not hushed. The house learned to publicize

Opposite: A look from Lanvin's Autumn/Winter 2025 collection, Peter Copping's debut for the house. Here, a modern reading of Lanvin's codes through the softened structure and long, fluid line.

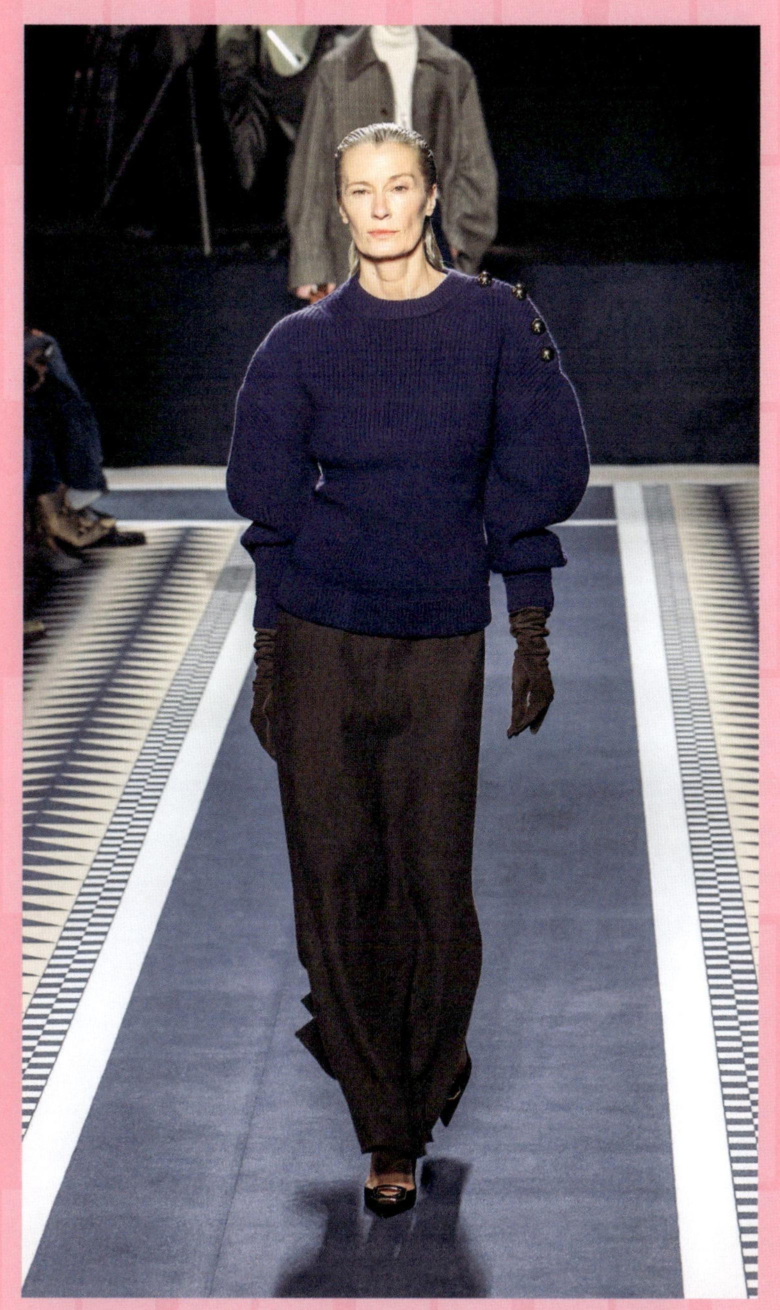

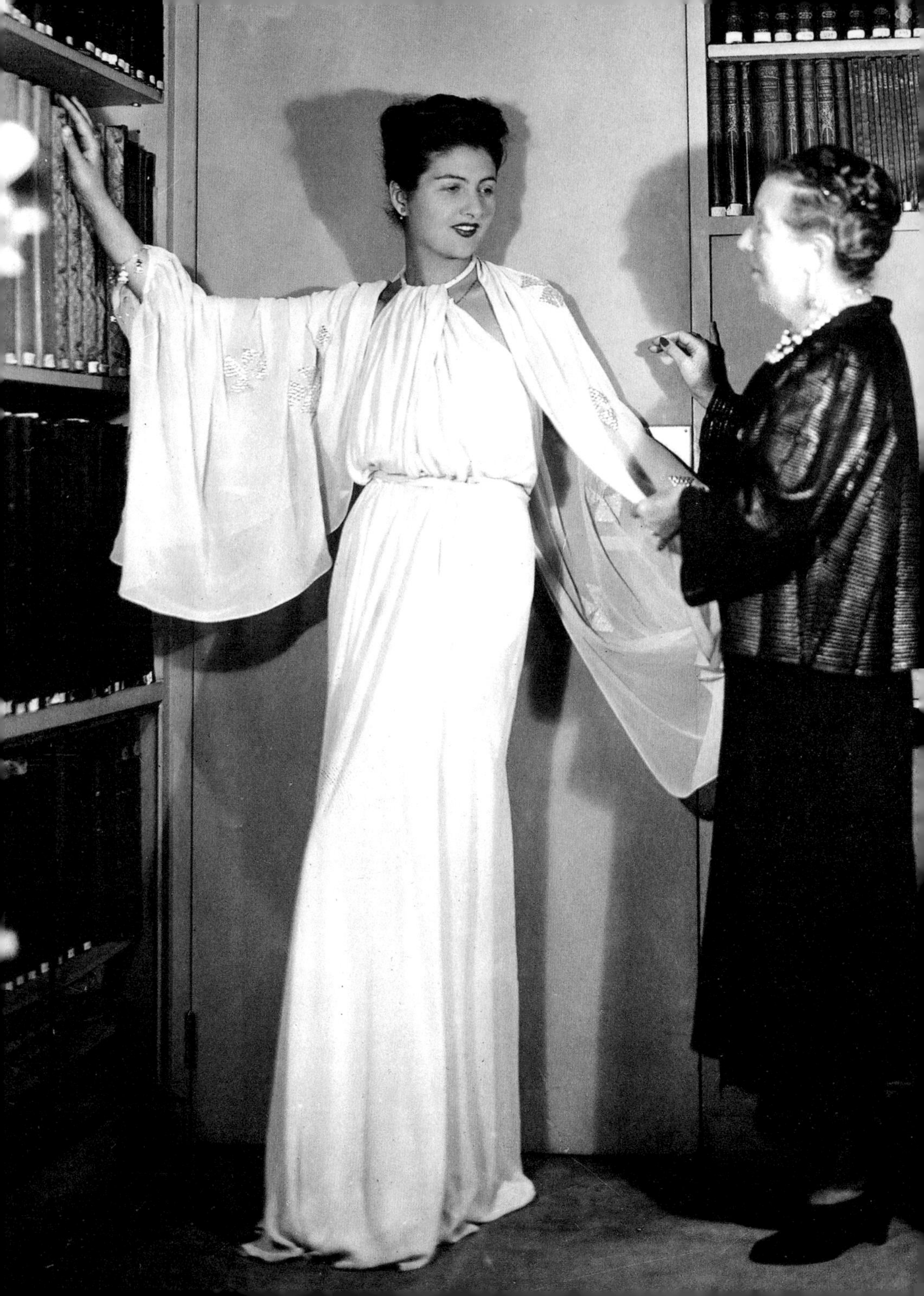

its taste with unique catalogues, invitations, a bottle design for Arpège that carried the address further than any garment could travel. Tourists came to see the façade and buyers came to learn the system.

This was Lanvin's impact on Paris: she proved that a couture house can have its own colours, its own workshops, its own scent, and also that a Paris label can define a life, not just a season. The city maintains this invaluable lesson: make a world, keep the quality inside it and let the style circulate – from workroom to window to street – without losing its centre, though.

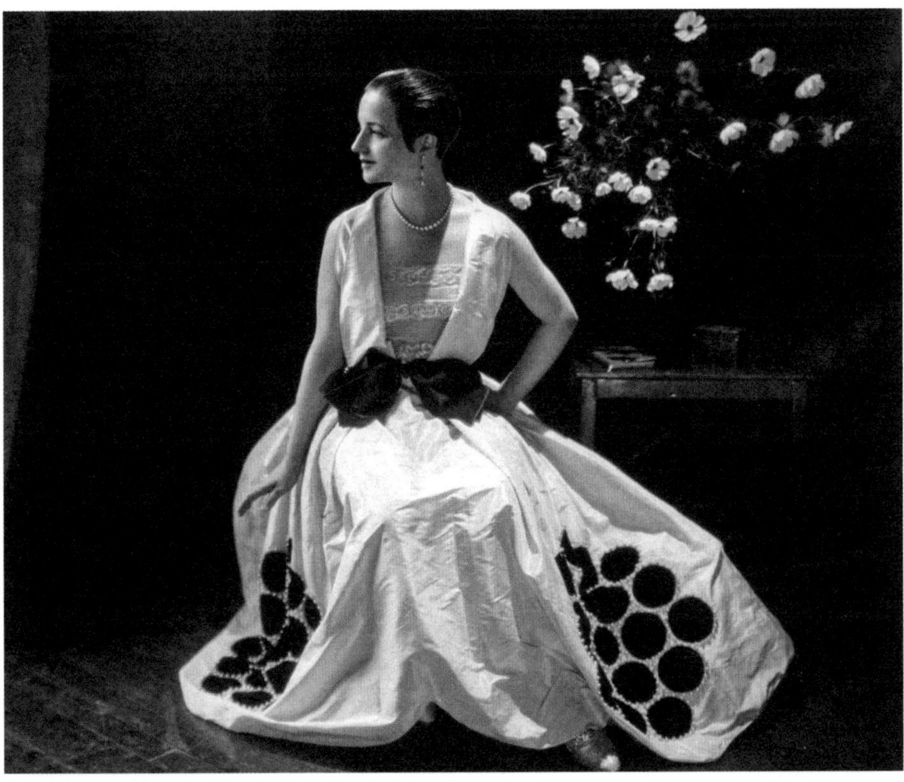

Opposite: Jeanne Lanvin adjusts a draped gown on a model. The open sleeves and fluid construction show the *robe de style* evolving towards a lighter, more modern line and although this creation is gorgeous, I am secretly inspired by JL's fit too: I feel like I could wear this every single day.

Above: This gown highlights the House's balance of ornament and restraint – a signature that Lanvin kept for a very long time.

MADELEINE VIONNET

The young seamstress Madeleine Vionnet arrived in Paris in 1900 after training in London, but she learned fast and opened her own house in 1912. War closed the doors, but she returned in 1923 and turned the city's focus from decoration to gravity. This move is simple to explain but radical in effect: she cut on the bias (diagonally), so the fabric followed the lines of the body. She draped the fabric straight onto the mannequin until the fall looked inevitable: no armour, no padding. When the wearer walked, the outline didn't break; when they sat or turned, the dress kept it together.

Dancers and actresses loved the designer's creations because the bias cut breathes and stretches on the diagonal, turns without riding up and catches the light along the curve instead of across seams. A Vionnet gown could be rolled, unpacked, shaken once, and it would find itself again: stage-ready, camera-ready, travel-ready. That usefulness is what sold modernity: ease that read formal, movement that looked very composed.

What changed in Paris was how people worked with cloth. Students started pinning on the stand, instead of drafting everything flat, and shop windows learned a new trick: one clean gown on a still figure can suggest movement without a single ruffle. Madeleine Vionnet was consistent about proportion, ruthless about clarity and uninterested in seasonal gimmicks. That reliability builds trust with both clients and editors, which is its own Paris currency.

Opposite: A bias-cut Vionnet gown displayed on a mannequin. The drape shows how she allowed fabric to fall on the body without padding or structure, relying only on the cut to create movement.

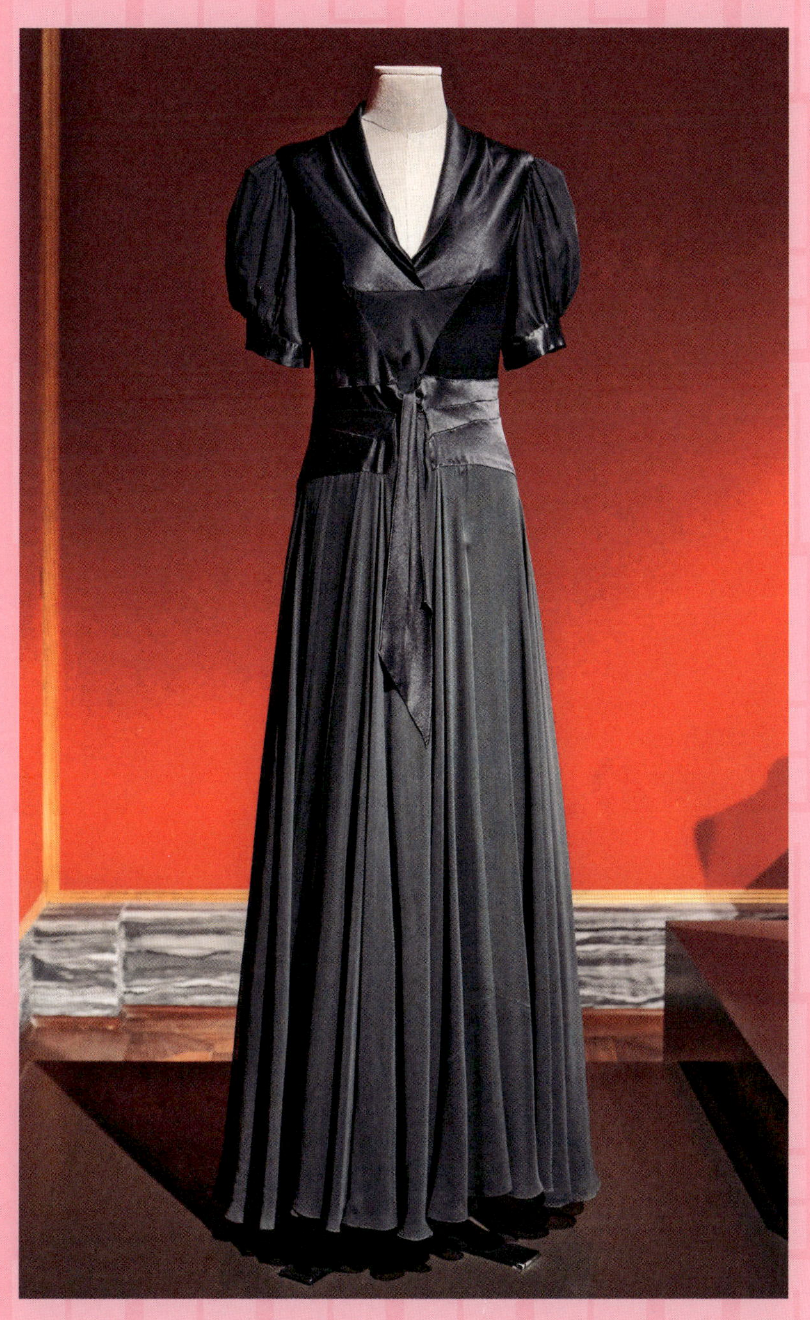

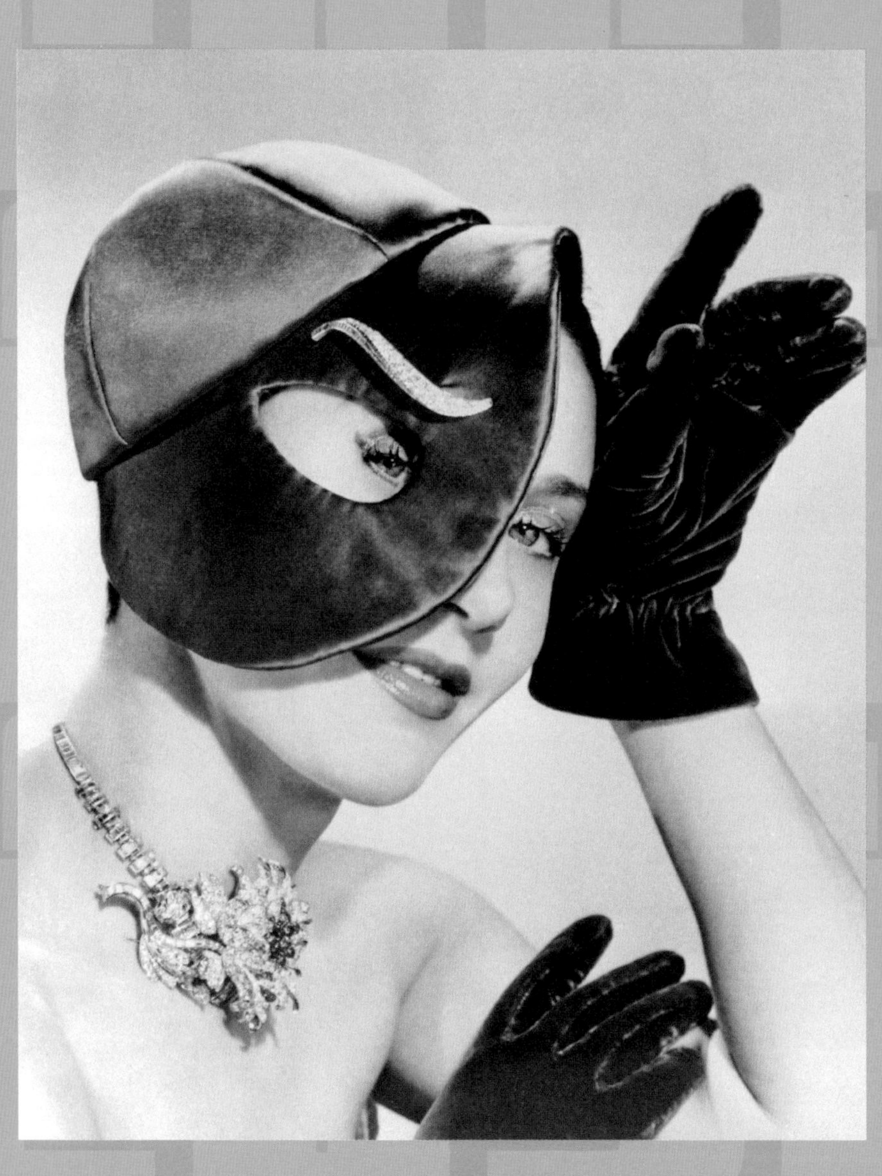

Elsa Schiaparelli

Designer Elsa Schiaparelli brought surrealism to the cutting table and kept it standing upright. A lobster could cross a skirt, a skeleton might rise in *trapunto* (a quilting technique), a shoe could become a hat – but the joke landed because the tailoring held. From 1927 to 1954 she turned wit into an organized system: zips as headlines, embroidery as punchlines, and shocking pink as voltage, not just a colour.

With fellow artists Salvador Dalí and Jean Cocteau, she proved that fashion could argue with art on equal terms by collaborating constantly and talking daily, and the atelier made sure the argument survived motion and light. Schiaparelli didn't do novelty for novelty's sake but she issued permission – to look twice, to join intelligence with humour, to remember that imagination needs engineering. That's why the images still read as modern: optical tricks that stay crisp up close, hardware with manners, and humour as silhouettes. In other words, fashion surrealism.

Opposite: A model wears a visored Schiaparelli evening hat with a peephole. A diamond clip from Van Cleef & Arpels forms an eyebrow over the peephole, to provide a surrealist look.

André Courrèges

Initially, André Courrèges trained as an engineer, then worked for Balenciaga before opening his own house in 1961. He designed for real life, but the kind of life that moves fast. In 1964–65 people named his fashion language "Space Age". What they meant by that was simple: shorter skirts, clean cuts, lots of bright white matched with silver. Geometry played a huge role in Courrèges' designs. They looked fresh on new TV screens and in daylight, not just in the bourgeois salons.

The designer also pushed ready-to-wear early on, so the look he created didn't remain rare. Shops could carry the same neat clothes you saw in Paris shows and the quality remained steady. The press loved it because the clothes photographed really well; buyers loved it because the sizing and make were reliable. Very quickly, the white boot and the short, sharp jacket became city basics, and not just novelties.

André Courrèges gave the capital a modern uniform for youth and proved that "futuristic" could still be practical. His influence can be seen any time a designer treats white like architecture, keeps lines simple and lets a mini-skirt look strong rather than cute.

Opposite: André Courrèges fits a geometric dress in his atelier. The clean structure, white fabric and sharp angles show the beginnings of his Space-Age language – the beginning of the sci-fication of fashion.

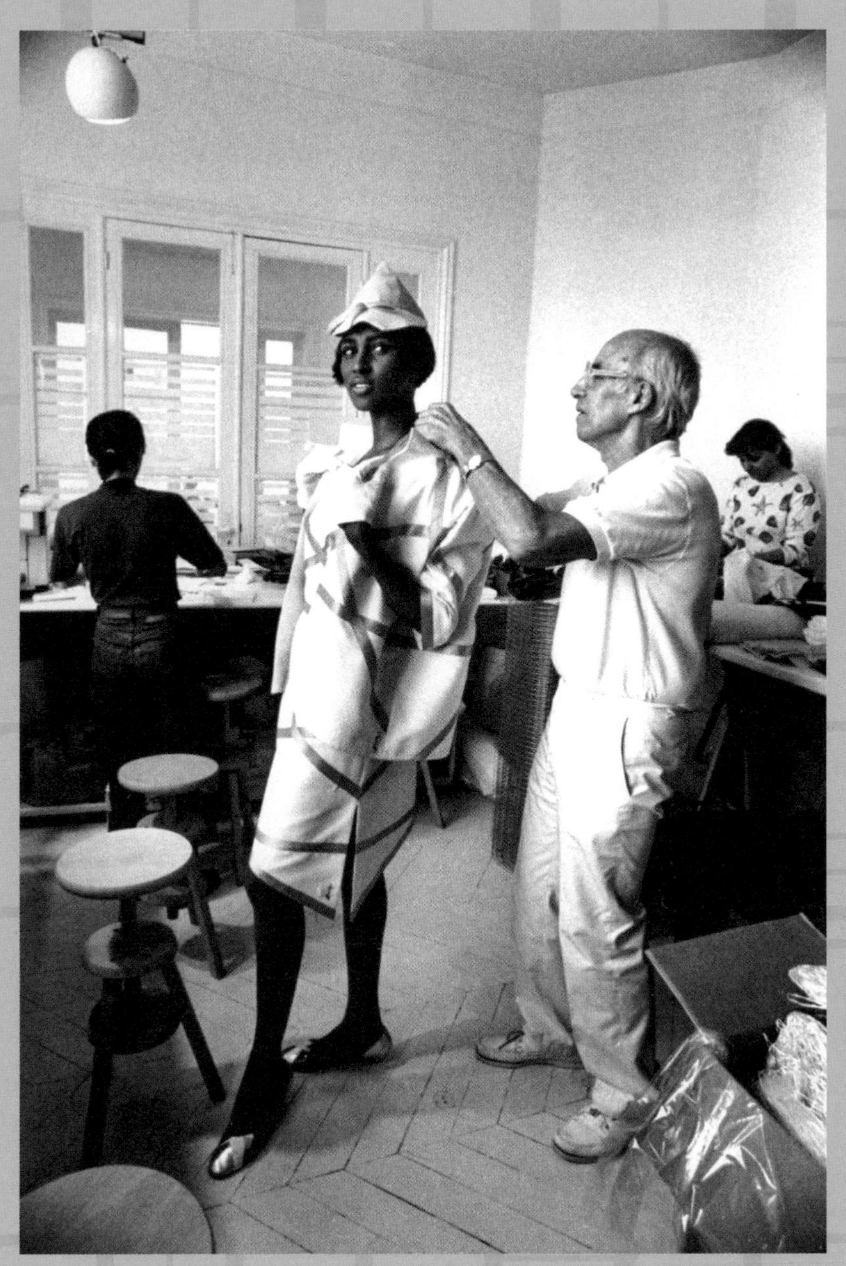

Trained as an engineer, Courrèges treated clothes like moving structures. Every seam had a function and every angle was the result of calculation.

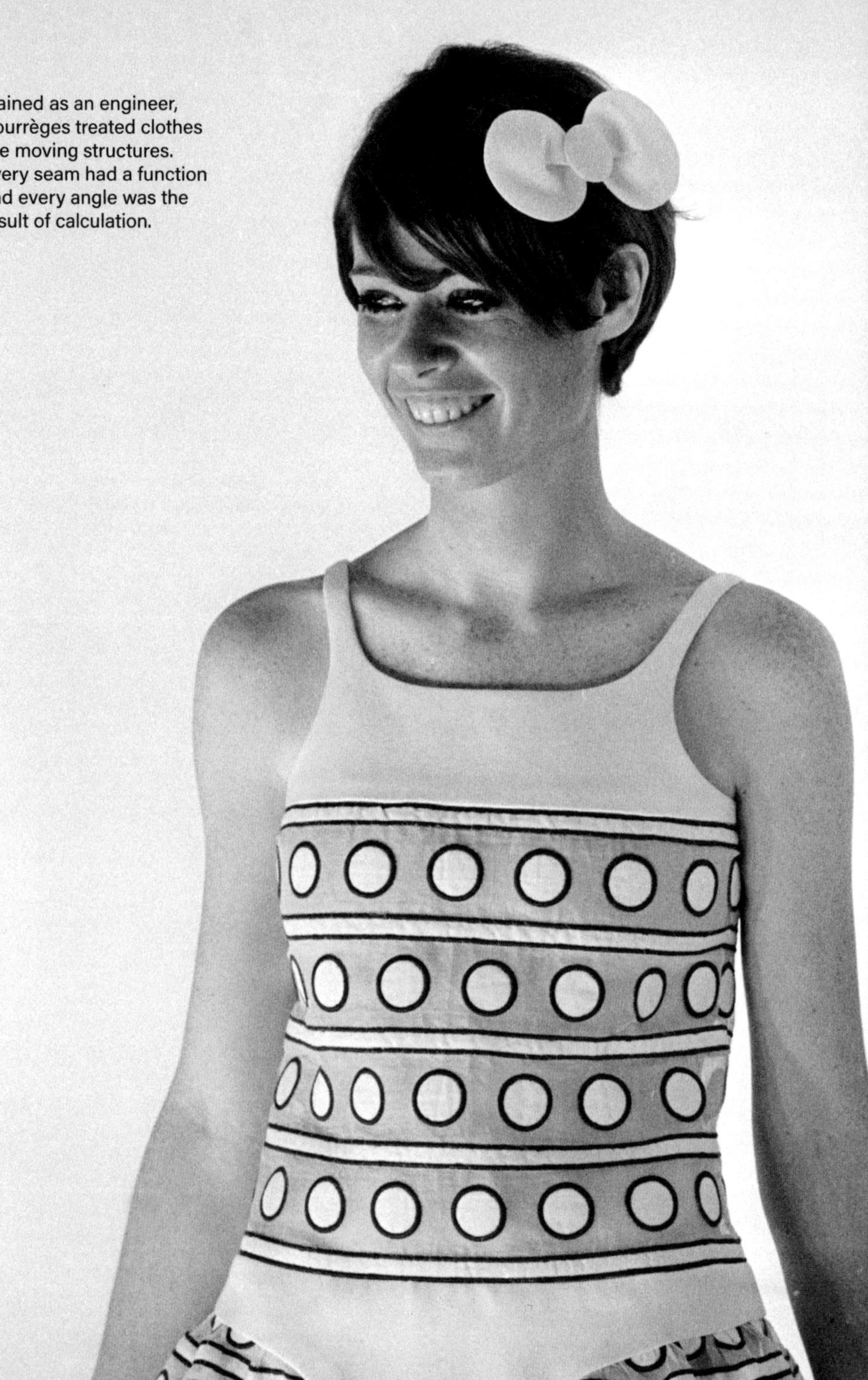

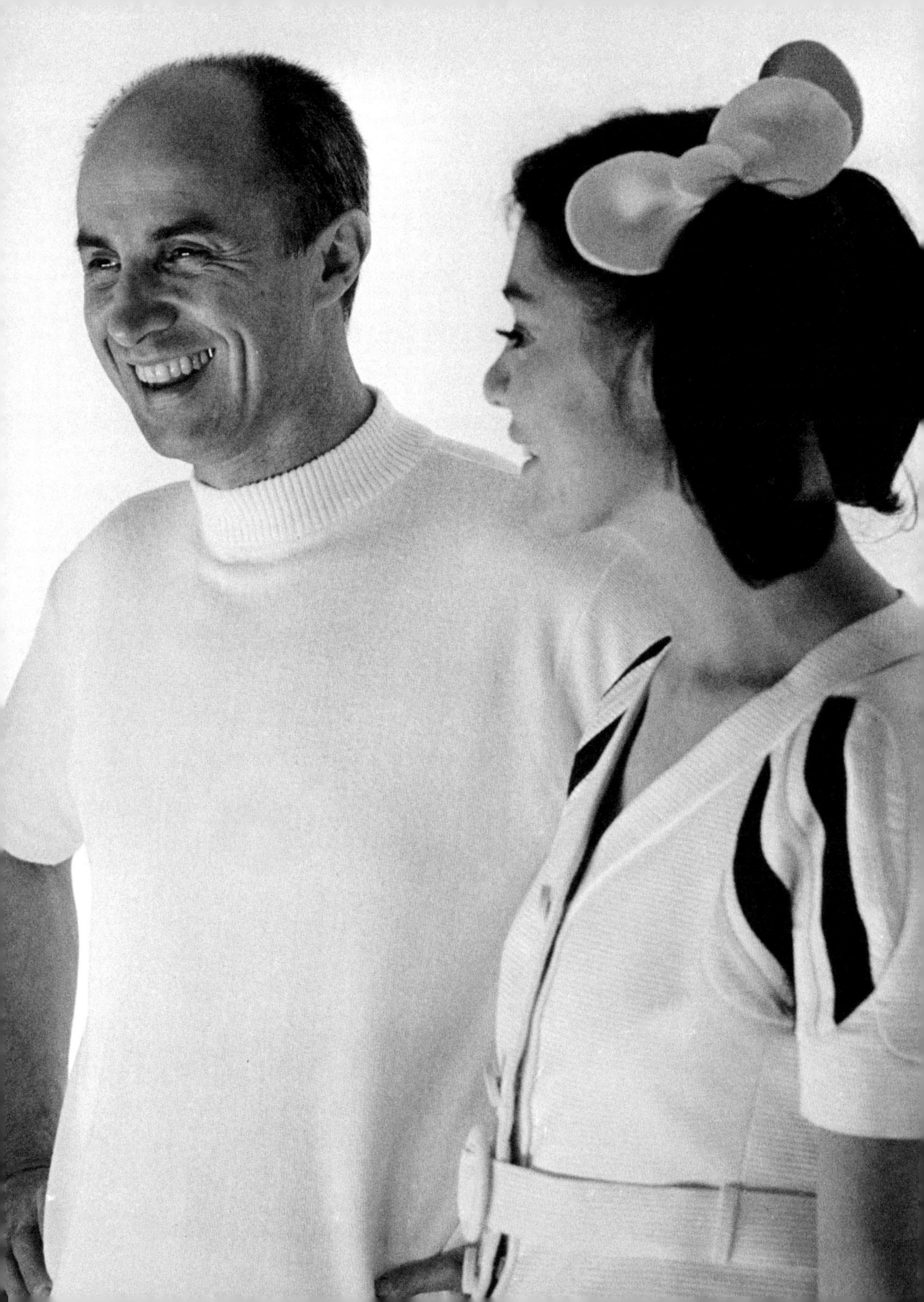

PACO RABANNE

Designer Paco Rabanne studied architecture, learned jewellery-making hands-on at the workbench, and in 1966 opened his Paris house with a jolt: "12 Unwearable Dresses in Contemporary Materials". His first show built dresses from metal discs, plastic plates and aluminium, all linked like jewellery with rings and wire: no fabric, no thread. The title was tongue-in-cheek: they were wearable, just wildly unlike normal garments, being cool to the touch, bright, clinking softly and throwing light as you moved. Overnight, Paris understood that a dress could be made like an object, not a textile.

Rabanne kept the idea practical by using repeatable modules like rings, plates and clips, so radical pieces could be produced with care, not as one-offs. Pop culture did the rest: singers, films and clubs adopted the shine and the image travelled fast. His legacy on the Paris scene is that he widened what "fashion material" means and showed that concept leads and medium follows. He let nightlife be a laboratory and made industry techniques part of couture craft.

The city gained a new permission in fashion design: to treat the body as a light source and hardware as construction. You can still see echoes of Paco Rabanne's work whenever a dress behaves like jewellery, when transparency is structure rather than a tease.

This lesson lands for everyone: if the concept is clear, the form can change.

Opposite: This is the best photo of Paco Rabanne that you'll see today!

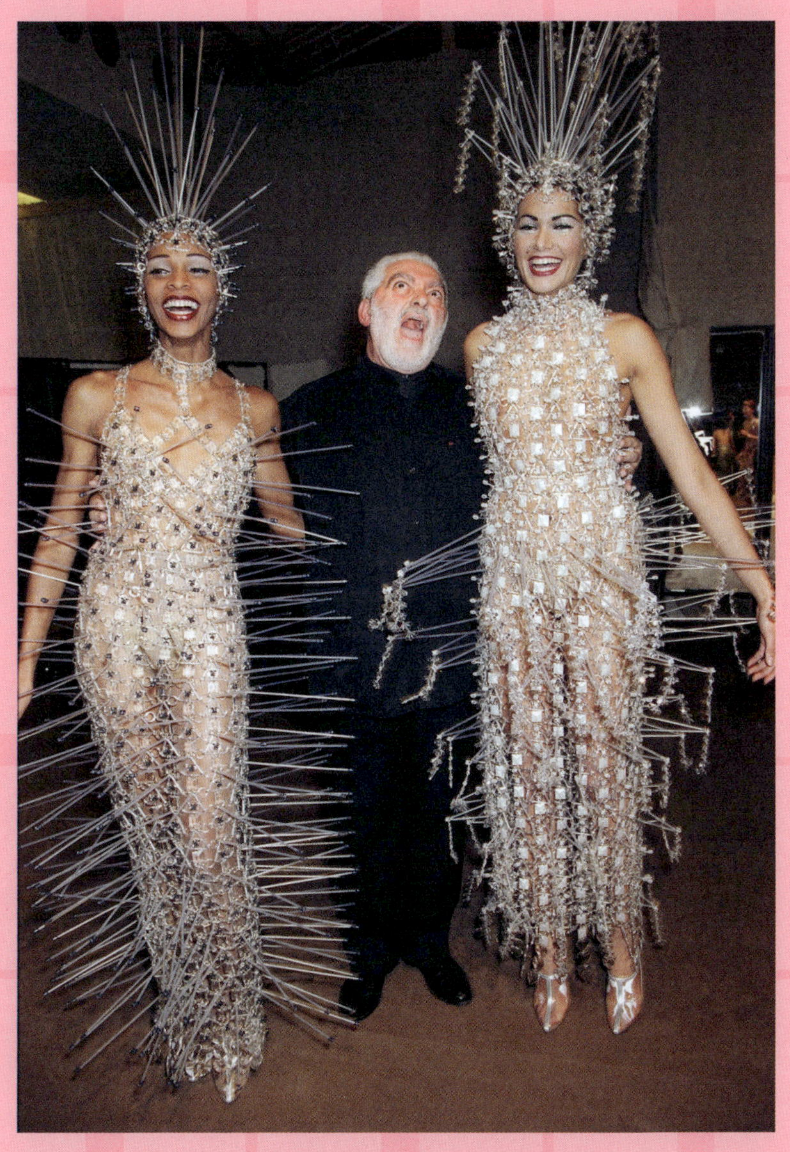

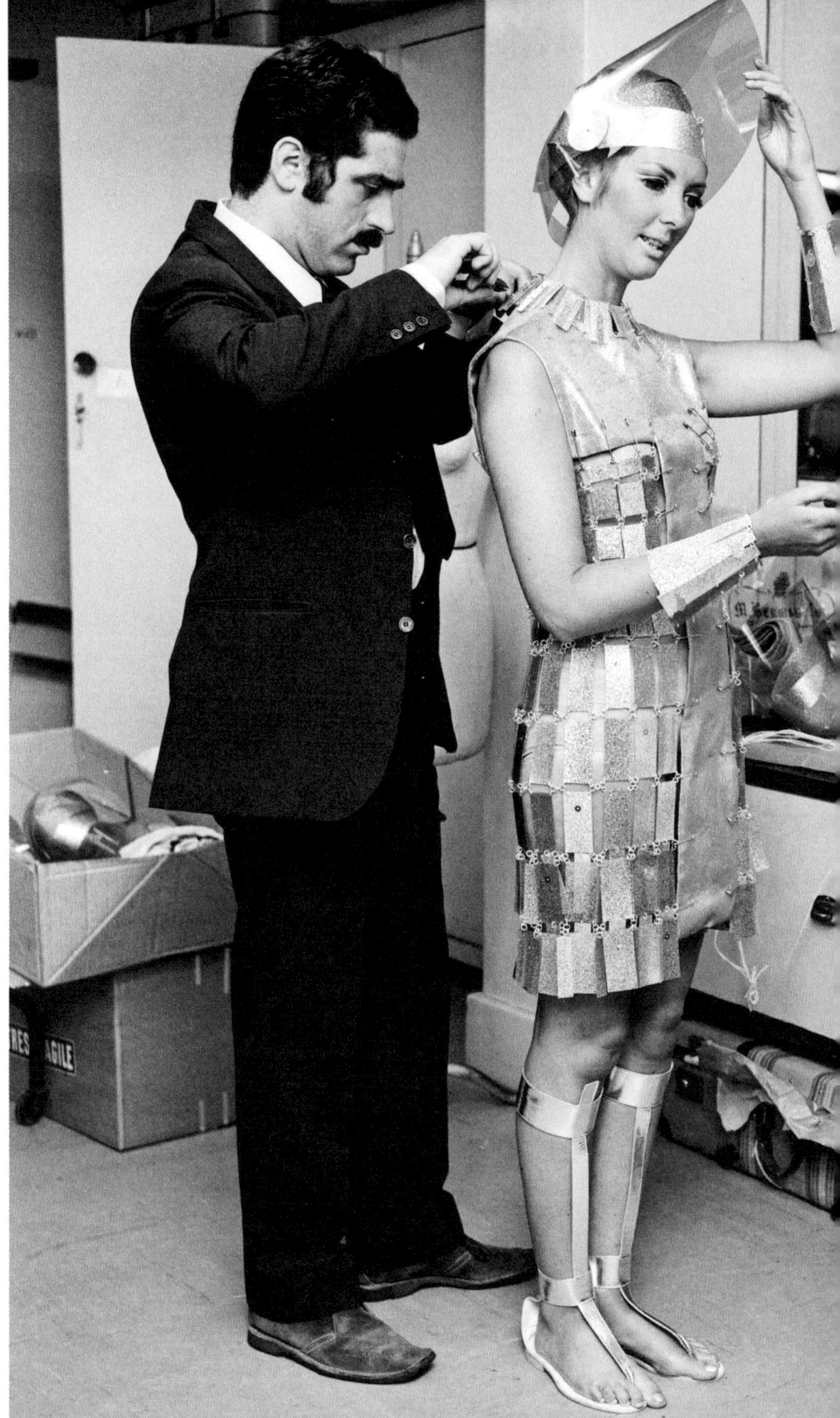

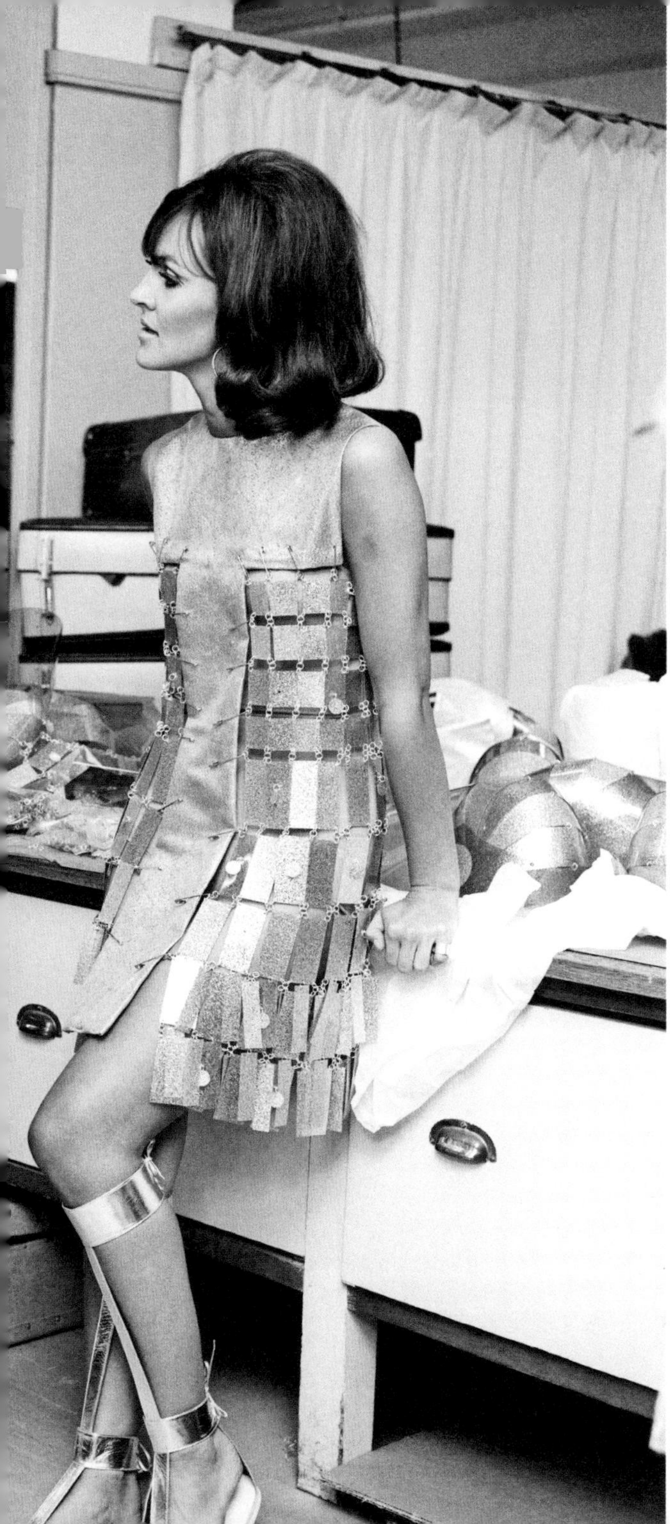

Left: Paco Rabanne fits metal-plate mini-dresses in the studio: the modular construction and rigid shine show how he replaced fabric with components assembled like armour.

Christian Lacroix

Christian Lacroix brought joy to a city that often prefers restraint. He studied art history, learned theatre costume and worked at Jean Patou before opening his own house in 1987. Paris had been quiet; he answered with colour, bows, sparkle and bold shapes, but the cutting remained strict. The clothes look festive because the engineering is tight. That's why the images still sing: the line holds, while the surface celebrates.

The "Pouf" dress became his signature: short, lifted, light on the legs. It made any entrance feel like a party and still fitted securely. He pulled inspiration from Provence and the South – fêtes, opera, carnival – and turned those memories into city clothes. The mood was happy, not foolish. You can dance in it ... You can be seen in it ... You keep your posture ...

Lacroix also spread the spirit beyond the couture room. Ready-to-wear, accessories and the perfume C'est La Vie! carry the idea to people who will never sit at a salon show. Not every business step lasts, but the point is clear: fantasy works if the atelier is simply disciplined.

Lacroix proved that history and theatre can be tools, not costumes, when the making is exact. That's the legacy: exuberance with balance, a city allowed to celebrate and still look sharp.

Opposite: Christian Lacroix returned religious iconography to Paris fashion without irony. He grew up surrounded by Provençal pageants and Catholic processions, so these crosses came from memory, not shock value. Paris understood it instantly – for him, embellishment wasn't simply decoration; it was storytelling.

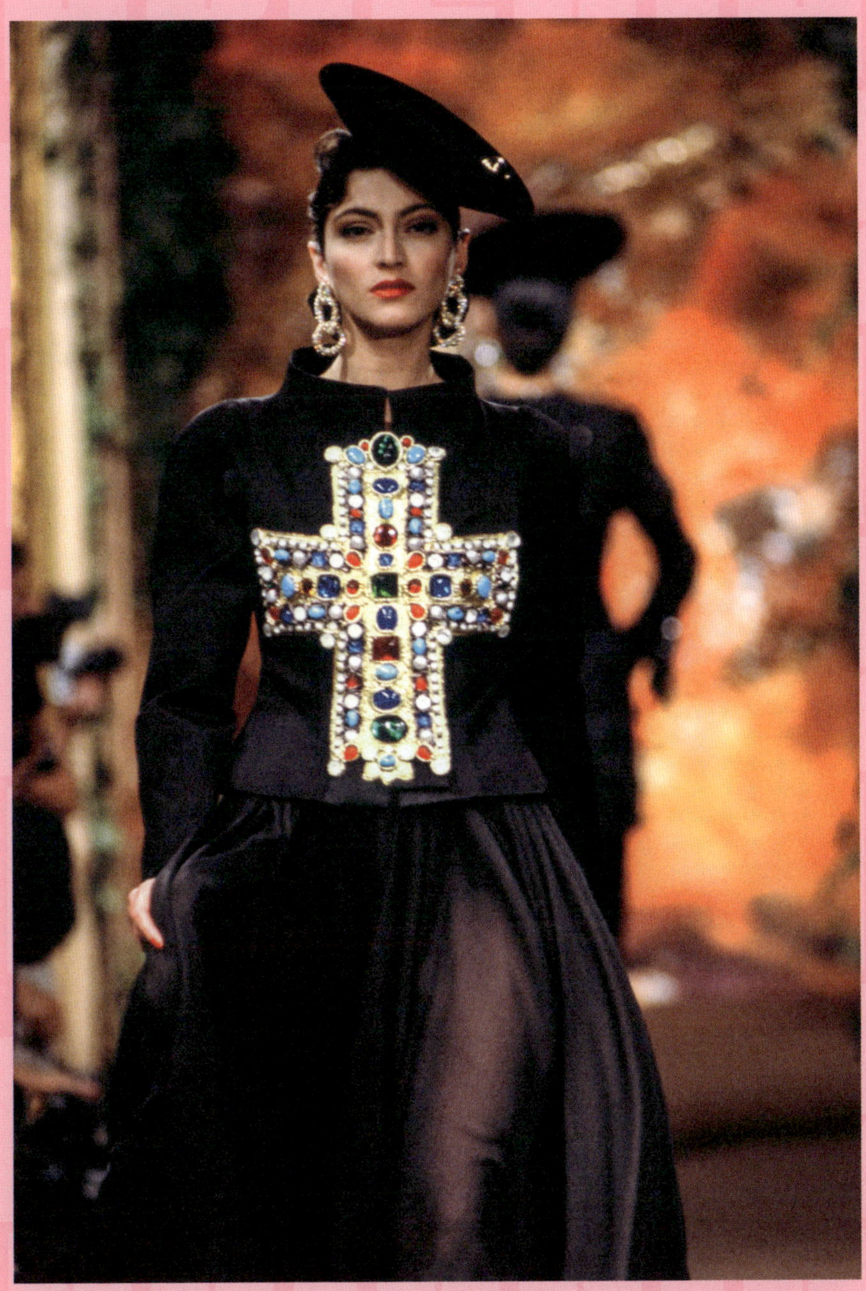

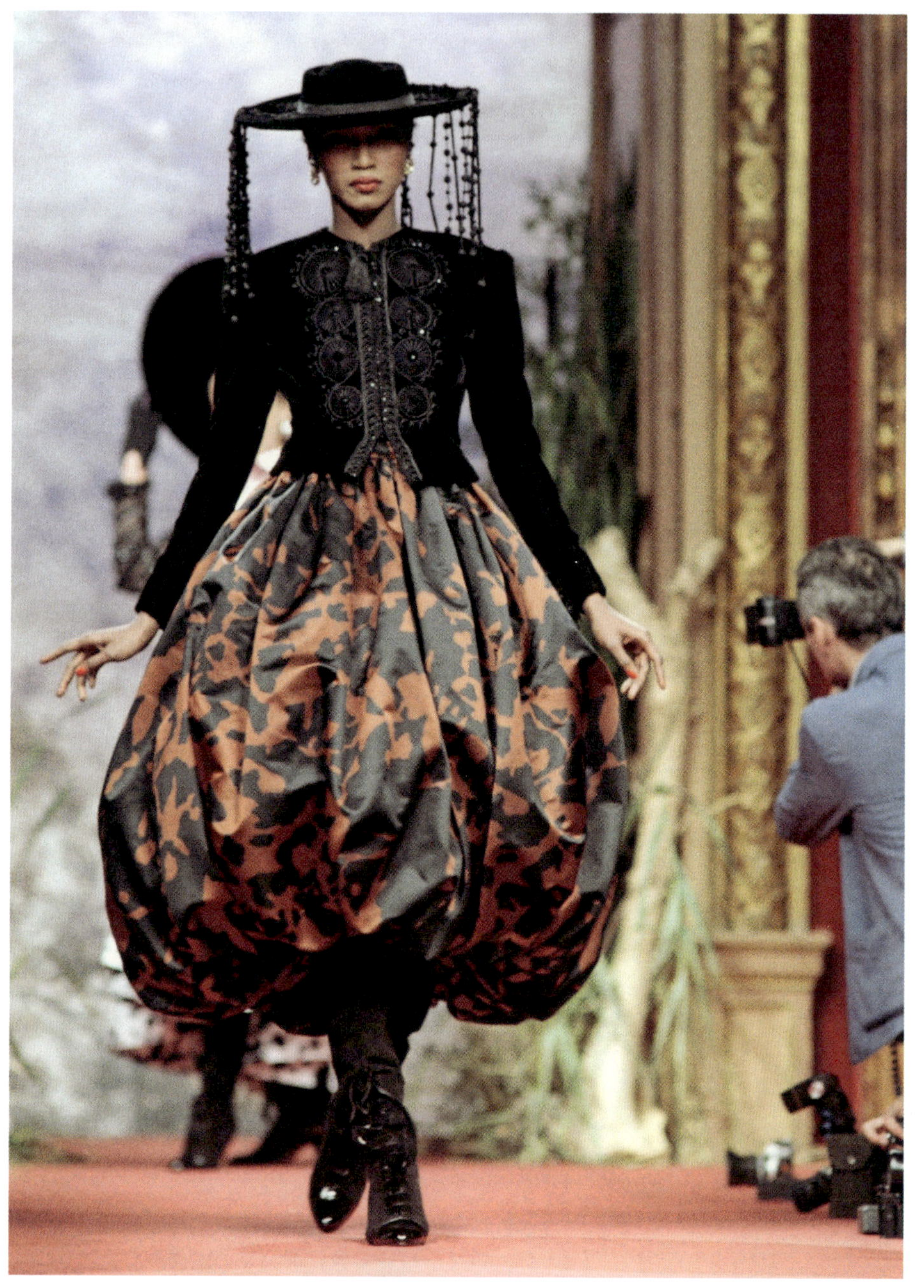

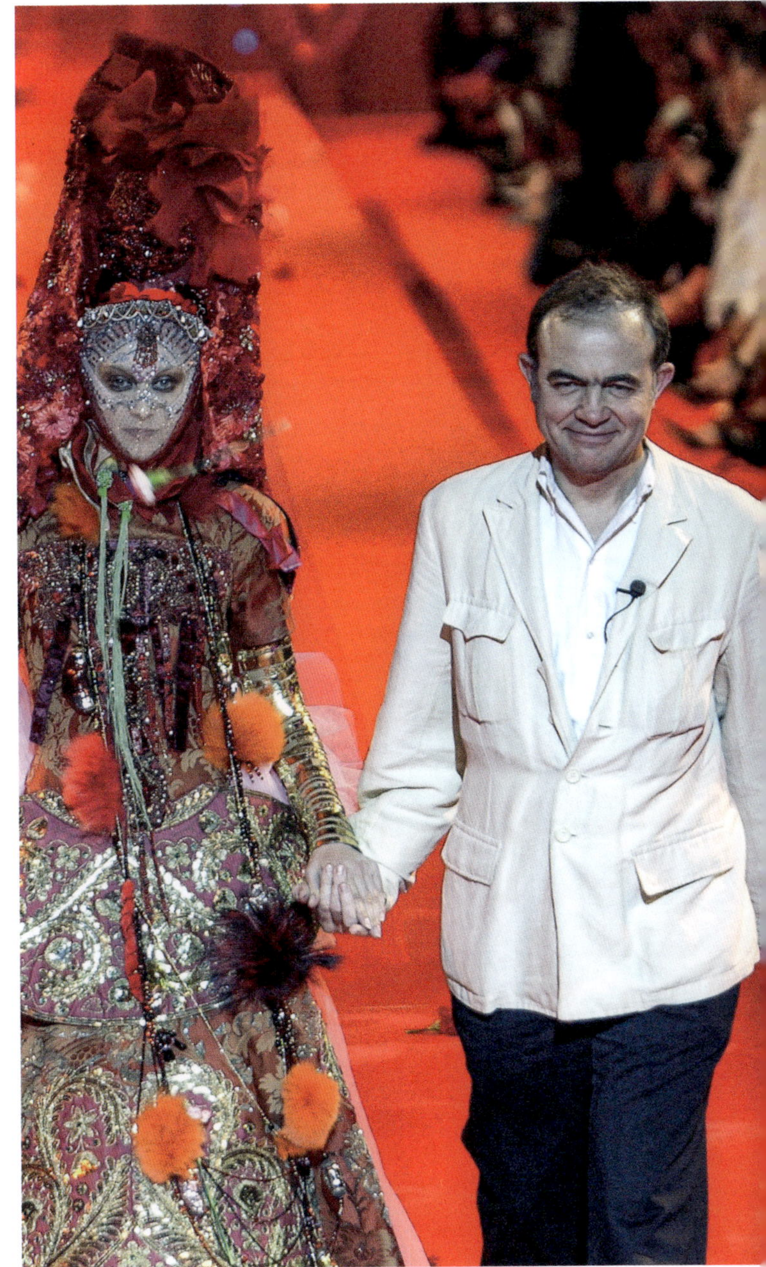

Right: One of the most beautiful and complex Lacroix brides, built like a moving tableau: layers of folklore, theatre and ornament wrapped up into a single exit.

Opposite: Lacroix studied eighteenth-century dress patterns at the Musée des Arts Décoratifs in Paris and reinterpreted them as modern couture engineering. Here, the bubble shape looks playful but is anchored by a strict inner structure – typical Lacroix: joy supported by architecture.

KENZO TAKADA

In the late 1960s, the Japanese designer Kenzo Takada arrived in Paris and opened a small shop called Jungle Jap. By 1970 the Kenzo label had gone live. Paris was still a little stiff, but he definitely opened the windows to a more relaxed look. Prints mixed kindly. Stripes flirted with florals, unheard of until now. His fashion shows felt like a street party, not a ceremony. Models smiled and walked together. He taught Paris that looseness can still read with clean lines.

Kenzo focused on day clothes first because that's where life happens. The cut stays modern and direct, so all the travel in his references never slides into costume or cultural appropriation. You see cities talking to each other in one look: Tokyo, Paris, anywhere really, and somehow it still makes a great deal of sense.

Kenzo turned fashion into community without dropping the standard. He gave Paris a public smile: prints that mixed and matched, layers that kept moving. The legacy is simple and strong: it is clothes that welcome you in, walk all day and look great in daylight.

Opposite: Kenzo Takada often photographed clothes outside the salon because he wanted fashion to breathe with real light on real streets. This approach meant Paris recognized that joy and colour could exist outside the couture salons.

Overleaf: Kenzo (centre) broke the unspoken rule that runway casts should be uniform. His shows mixed faces, energies and body languages, something Paris had not seen before on this scale.

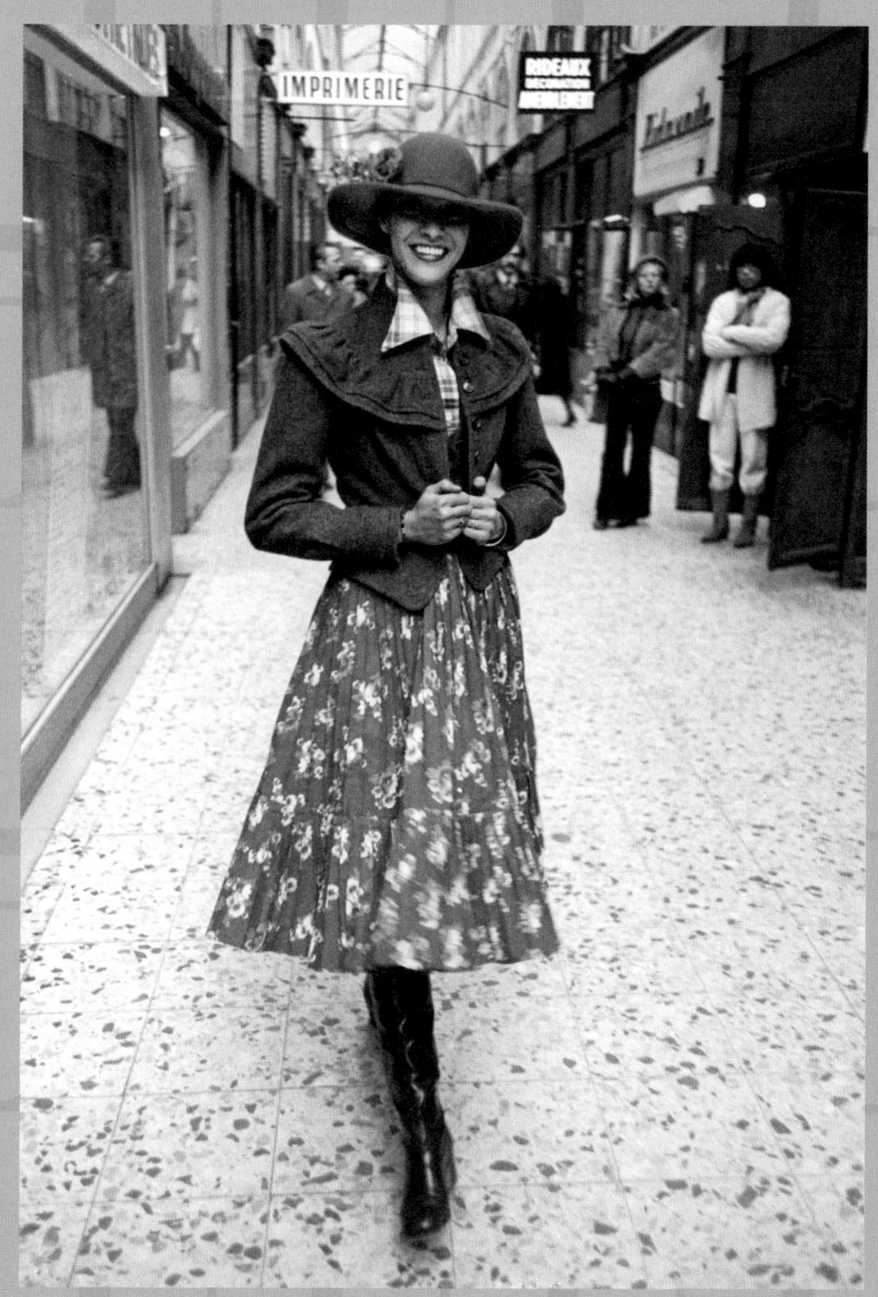
IMPRIMERIE
RIDEAUX
DÉCORATION
AMEUBLEMENT

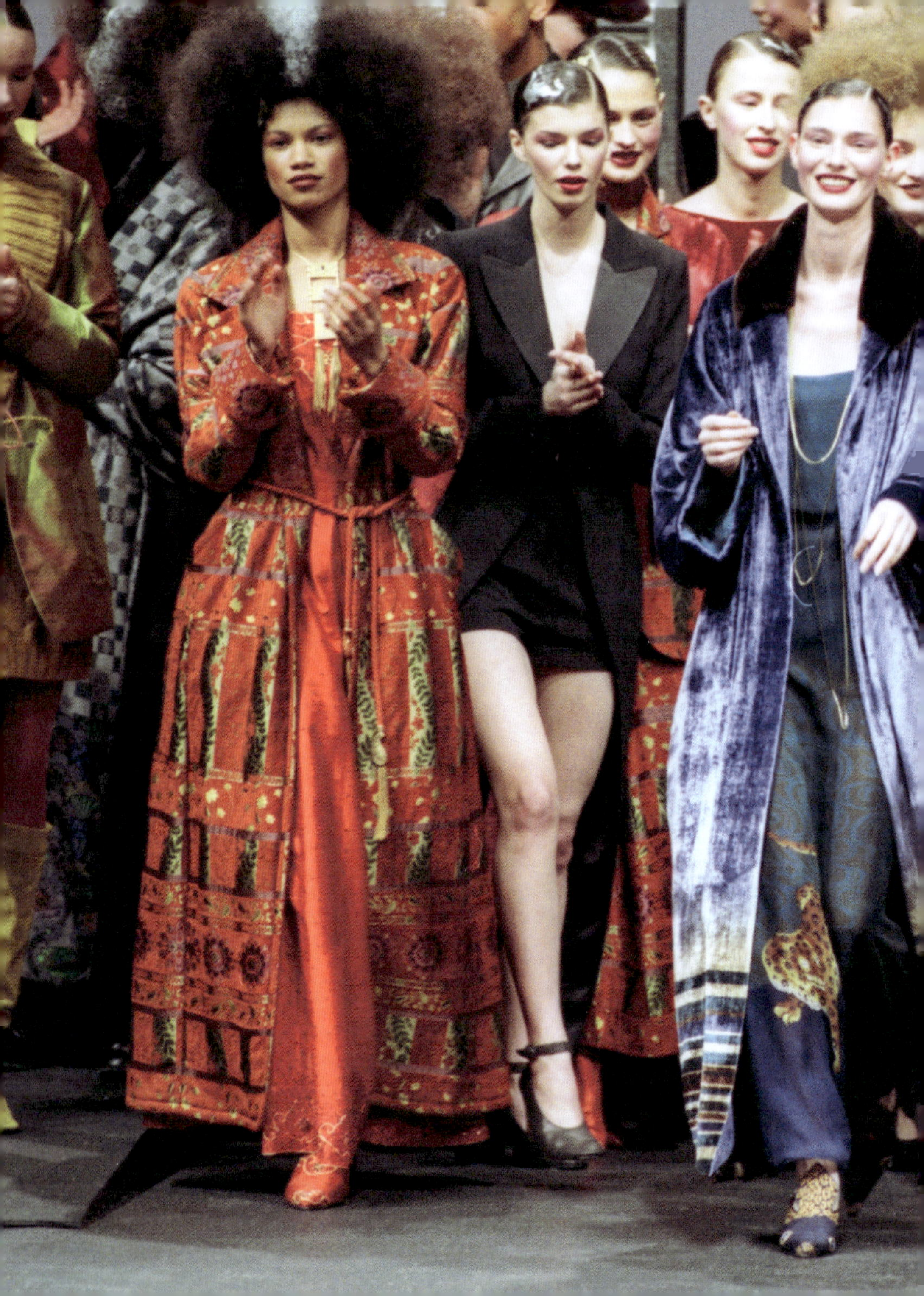

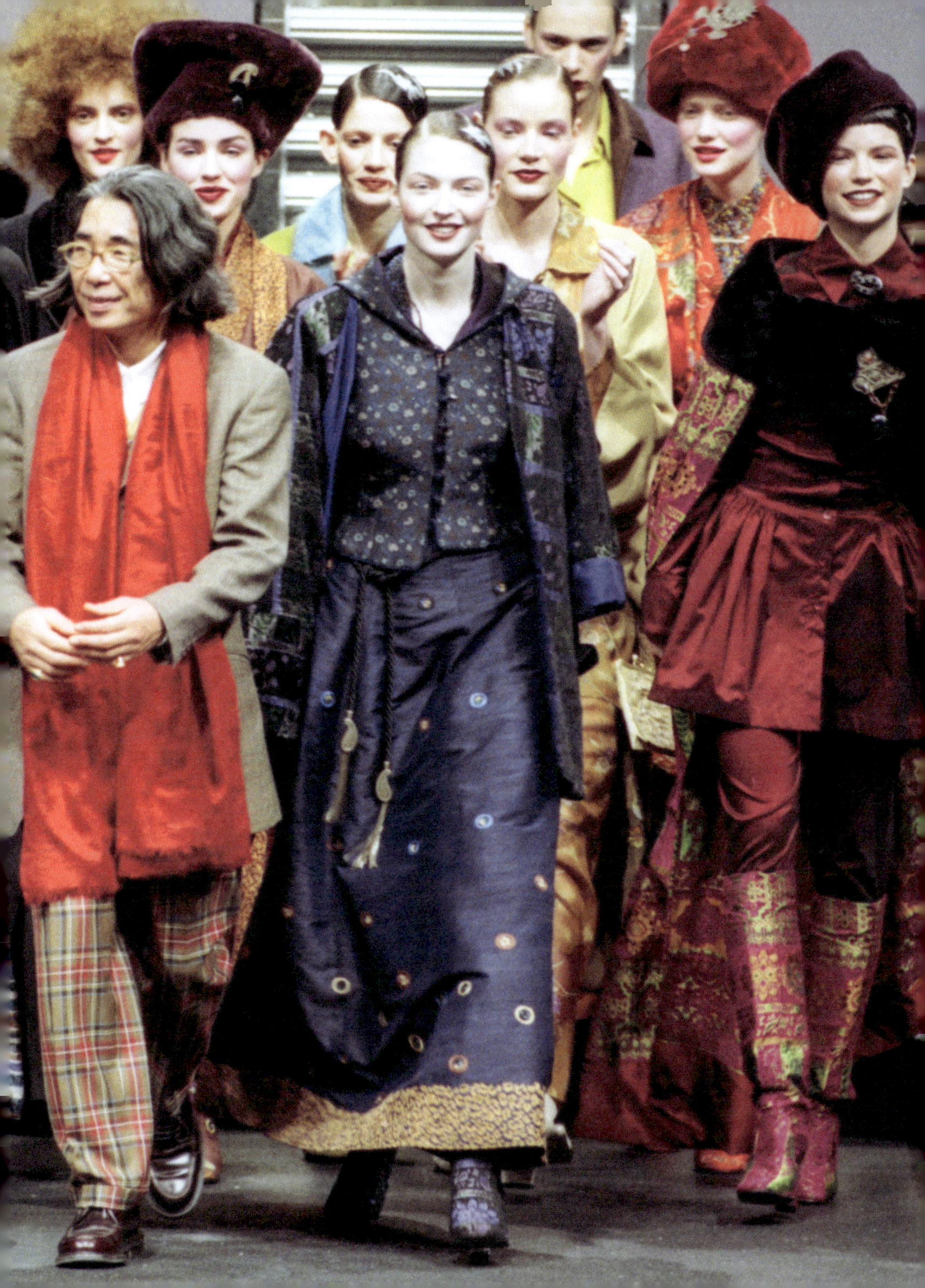

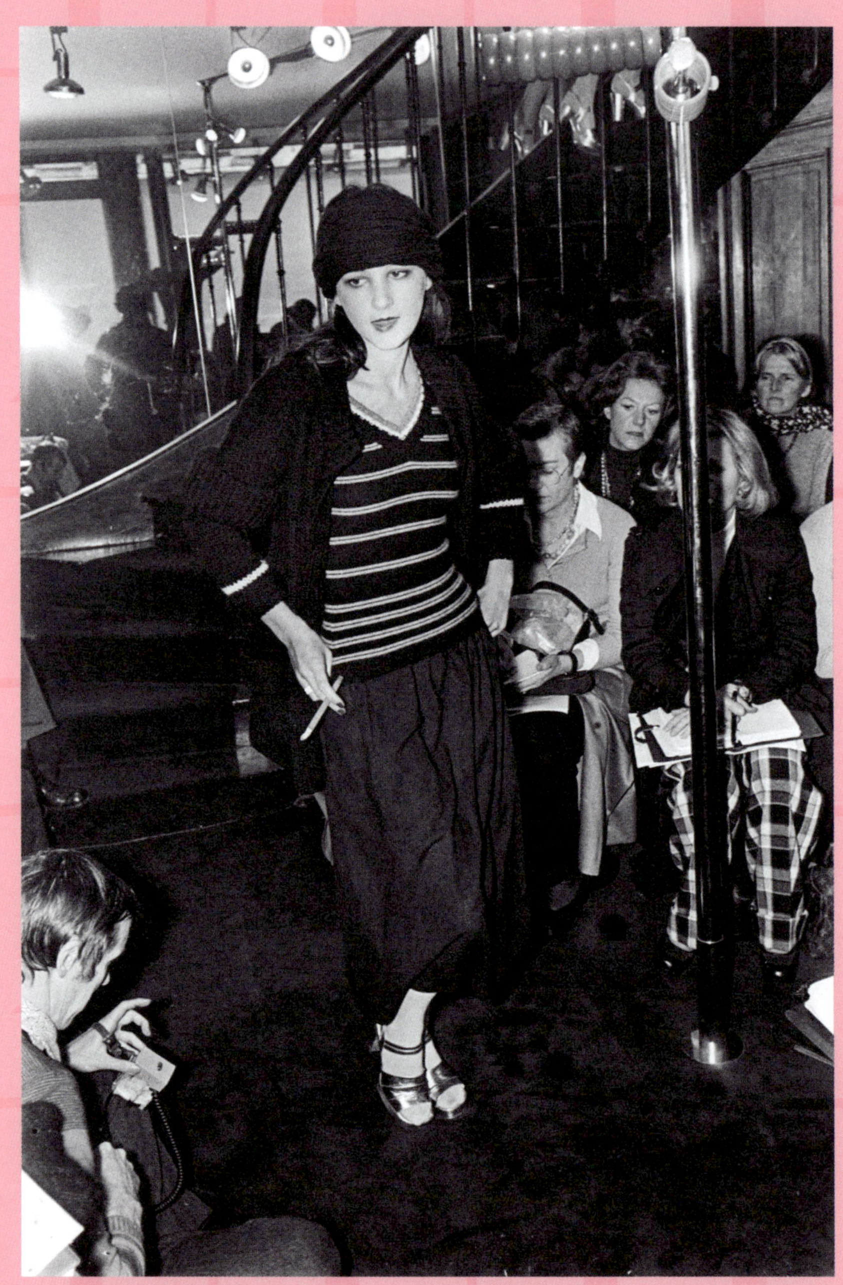

SONIA RYKIEL

Sonia Rykiel's big moment was the 1960s and 1970s, and right from the start, it felt Left Bank. She took knitwear out of the shadows and placed it firmly at the centre of Paris life. A single sweater could take you through the day: desk at noon, drinks at six, last train home. The sensuality is owned by the wearer; everyone else is just catching up. Stripes drift in and out like conversation and the famous "Poor Boy" knit became shorthand for intelligence you can pull on.

Rykiel's shows looked like Saint-Germain itself (bookshop energy, friends, laughter), so nothing really needed translation. Paris warmed to the idea: daywear could be soft and sharp at once. Boutiques started stacking sweaters as in a library; women built a wardrobe they could rotate without changing their voice. That's the legacy: ease with backbone, a city that learned that you can say a lot – quietly – in knit.

Opposite: The Sonia Rykiel story begins in the early sixties when she designed a dress for herself because nothing in the shops felt right. She put it out into the world and it moved fast – Audrey Hepburn famously bought 14 of these dresses in one visit to the salon. Paris recognized the signal: a new kind of sensual, intelligent ease had arrived.

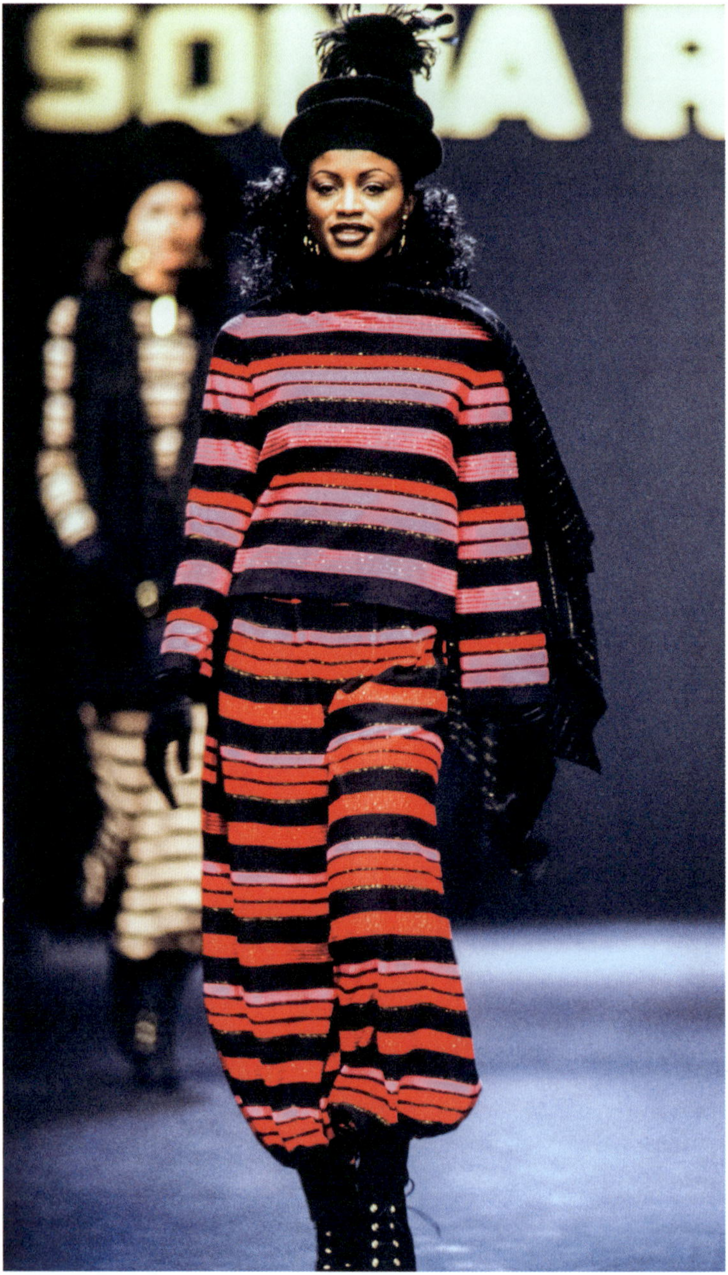

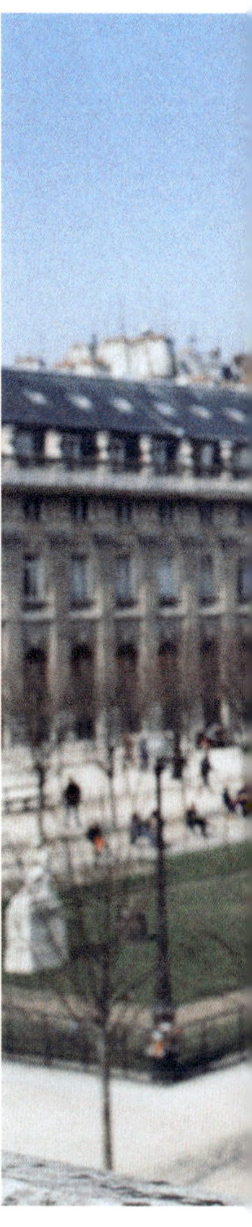

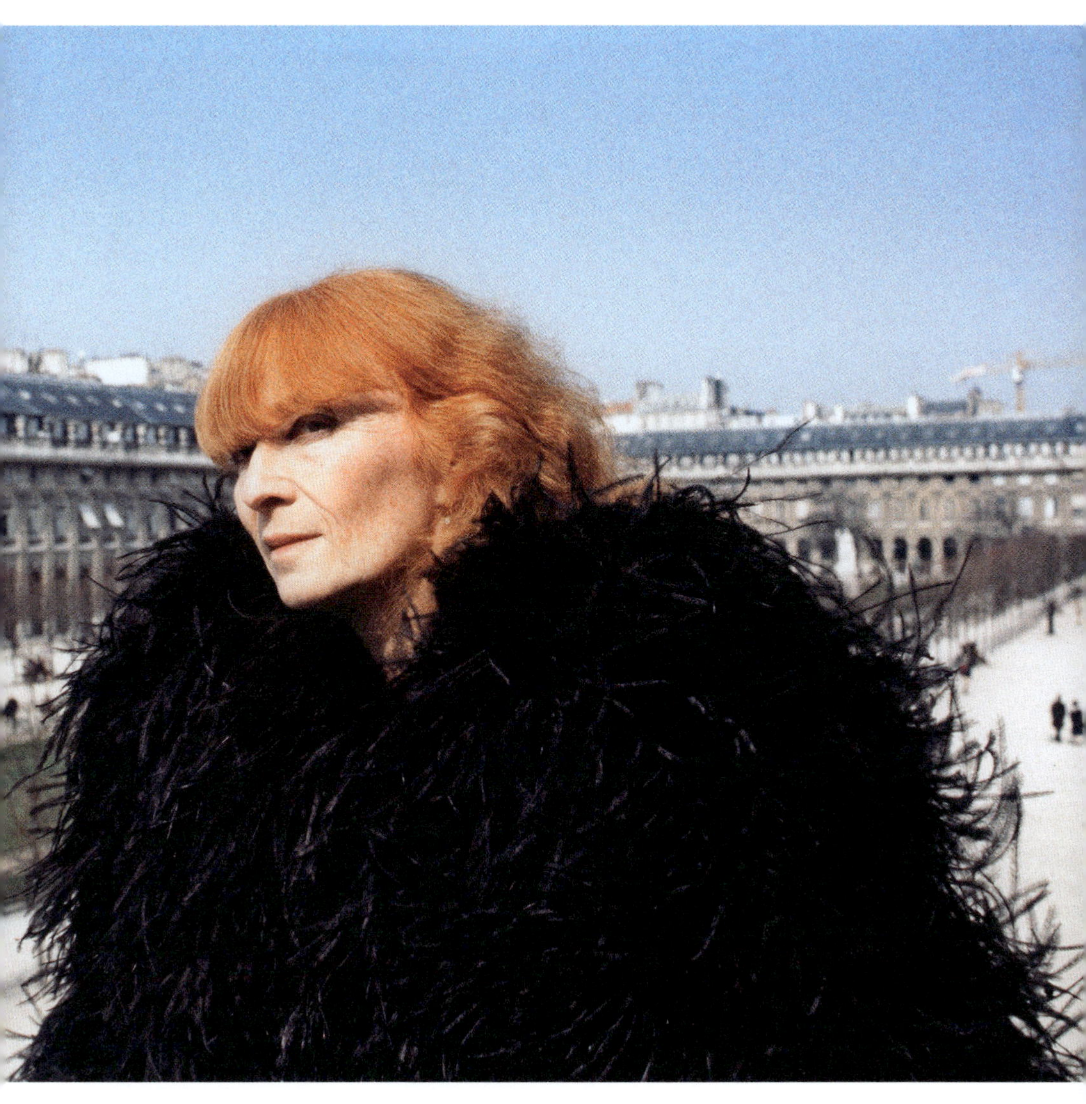

Opposite: Sonia Rykiel's stripes soon became a signature. In her hands they represented character and attitude, a way for clothes to speak before the wearer did themselves.

Above: Fashion designer Sonia Rykiel poses at the Palais Royal garden in Paris, 1984.

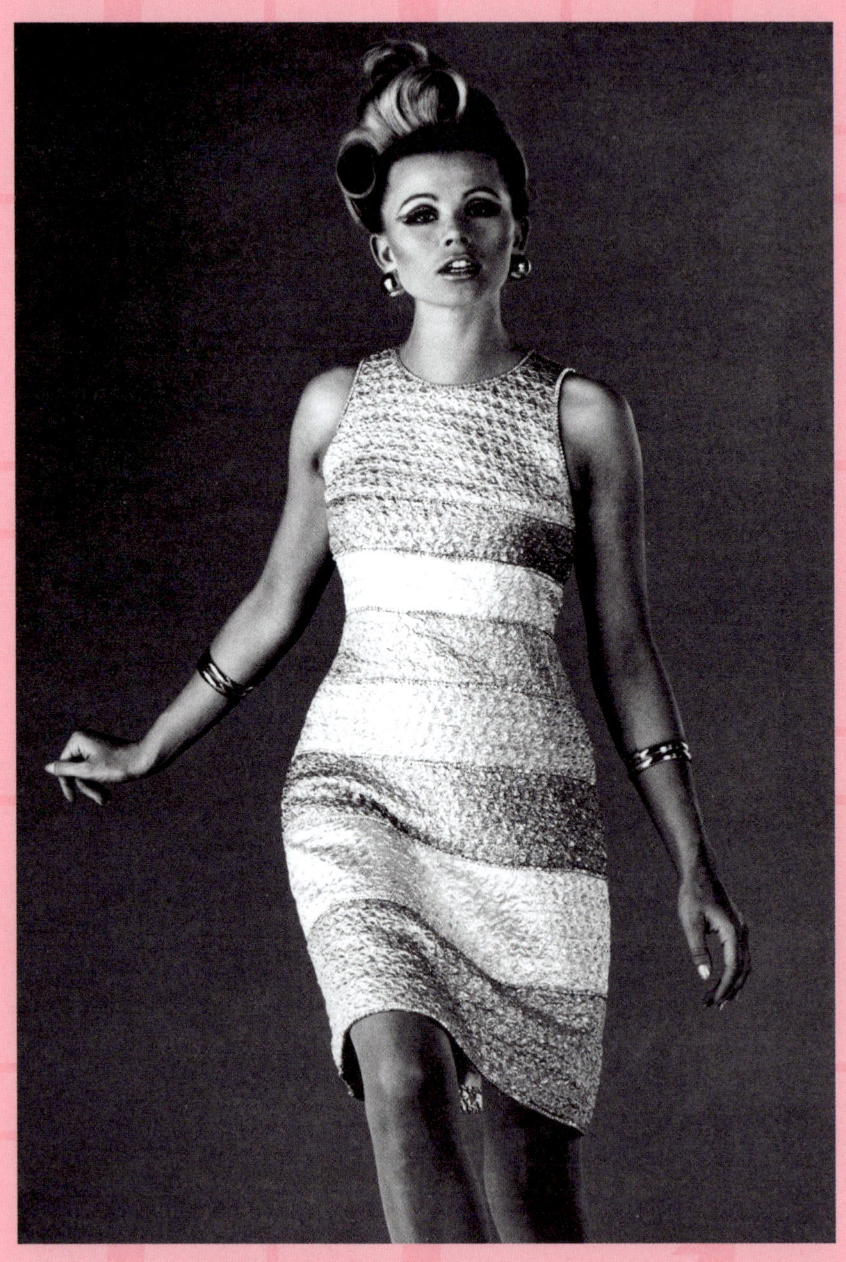

GABY AGHION (CHLOÉ)

Gaby Aghion defined the 1950s and 1960s in Paris by giving ready-to-wear a mind of its own. She didn't copy couture; she asked for clothes that felt like good decisions at nine in the morning but also at nine at night. Silk that moves, sleeves that don't fight, waists that let you breathe – and all of it sold in sizes so you could walk out in it today.

Aghion built the House of Chloé as both school and stage: new designers learned the handwriting, the identity stayed steady, the mood was romance with brains. Day dresses carried meetings, galleries, dinners and never turned costume. Paris got the message that prêt-à-porter could be culture, not consolation. Behind the scenes, she tightened the rhythm – reliable deliveries, clear drops – so shops could plan and women could rely on what they love. The result travelled: the Left Bank's ease became respectable on any street and the city treated daylight dressing with the same attention it once reserved for evening. That's Aghion's impact – a template for modern femininity that is light, intelligent and ready when you need it; a label that teaches Paris to take ease seriously because it's made seriously.

Opposite: Fun fact – early Chloé was shaped by Aghion's own wardrobe, dresses she wished existed for her functions. Also, many of these early fittings took place in friends' apartments.

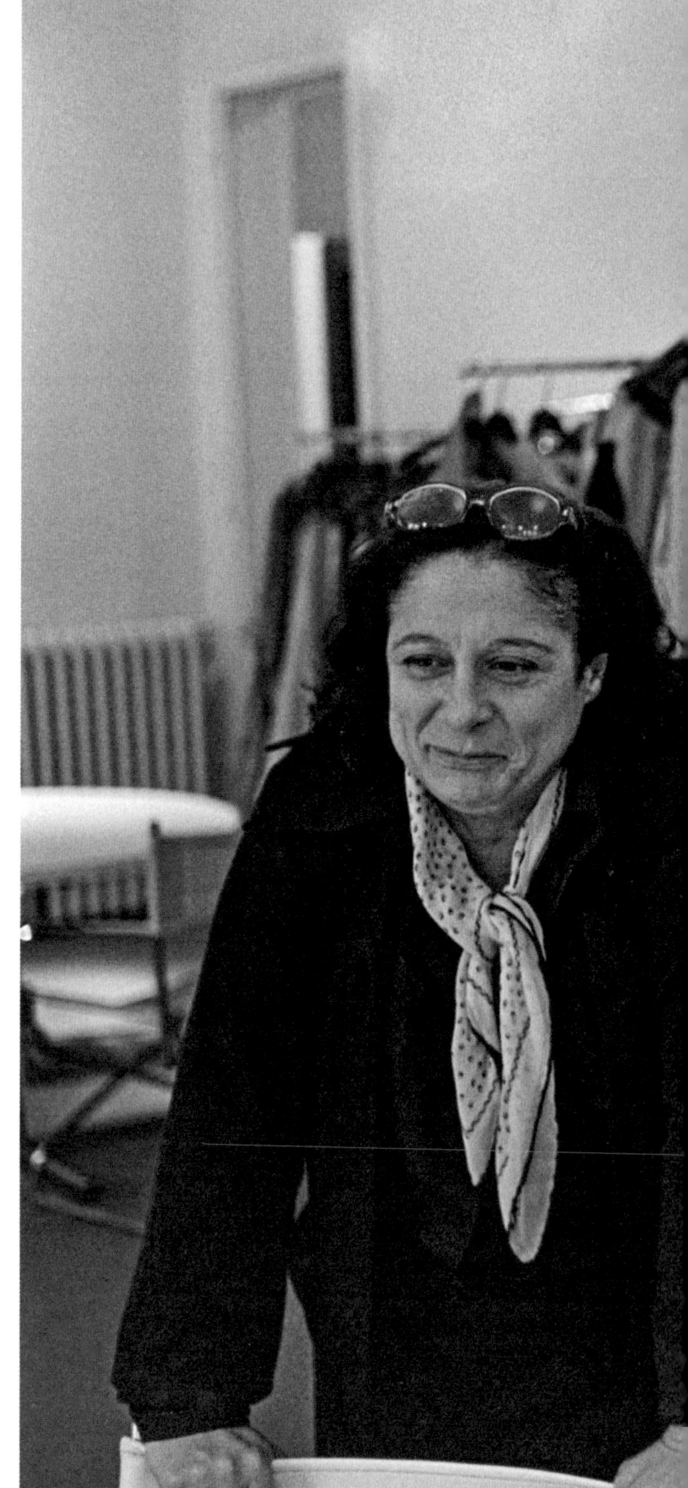

Right: Gaby Aghion with a young Karl Lagerfeld inside the Chloé studio. She trusted the designer early, giving him space to experiment with the lightness that became the house's signature. Their partnership shaped the Chloé attitude: intellect without stiffness, charm without decoration.

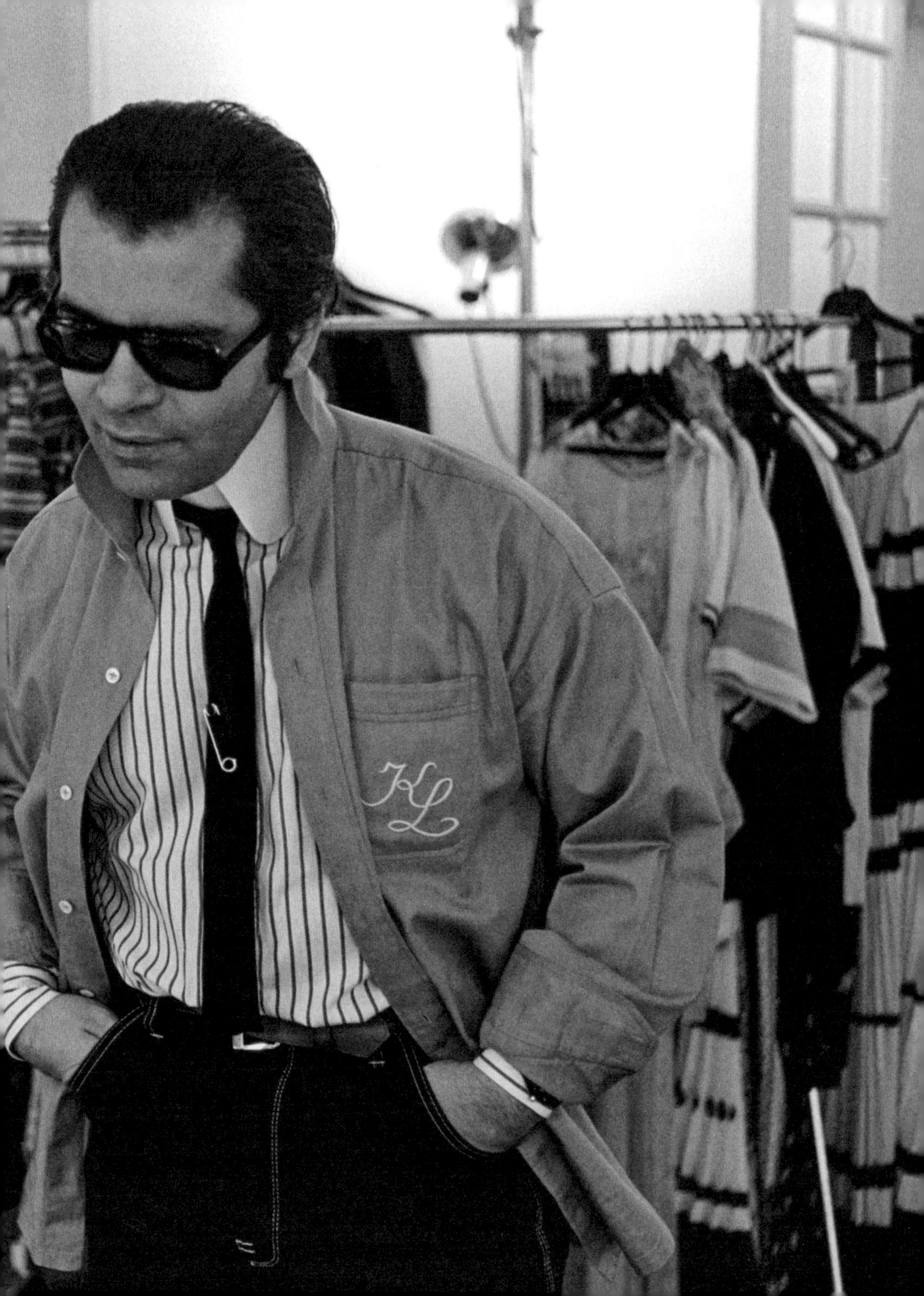
KL

CHAPTER 2:

LES ENFANTS TERRIBLES

Night energy stepped into day and refused to leave. Some designers turned the body into an engine; others stripped away shape to show meaning; a few rebuilt glamour from the ground upwards. The shocks lasted because the tailoring held. Deconstruction came with manners, romance with engineering, humour with pattern cutting. All of them used friction to teach Paris a new point of view.

THIERRY MUGLER

Thierry Mugler turned Paris into an event. A former ballet dancer from Strasbourg, he brought that stage thinking into his clothes: widened shoulders, clamped waists, hips like wings and seams cut as strictly as a uniform. His shows became the city's nights out – Cirque d'Hiver, Zénith, supermodels, lights, live acts – and yet the jackets snap shut and the corsetry never budges. He designs a walk, a camera angle, a posture. In 1992 he launched an iconic scent called Angel that helped invent the modern gourmand perfume (sweet, edible notes) and proved that a fashion mood can live in a bottle and circle the globe. The same year he directed George Michael's "Too Funky" video: Mugler costumes, Mugler attitude, broadcast literally everywhere. He treated pop culture as a runway extension and Paris learned to claim that territory with him.

Mugler kept crossing worlds without losing his line: opera and theatre costumes; later, Cirque du Soleil; years after his runway peak he was still shaping images (think Beyoncé's tour looks or the "wet" latex dress moment that re-lit his name for a new audience). The point isn't nostalgia; it's range backed by engineering. Even the most outrageous pieces, insect carapaces, motorcycle bustiers and chrome trims sit on disciplined tailoring. Therefore, the spectacle ages into iconography instead of costume. If you ask me, that's pure fashion genius!

Thierry Mugler's impact on Paris was to prove the city can host stadium-scale fantasy built with couture precision. He expanded what a fashion house can do: runway, film, perfume, performance, while keeping fit was a non-negotiable.

Opposite: Model walking for Thierry Mugler in a couture leather jacket, Paris, 1988.

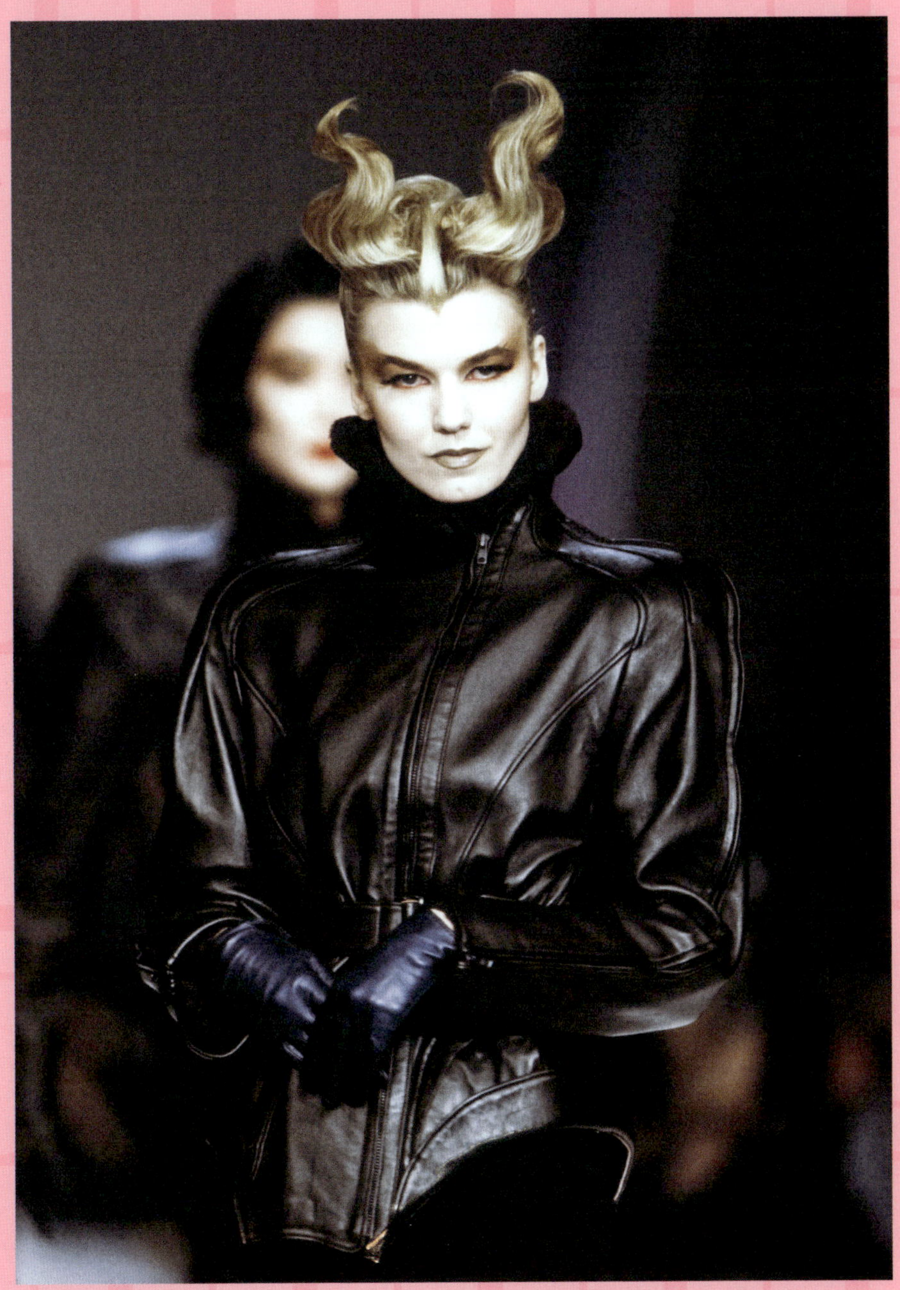

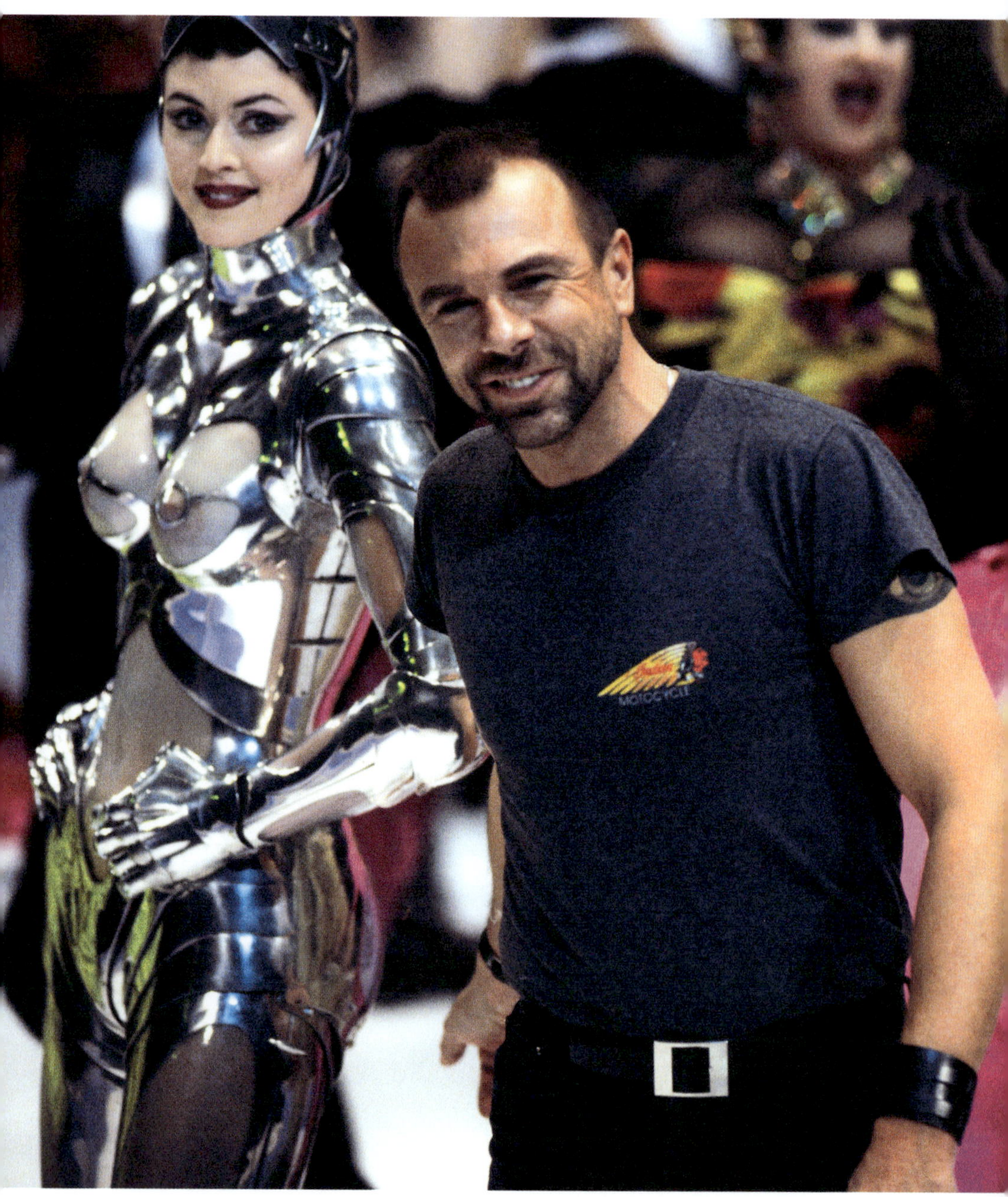

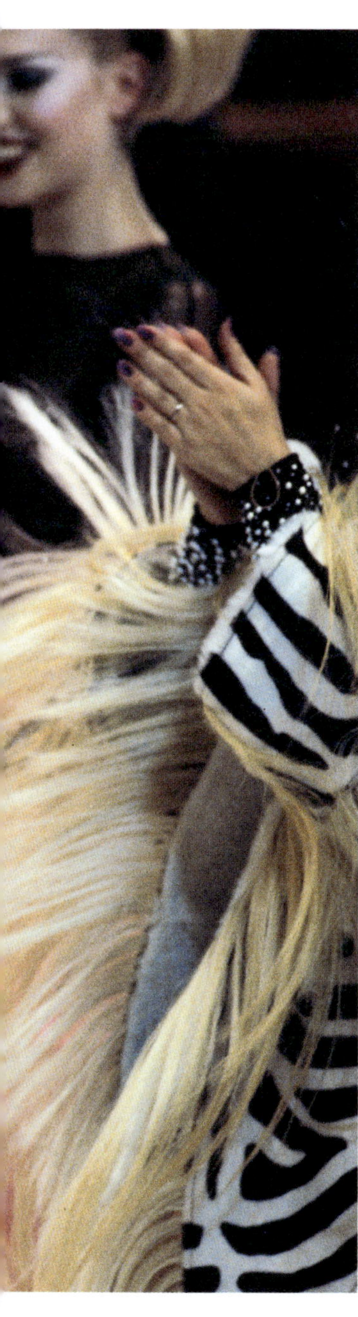

Left: This photograph is from Thierry Mugler's 20th anniversary show in 1995, the moment he unveiled the chrome armour that became one of the most recognizable looks in fashion history.

JEAN PAUL GAULTIER

Jean Paul Gaultier grew up glued to Paris couture magazines and slipped sketches to Pierre Cardin before he was 20. By 1976 he was showing under his own name and instead of repeating haute ideals, he flipped them. In 1984 he sent men in skirts down the runway. Then in 1990, Madonna's Blond Ambition Tour turned that iconic conical bra into global shorthand. He designed costumes for *The Fifth Element* (1997) and for music videos, blending pop culture and couture so tightly, they felt like one ecosystem.

Gaultier treats casting as part of the design. He chooses models of different ages, bodies, genders and backgrounds, so the runway itself makes the statement, not just the clothes. His shows look like the city: drag queens, street kids, celebrities, couture clients, older women, different races, a crowd, not a club. He borrows from sailor bars, banlieues, North African tailoring, punk, then cuts it like a suit. It reads theatrically and yet human at once because the craft is strict and the humour is real. Perfumes like Classique and Le Male carry the brand to millions, while the shows keep the courage alive.

Gaultier's impact on Paris was to open the door without lowering the standard. He proves that inclusivity can be chic, wit can live with high craft, and gender can be played with rather than policed. In taking street codes to couture and couture codes to the street, he rewrites how the capital sees itself. Decades on, designers still study his casting, his silhouette and his attitude. The legacy is not just a cone bra or a striped shirt; it is a city that finally mirrors its own streets with joy and precision, and there's nothing more beautiful than that.

Opposite: An early iteration of Jean Paul Gaultier's iconic cone work (before Madonna turned it global). He was already testing how far he could bend historical underpinnings into humour, and the audience understood they were watching a new fashion wave forming in real time.

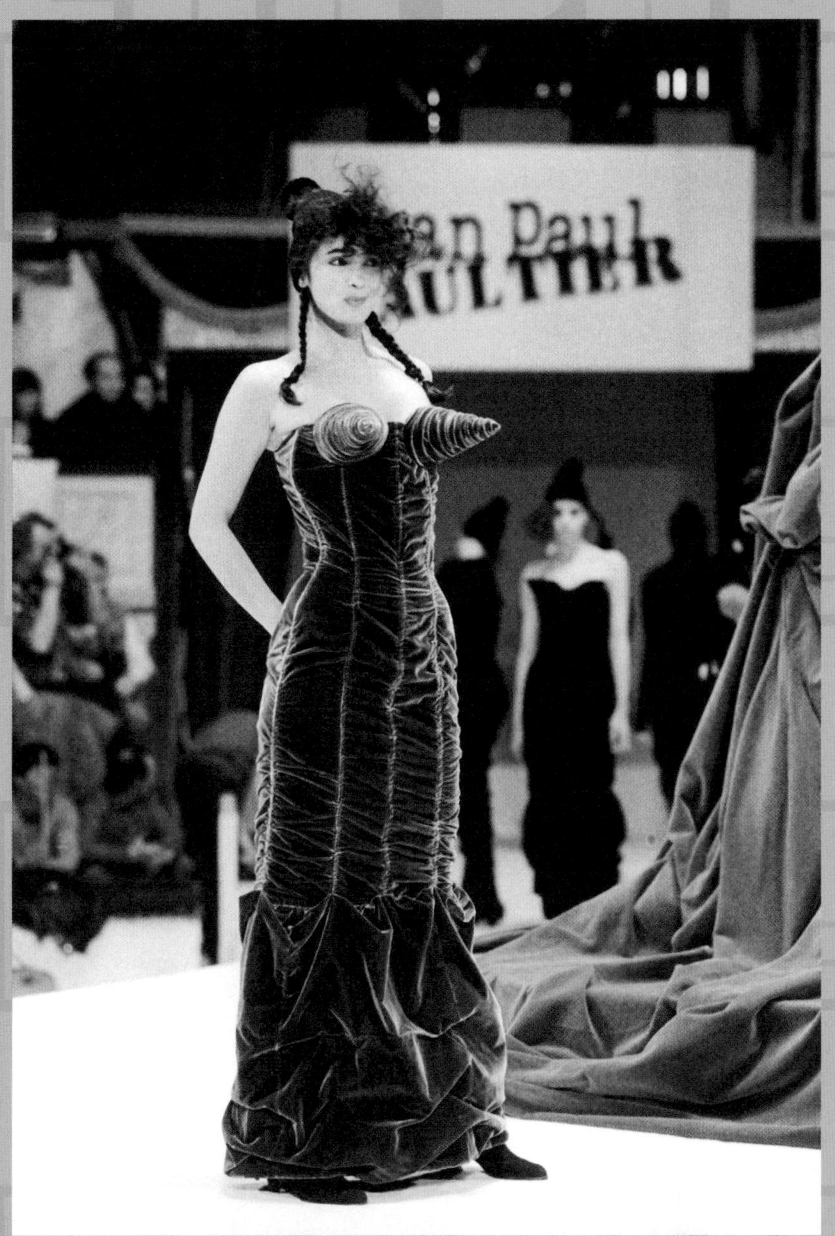
an Paul
AULTIER

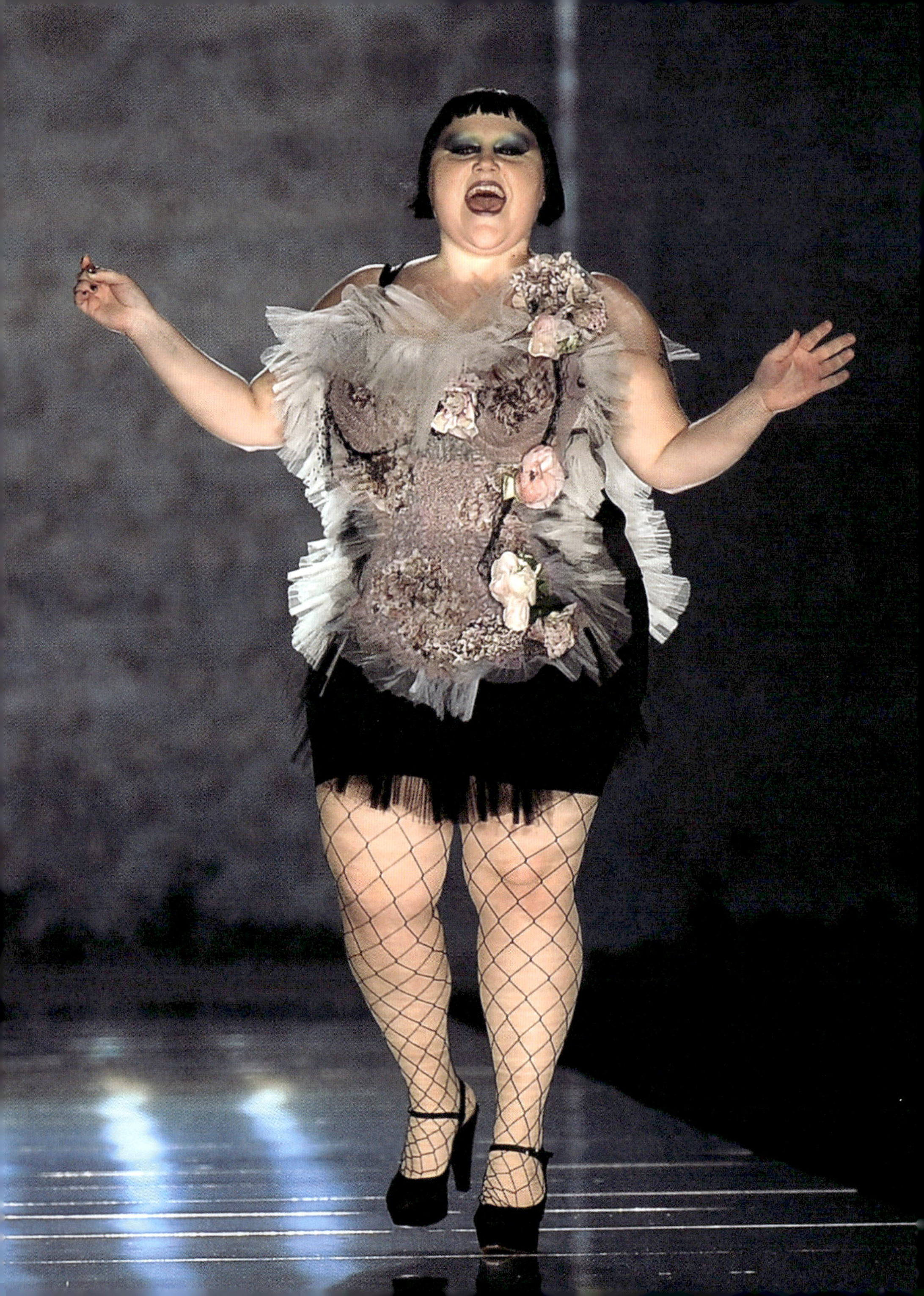

Opposite: This moment from Gaultier's Spring/ Summer 2011 show, with Beth Ditto on the runway, shows how naturally he folded real personalities into his collections long before inclusivity became an industry script.

Right: It's no secret that JPG brought club into couture. The designer has been hugely inspired by nightlife in his designs and brand identity.

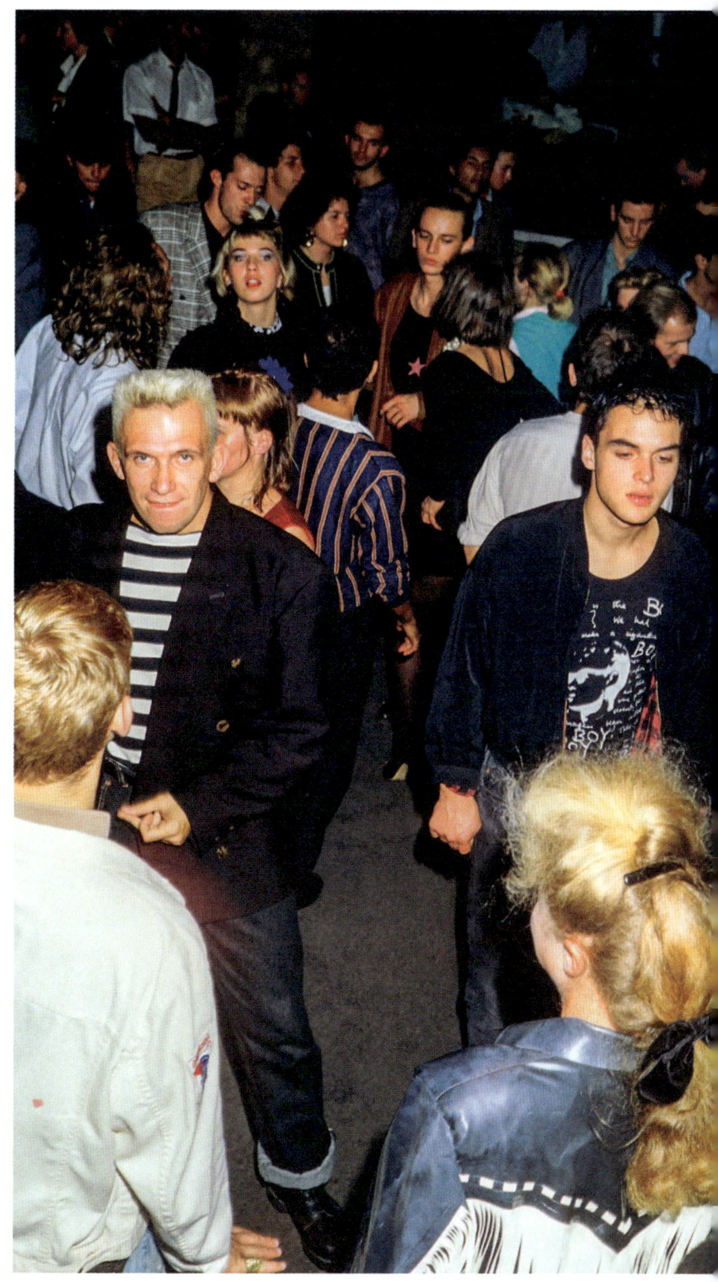

REI KAWAKUBO

Rei Kawakubo landed in Paris from Japan in 1981 and the room went quiet: black, holes, asymmetry, volume where volume "shouldn't" be. Early reviews describe this as "Hiroshima chic". Buyers who try the garments on feel a new freedom: no waist, no fixed centre, movement created by subtraction. She returns season after season, builds a Paris base and a cult form really: students tracing patterns at night, editors rethinking their vocabulary. Les enfants terribles love it.

Kawakubo redesigns the frame around the product as well. Stores look like laboratories, with plywood, strange lighting and no clear hierarchy. Her shows strip away fuss. Pattern cutting reads like a thesis: sleeves shifted off, jackets rising like tents or falling like cloaks. This is not only anti-fashion; it is a new discipline where absence is design and tension can be beautiful.

Comme des Garçons is not only a label. Its mom, Kawakubo, builds it into an empire of sub-brands, concept stores and magazines. In London, she opens Dover Street Market, a retail model that feels like an exhibition as much as a shop, and gives platforms to designers like Junya Watanabe, who flourish under her gaze. What begins as a radical collection in Paris becomes a whole ecosystem where design, business and culture work together.

Kawakubo's impact on Paris was to widen what the city can call luxury. She proved you can charge couture prices for intellectual risk when the garment stands up to wear. Gender, size, finish all become variables. Buyers recalibrate sizing, stylists learn to build looks from volume outwards and young designers pin straight to the form before they draw. Rei Kawakubo's legacy is not just a silhouette but a system: subtraction, nerve, structure and an empire that keeps multiplying the question of what fashion can be.

Opposite: Rei Kawakubo, the mother of avant-garde.

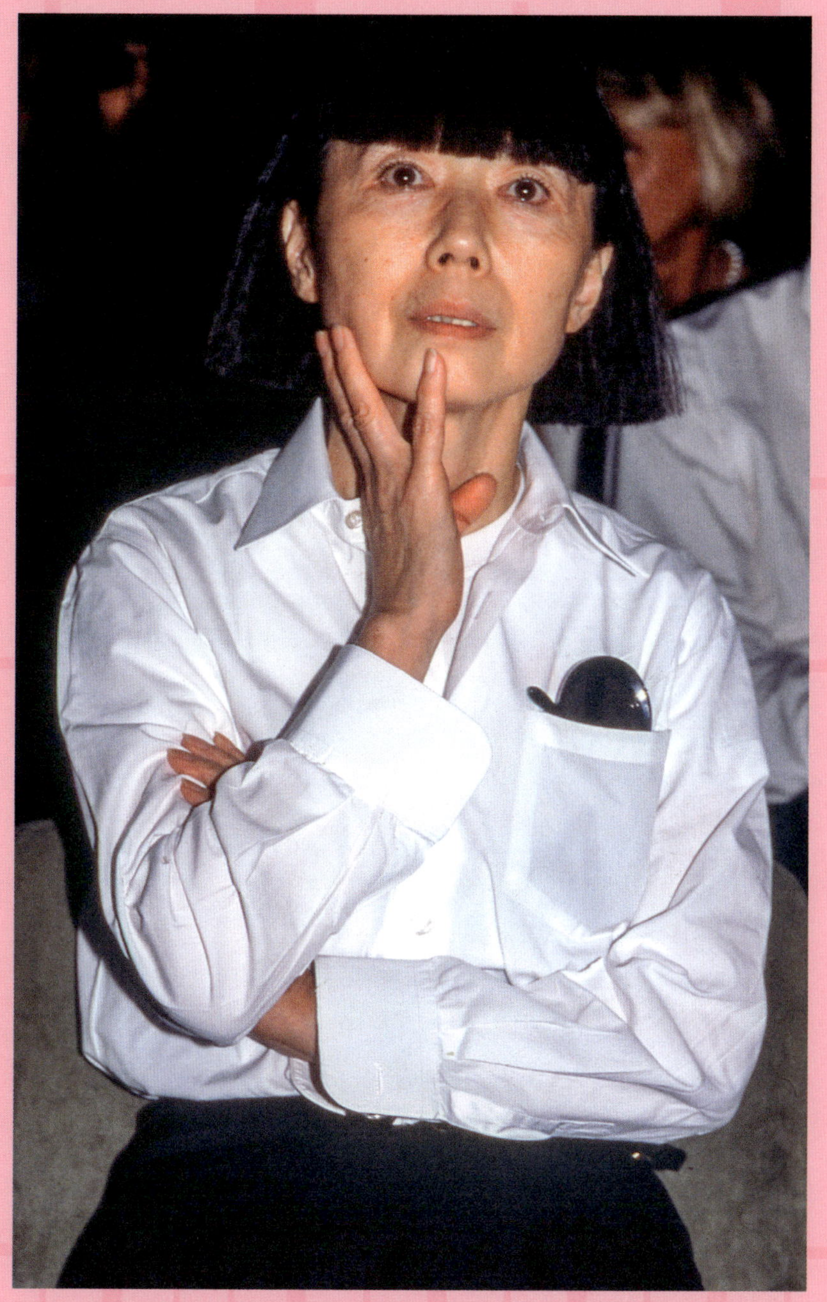

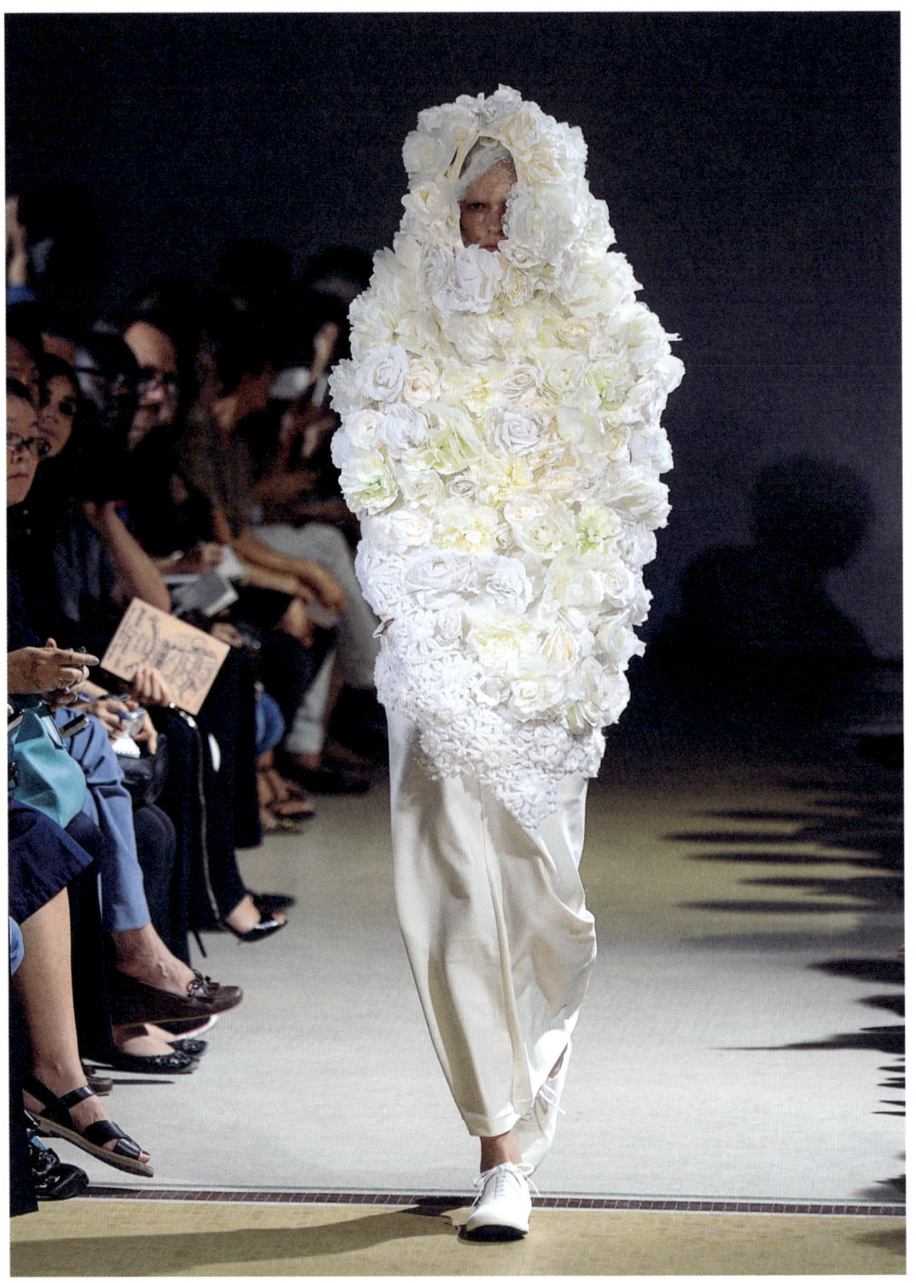

Opposite: From Comme des Garçons' Spring 2012 collection, this silhouette shows Rei Kawakubo's refusal to treat the body as a fixed outline; the roses turn into armour, a soft barricade that rewrites the rules of proportion entirely.

Right: From the 1997 "Lumps and Bumps" collection, this look shows Kawakubo challenging the most sacred rule of fashion – that clothes should flatter the body; instead, here the body submits to the garment.

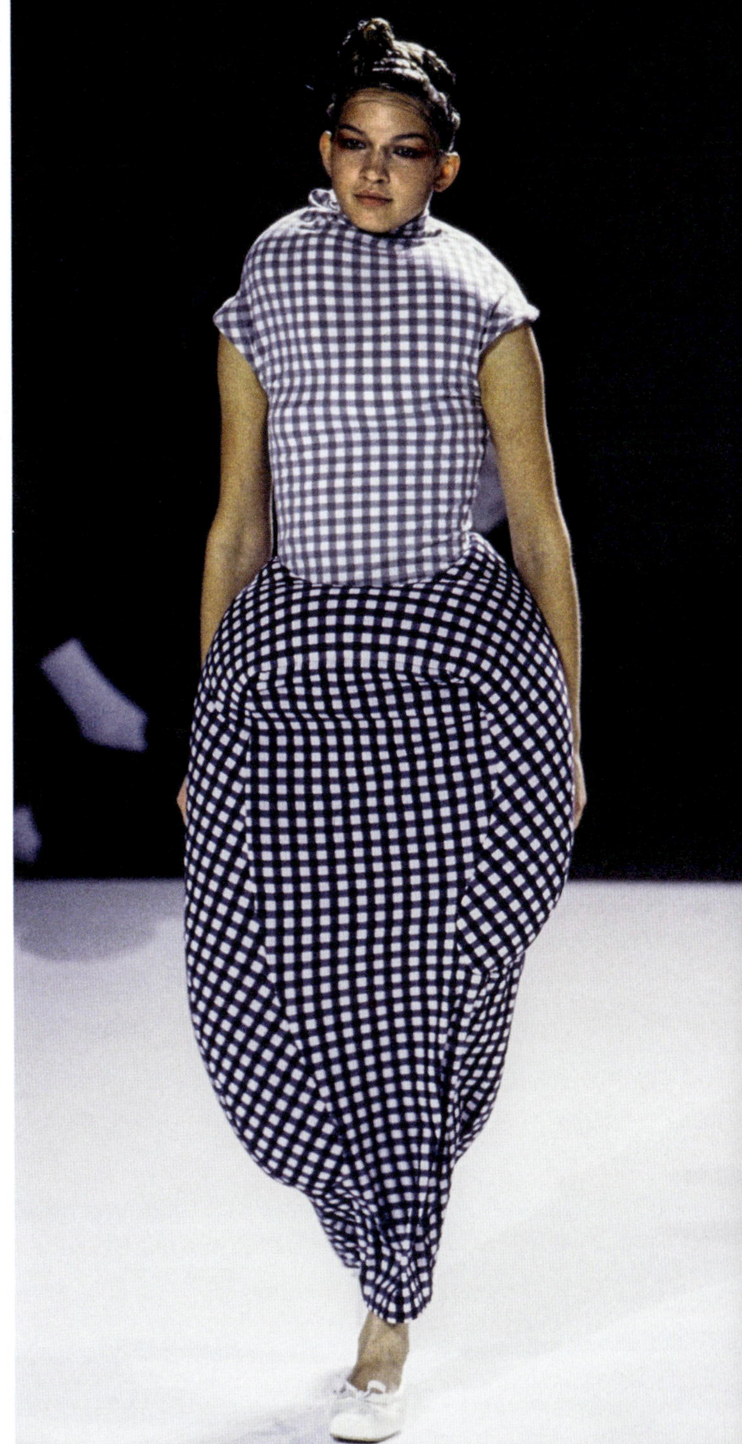

YOHJI YAMAMOTO

Yohji Yamamoto arrived in Paris in 1981 with a different tempo: long coats, deep black, soft shoulders, slow movement. Where the city expects a waist, he lets it go. Where others chase surfaces, he works in the shadows. From across the room the clothes look relaxed; up close, they are exact. You walk, you sit, you turn, and the silhouette stays. Through the 1980s and 1990s his shows played like quiet theatrical exhibitions: flat shoes, loose hair, minimal music. Layers hide and reveal. Trousers skim rather than grip. Men and women's garments are cut with the same hand, so the armour falls away on both. Critics call it poetic. The ateliers know it is hard geometry in soft cloth. Wim Wenders' documentary with Yohji, *Notebook on Cities and Clothes* (1989), captures the mood: thought in motion, cut into shadow. It is a must-watch if you're into anti-fashion.

Yamamoto's path in Paris is entwined with Rei Kawakubo's. They arrived in the same year, were close in life for a time and kept a long, thoughtful dialogue between their studios. He speaks in drift and softness; she answers with tension and subtraction. The press often treat them as a pair, but they guard separate identities. This pairing works because the contrast is clear: her clothes question the body's map, while his give it room to breathe. Each sharpens the other's argument and the city learns to read both languages. They're just two complementary parts of the same movement.

Yohji Yamamoto's impact on Paris is to slow the eye and sharpen judgement. He proves that oversized can be precise, monochrome can be luminous, and drape can be a test of mastery.

Opposite: Yohji Yamamoto treats clothing as moving architecture: quiet, sculptural and built to give the body mystery rather than definition.

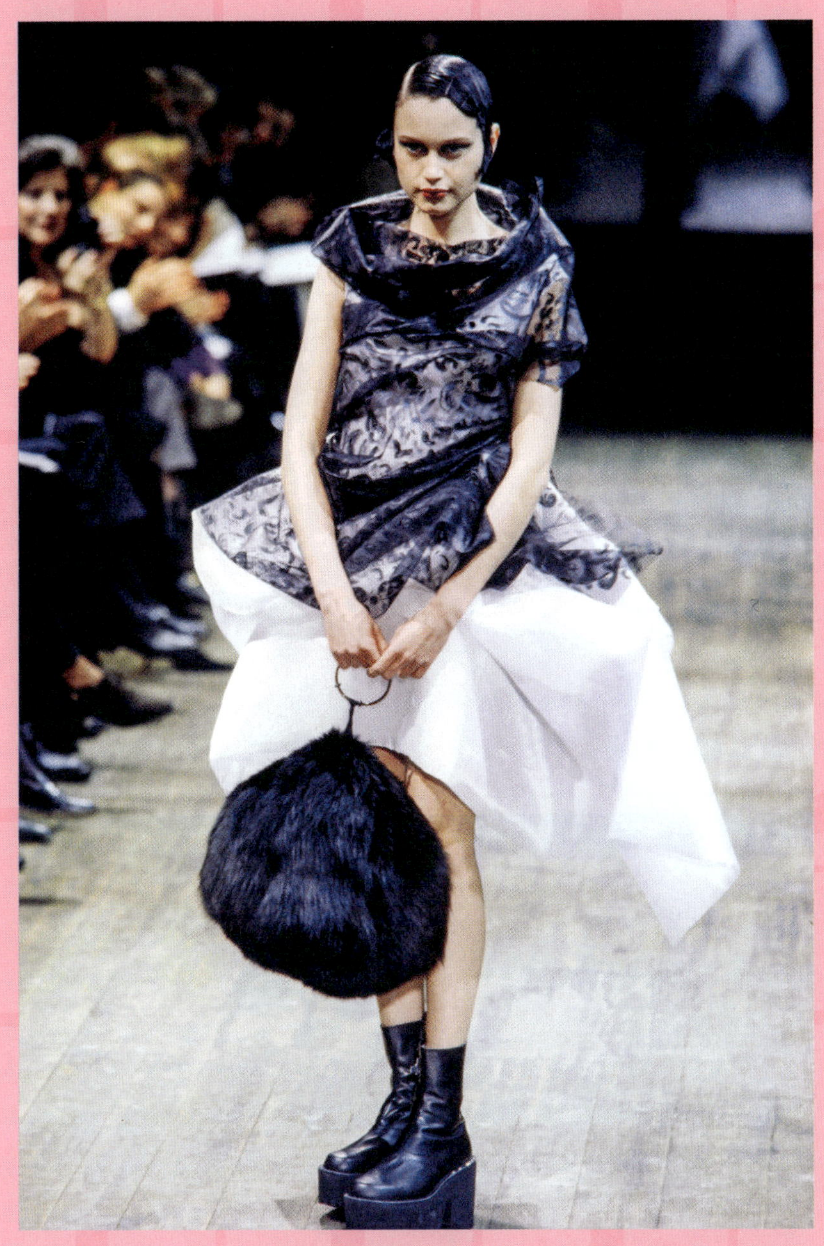

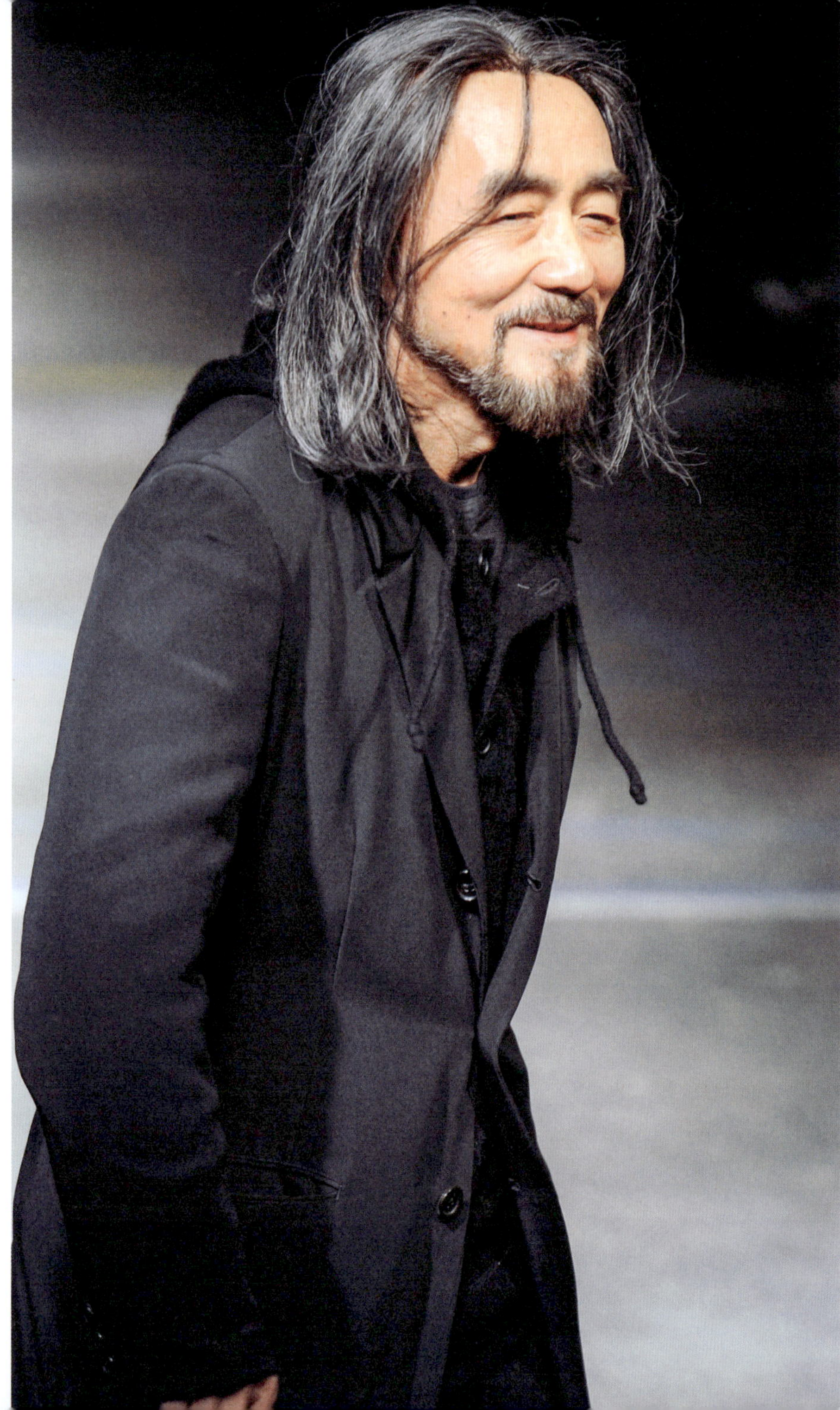

Editors and buyers start reading pattern-making in three dimensions. Students and stylists adopt the black uniform that still defines the Paris backstage. His legacy is a grammar of space and silence, clothes that give the wearer room to think and a capital that learns restraint can be power.

Below: Yamamoto's Spring 1983 Ready-to-Wear Runway.

Opposite: Yohji, the father of dark wave fashion.

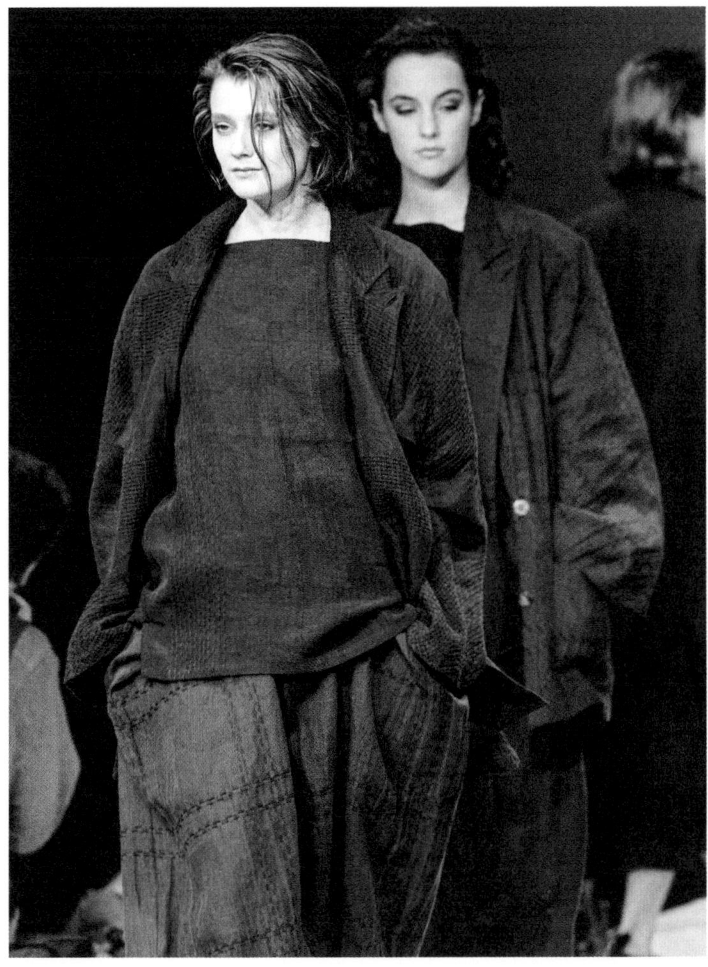

MARTIN MARGIELA

Martin Margiela arrived in Paris from Belgium in 1988 and started his own label after working for a time for Jean Paul Gaultier. His first shows didn't take place in the same designated fashion week locations, but abandoned warehouses and on the street, with kids from the neighbourhood sitting right in the front row. He didn't have the budget to book the then top models that you would normally see walk every single show that mattered, so he covered up the girls walking his runaways with masks as a way of embracing anonymity – clothes matter on the runaway; the rest is just fuss.

Margiela took the clothmaking toolkit and turned it inside out: linings on the outside, hems unfinished, labels held by four white stitches. The anonymity (no designer bow at the end, faces hidden in press shots) wasn't a gimmick; it was a shift in power. The focus stayed on the clothes and on the team that made them.

Margiela's ideas go beyond styling. He pioneered the "deconstructed" look but also a new business model: small ateliers working like a collective, recycling and upcycling decades before it became PR. Margiela treated each show like a concept lab, yet kept sizing, deliveries and pricing disciplined enough for stores to carry. Paris learned that an avant-garde label can be commercially viable without losing its soul.

Proving that mystery can be a strategy by breaking down an image that builds a stronger brand, Martin Margiela turned the city's runway ritual into an experiment, while keeping the craft intact. The legacy is now a new template: clothes as investigation, brand as collective and Paris as a testing ground where invisibility itself becomes a signature.

Opposite: An outfit by Maison Martin Margiela's Spring/ Summer 2011 collection at Paris Fashion Week.

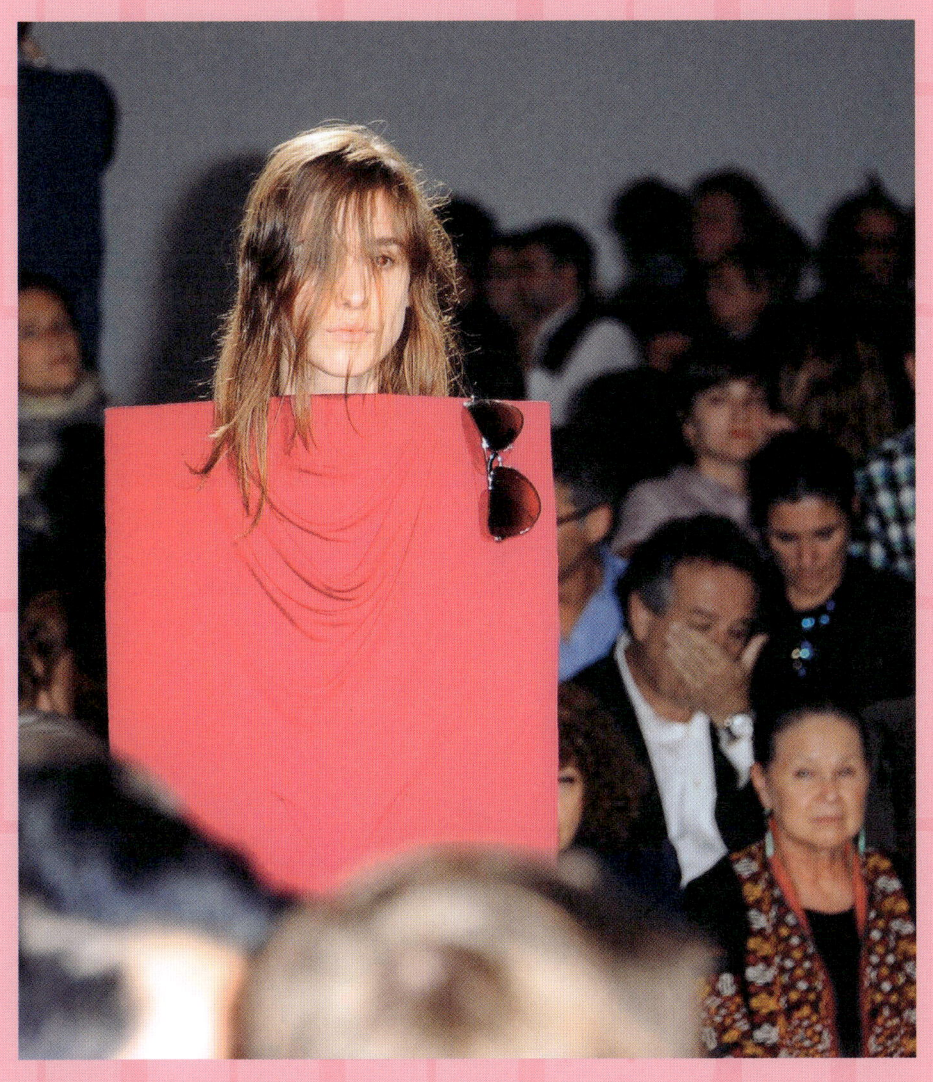

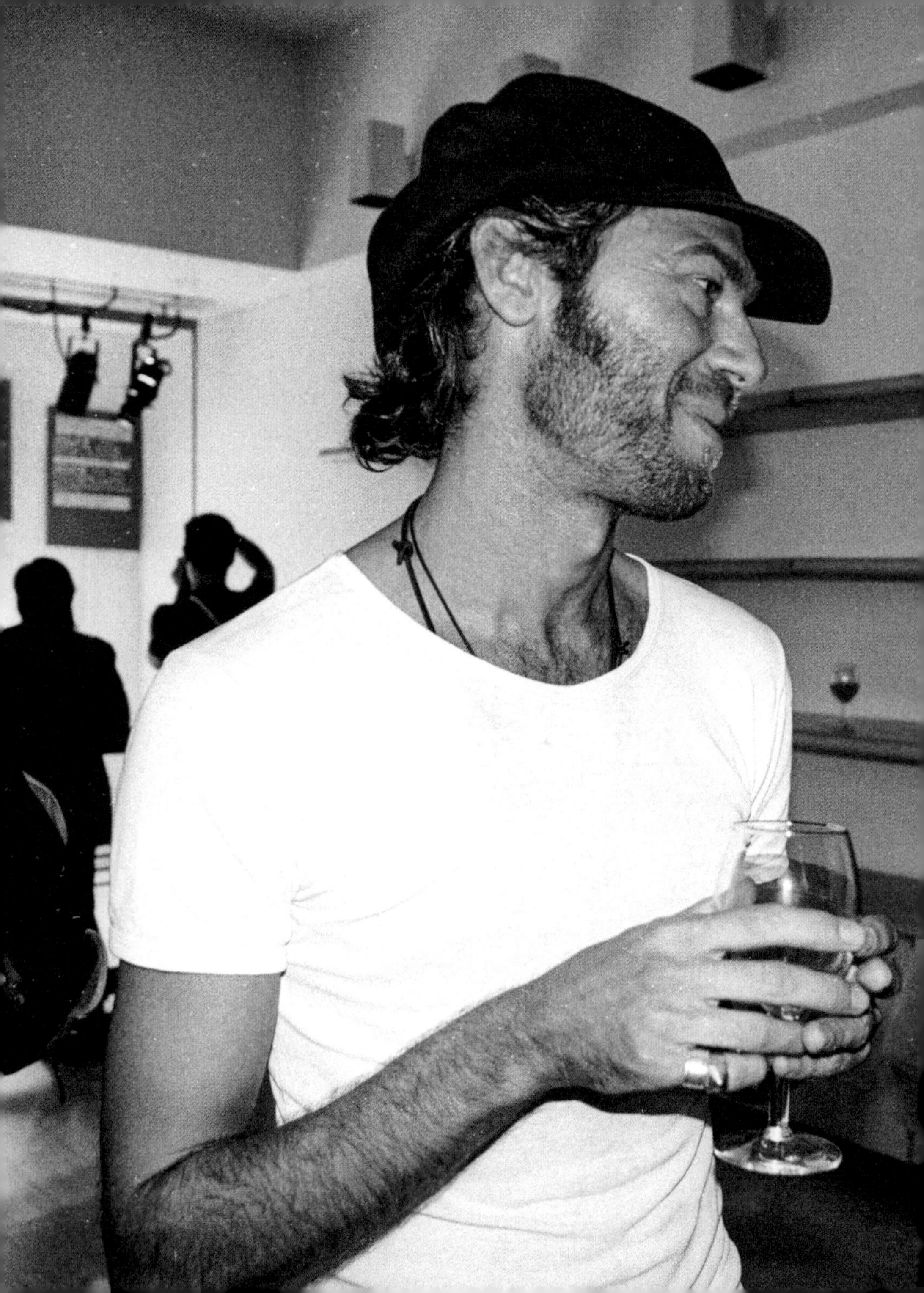

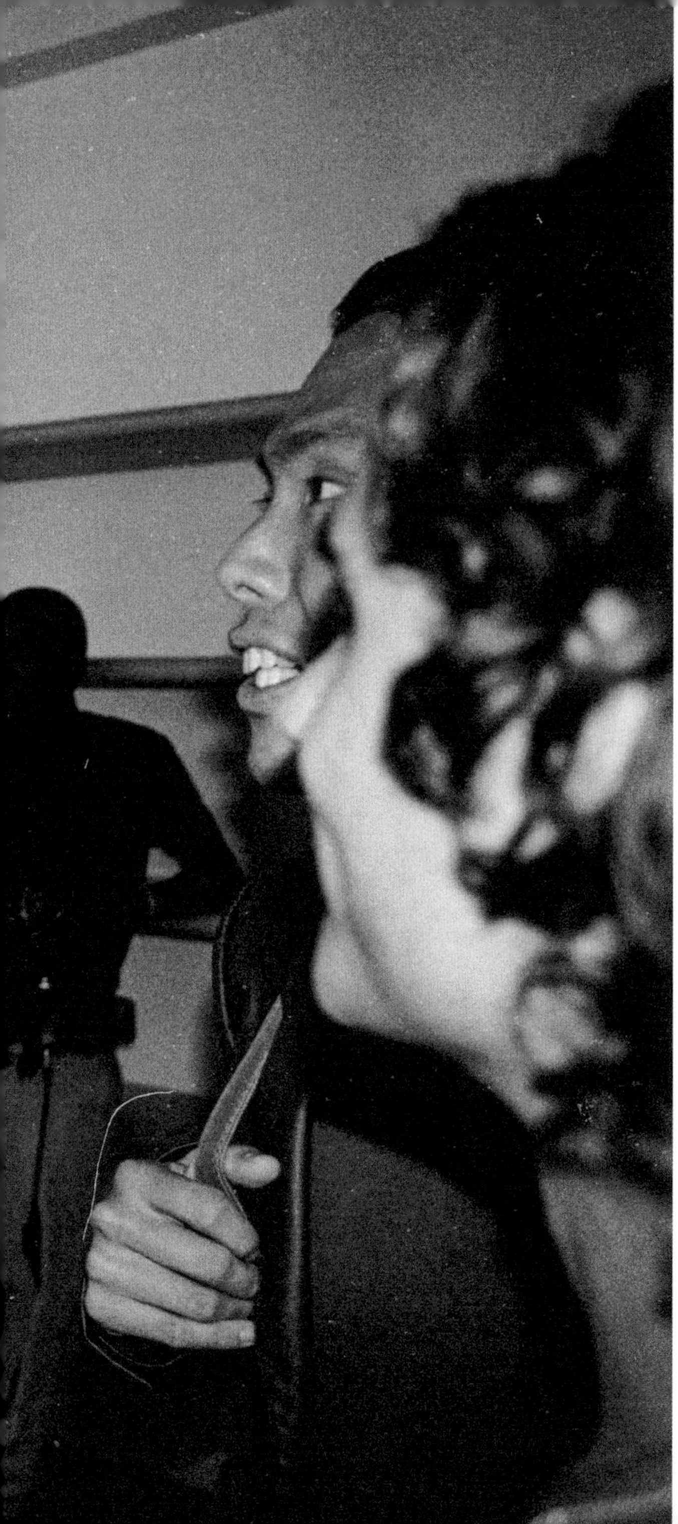

Left: This extremely rare photograph shows Martin Margiela having fun.

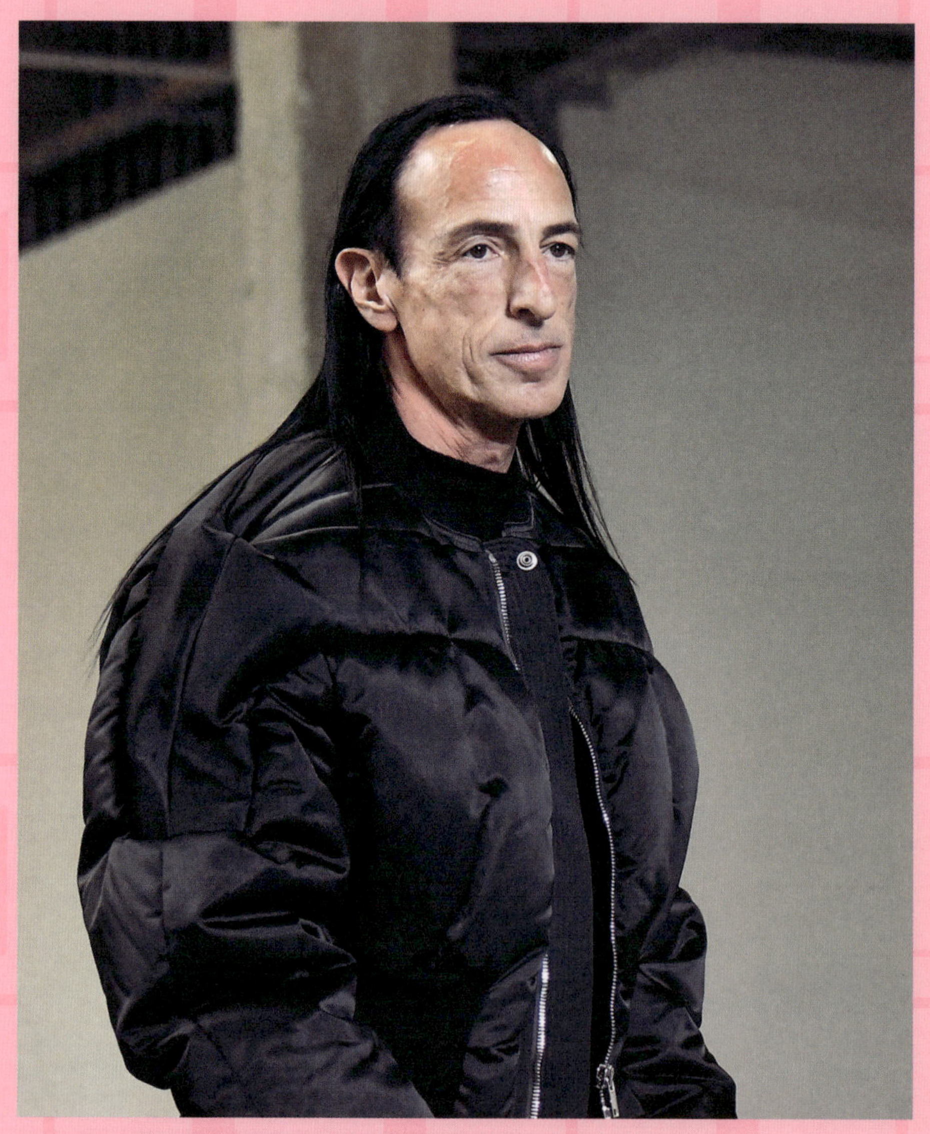

RICK OWENS

Rick Owens arrived from California in the late 1990s, showing first in New York and then moving his base to Paris in 2003. He brought a different mood with him: West Coast outsider meets Left Bank discipline. His silhouettes are long, draped, asymmetric and leather-heavy. At first glance they look like armour, but the fit is exact and the fabrics are luxurious. He builds a cult on brutal elegance and then slowly turns it into an institution.

Owens treats Paris as a full environment. He designs his own stores as concrete cathedrals, controls his image with partner Michèle Lamy, and keeps production mostly in Italy for consistency. Each show pushes spectacle: step pyramids, clouds of smoke, bodybuilders carrying models (you read that right!), yet the delivery schedules run like clockwork and the product in the stores matches the mood on the runway. He brings furniture, fragrance and a complete lifestyle into the brand without losing focus on the core cut. Needless to say, Owenscorp soon becomes a cult where "you're all freaks and you're welcome with me" – this, in his words, means a sanctuary for outsiders, a community that welcomes and embraces your inner weirdo.

An outsider can build a luxury house from the ground up without diluting its attitude. Rick Owens shows that darkness can be aspirational, experimental shapes can achieve mainstream reach and discipline can sit amid chaos. Editors and buyers fly in for his shows, not just to see the clothes but to feel a culture. Younger designers imitate his designs, his palette and his store architecture. The legacy is a model of total control: define your world tightly, deliver it consistently and Paris will make space for you – with absolutely no compromise required.

Opposite: A great portrait of the Lord of Darkness.

JOHN GALLIANO

British designer John Galliano landed in Paris in the early 1990s with a lot of talent but no money. His breakthrough show happened in a borrowed *hôtel particulier* (private mansion), models walked for free, hair and make-up were friends' favours, plus most of the looks were cut in black fabric because it was the only one he could afford. *Vogue*'s Anna Wintour and André Leon Talley helped him, and a small circle of patrons stepped in so the collection could happen at all. The room gasped: if he could do that with no money, how high might he actually fly with resources? They would soon find out.

Within a few seasons Galliano moved from survival mode to the Paris big leagues: first Givenchy in 1995, then Dior in 1996. He treated the runway as narrative cinema but still kept the craftsmanship intact. History, fantasy, bias cuts, uniforms, sailors, opera – on paper, this sounds excessive, but in the fittings it is disciplined dressmaking with a good dose of crazy. Under his watch, Dior's image machine scales: perfume, accessories and headlines feed each other and Paris rediscovers the show as a cultural event that can also drive a thriving business.

Opposite: If you were to ask ChatGPT to show you a classic Galliano look, this is what it would show you.

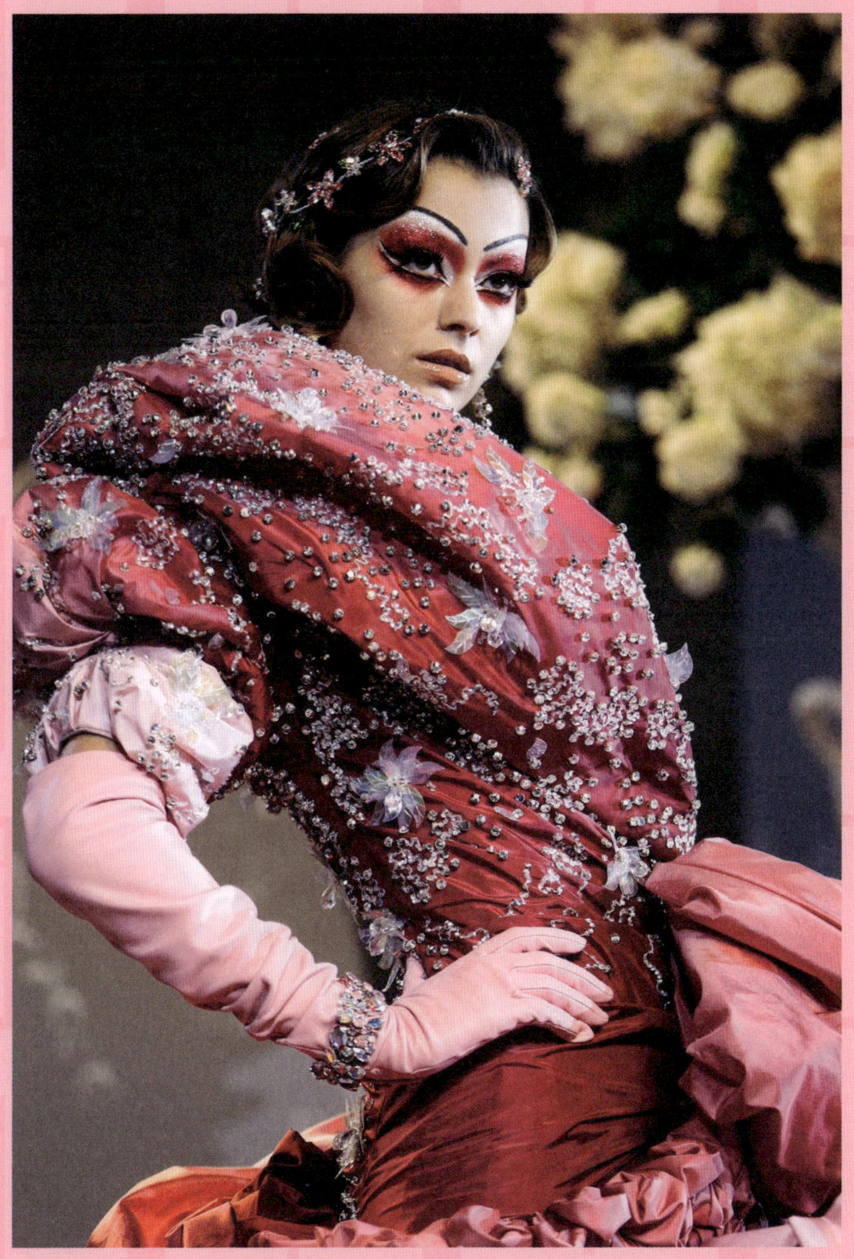

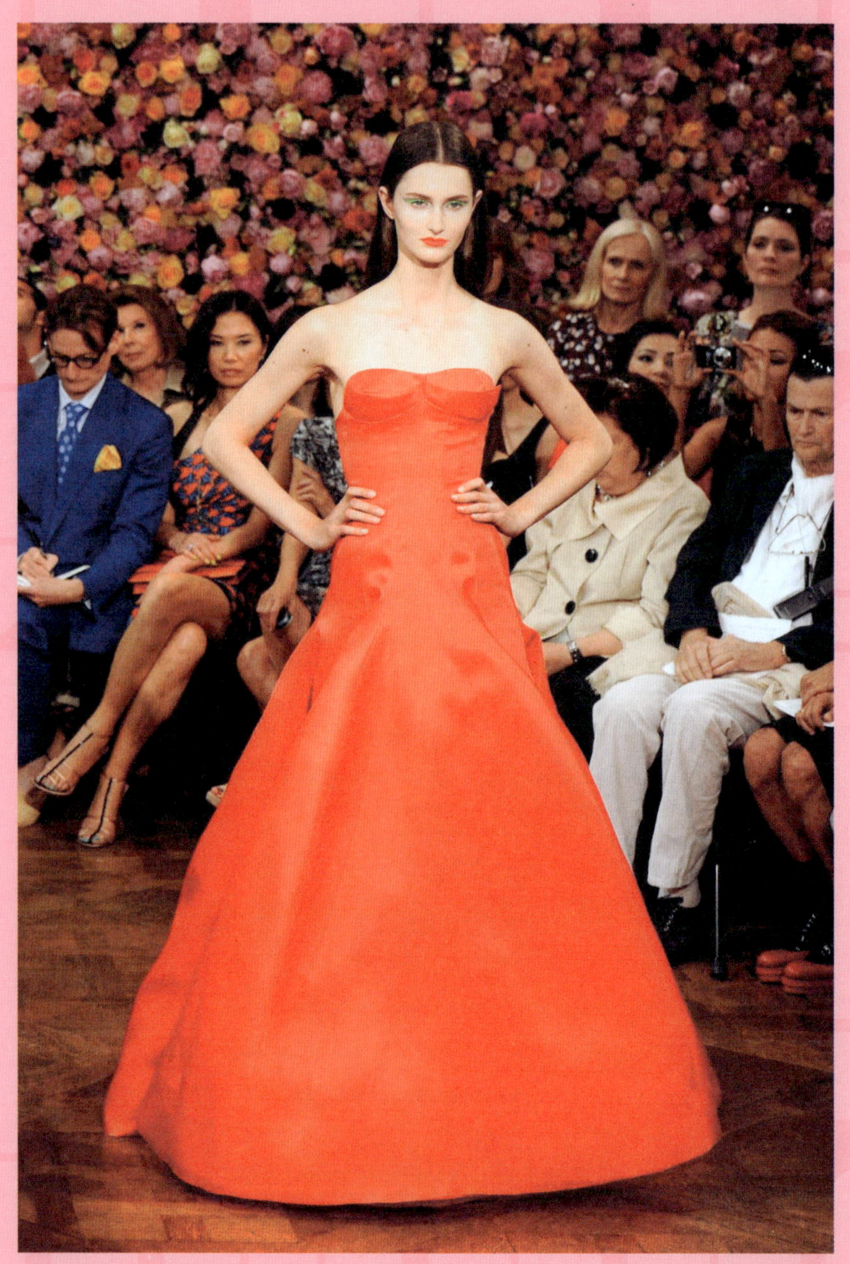

RAF SIMONS

Raf Simons began his career in Antwerp in the mid-1990s with a menswear label built on teenage energy and precise tailoring. He staged small, charged shows in industrial spaces, the models were students and friends, and his black-and-white uniforms came from necessity as much as aesthetic. Critics saw Helmut Lang references but also a new seriousness: youth codes treated like architecture. By the early 2000s his slim tailoring and subcultural casting had already managed to shape an entire menswear generation.

In 2012 Dior hired him to run their couture house. Overnight, he moved from cult shows to the world's biggest atelier. His debut collection stripped the grandeur back to clean lines and intimacy. Behind the scenes he brought a new tempo with a short development cycle and collaborative studio culture. Accessories and ready-to-wear sharpened under his watch, while the couture shows reached a younger audience.

Simons also opens the conversation between luxury fashion and the art world. He collaborates with artists and industrial designers, mixes street and couture casting, and treats each show as a museum installation rather than a closed salon. Documentaries like *Dior and I* (2014) make the process public, showing a couture house as a living team rather than a single sketching genius. His impact on Paris is to prove that a Belgian-trained menswear designer can guide the city's grandest couture house without diluting its DNA. He shows minimalism can scale and collaboration can be a business model. In doing so he gives Paris a new template for creative direction: less mystique, more method and a couture house wired to a bigger cultural circuit.

Opposite: Raf Simons for Christian Dior during the Haute Couture Fall/Winter 2012–13 season.

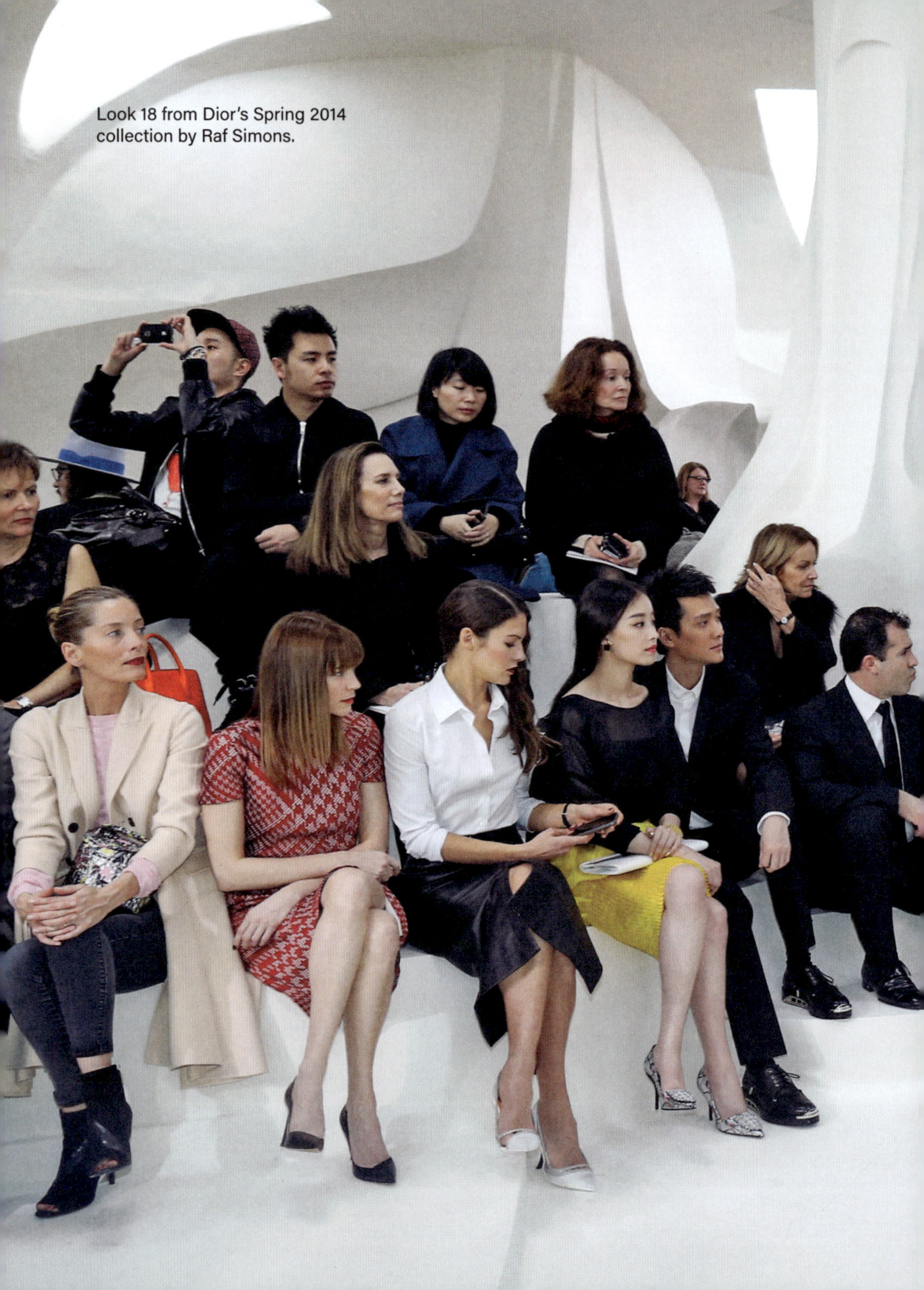

Look 18 from Dior's Spring 2014 collection by Raf Simons.

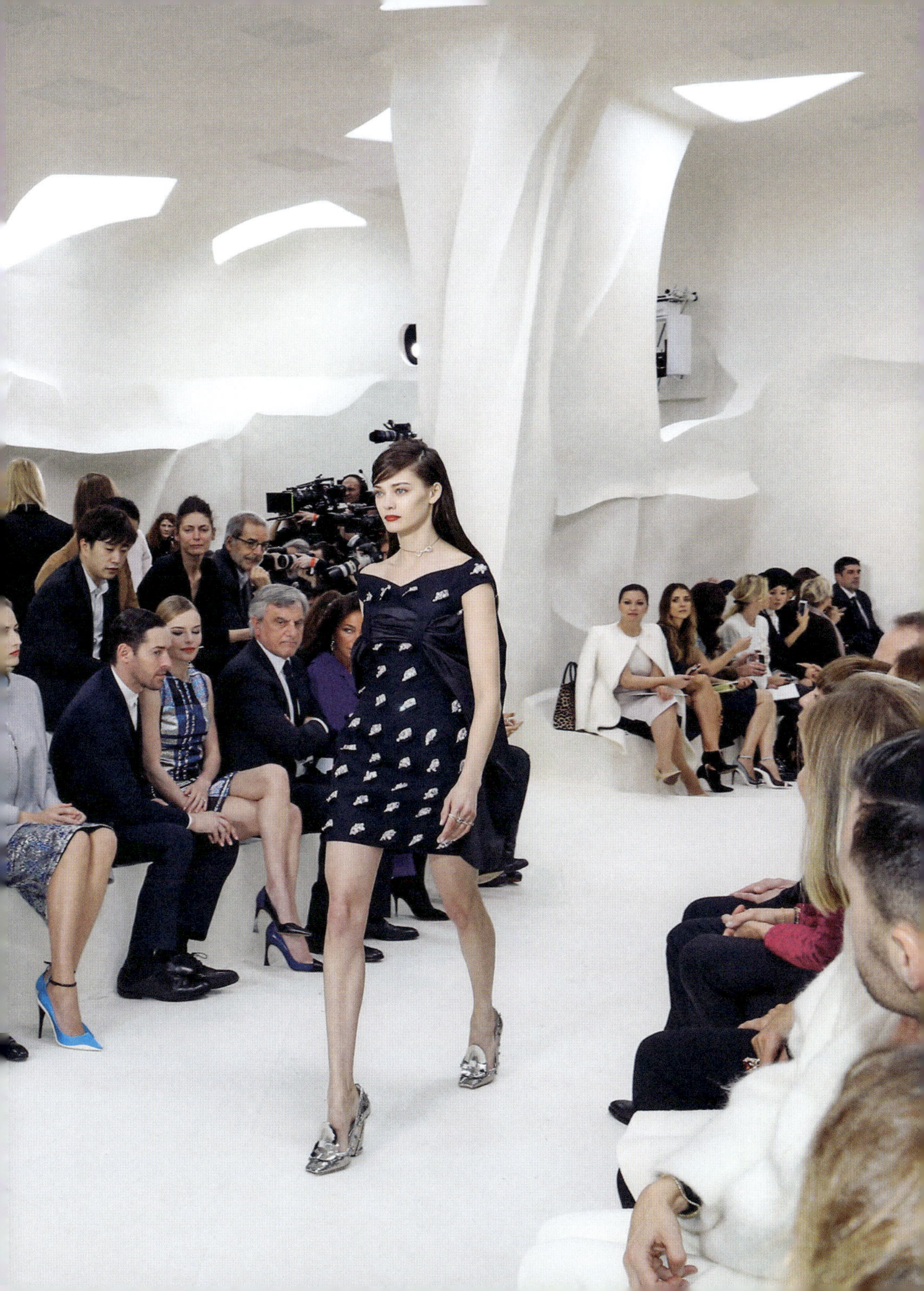

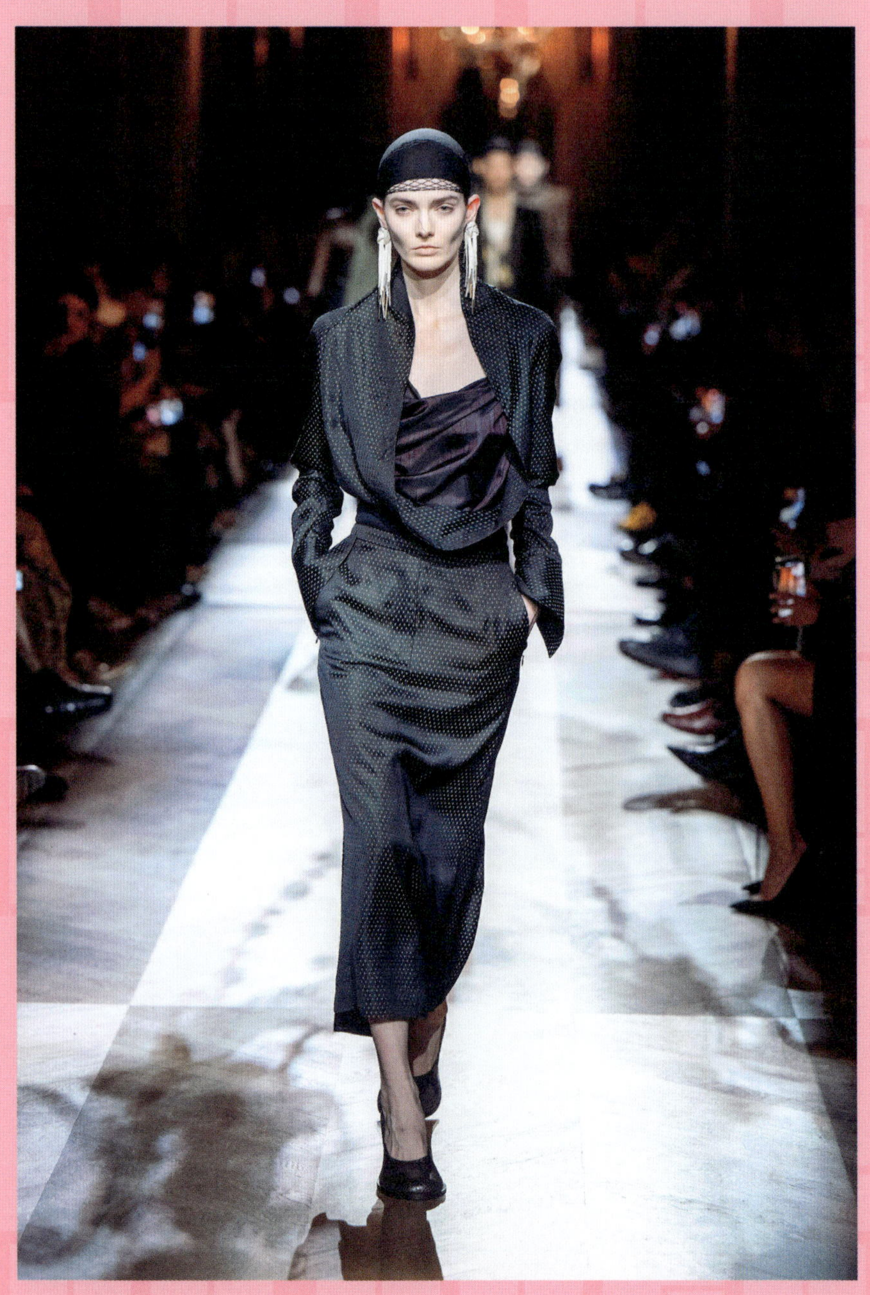

DRIES VAN NOTEN

Dries Van Noten emerged from the Antwerp Six in the late 1980s and stepped onto the Paris calendar in 1991. But he didn't try to shock. Instead, he built a reputation for intelligent layering, unexpected colour mixes and prints drawn from every corner of culture. The shows felt like mood boards you can walk through, rich in references but held together by cut. From the start he thought in terms of wardrobes, not one-offs, so buyers could build complete looks straight from the runway.

Textile work is his real signature. Van Noten revives forgotten weaving mills, commissions embroidery from India and was experimenting with finishes long before "heritage" or "artisan" became marketing hooks. Paris learned to see the fabric as a starting point rather than an afterthought. Editors came to his shows to scout not just shapes but also materials and combinations they hadn't yet imagined.

Van Noten also rewrites the business rhythm for a designer of his scale. Keeping his base in Antwerp, he stayed independent for decades, funding his own growth and protecting his supply chain, so quality stayed consistent. His stores feel more like curated apartments than flagships and his client base behaves more like a circle of collectors than seasonal shoppers. He encourages Paris to pay attention to textiles again, to show that print and colour can be as rigorous as tailoring, and to prove that a designer can build global influence from a quiet centre. Instead of spectacle, Dries Van Noten offers substance and the city still builds around that lesson.

Opposite: Among the Antwerp Six, Dries Van Noten stood apart because he made refinement rebellious: proving you could be radical through fabric, not shock.

Nicolas Ghesquière

Nicolas Ghesquière began his career as an intern at Balenciaga and took over the house in 1997 when he was barely in his mid-20s. At the time the label was a sleepy licensing name known more for perfume than clothes. Within a few seasons, Paris realized it had a new force on its hands. Ghesquière doesn't mine the archive literally; he reframes it for real life. His early collections mix couture-level jackets with easy trousers and then one accessory changes everything: the soft, slouchy Balenciaga "Motorcycle" (or "Lariat") bag. Editors are sent prototypes, Kate Moss carries it, and overnight the Lariat becomes the insider's bag that every big-city woman wants. What starts as a studio experiment becomes the blueprint for the 2000s It-bag economy.

That bag was also an astute business move. Ghesquière proved you can build a global accessories line out of a cult runway mood without diluting the brand. The teams now had a steady anchor product to fund fabric development and show ideas. Suddenly Balenciaga was not just a critics' favourite but a profit engine and a pop-culture reference.

In 2013 Louis Vuitton hired him to succeed Marc Jacobs as artistic director of women's collections, handing him one of the largest luxury businesses on earth. He repeated the pattern at a new scale with historic codes treated as material for a modern wardrobe and accessories that travel worldwide. Ghesquière's impact on Paris is to show that a designer can restore a sleeping house, ignite a global accessories craze and still build a serious ready-to-wear vision.

Opposite: Ghesquière's real superpower is treating sci-fi not as fantasy but as a blueprint for modern wardrobes, making the future feel genuinely wearable.

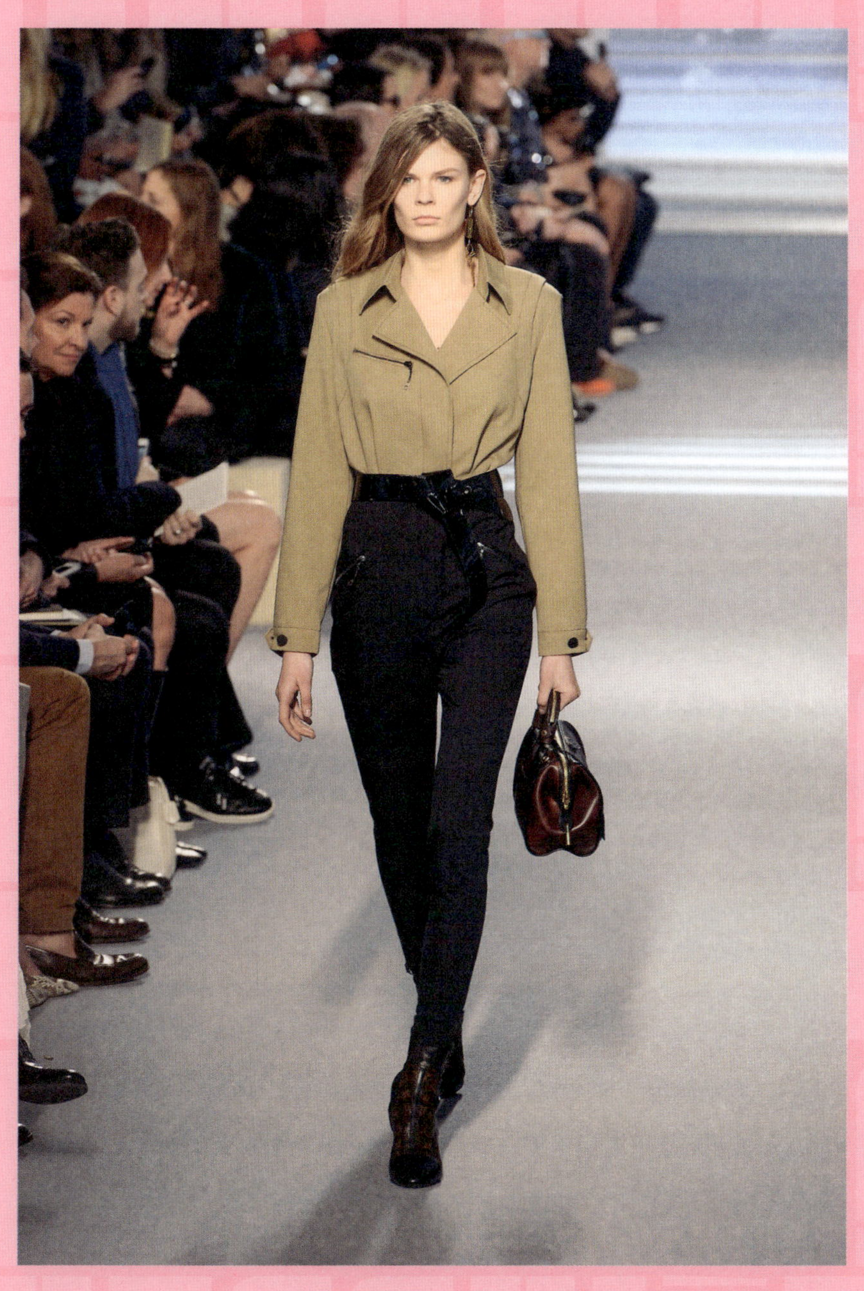

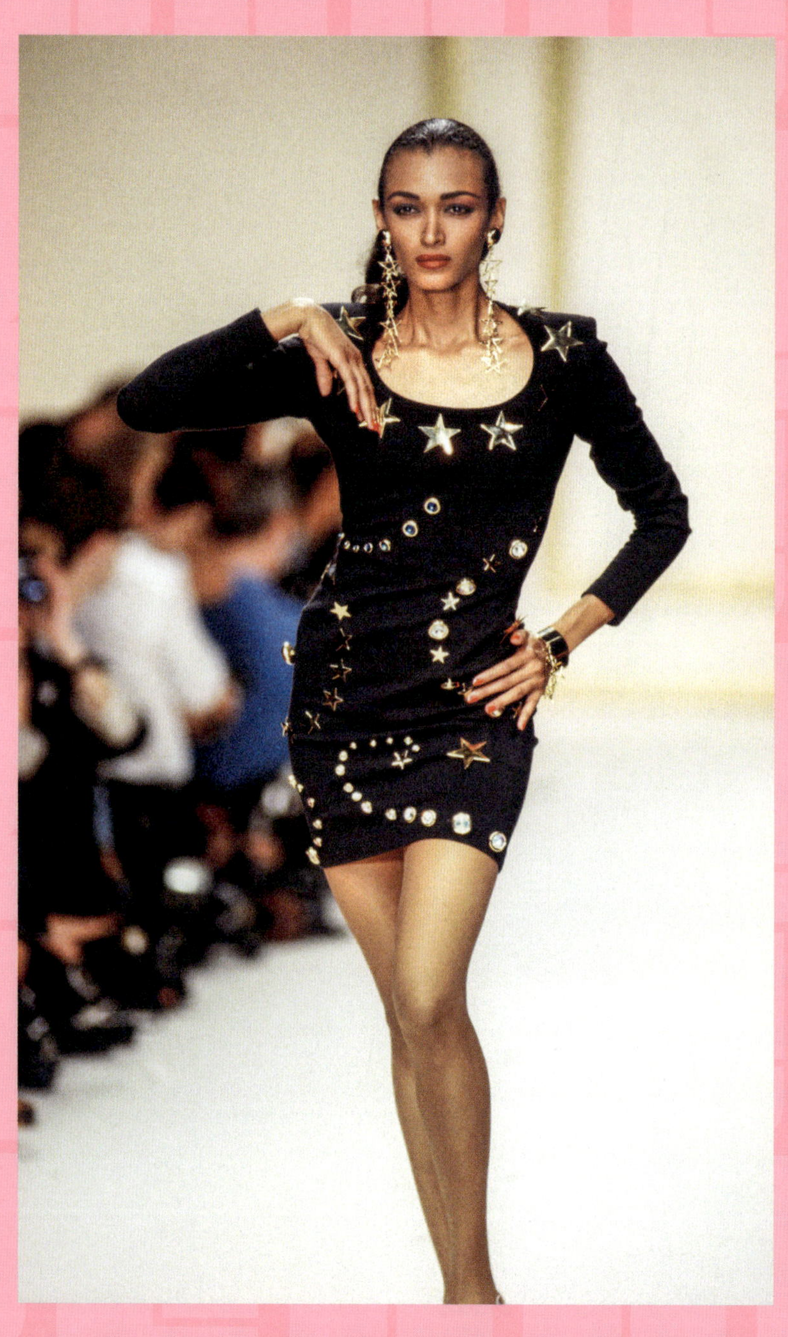

PATRICK KELLY

In 1979 Patrick Kelly arrived in Paris from Mississippi by way of New York with a suitcase, a sewing machine and no connections. He handed dresses to friends, hustled freelance jobs and started selling on the street. By 1985 he was showing his own label at the Louvre's fashion wing, the first American and the first Black designer admitted to the Chambre Syndicale. The leap was stunning but not accidental: Kelly had been dressing Paris club kids and editors for years, combining Southern wit with couture cut.

Kelly's signature was joy with edge – button-covered dresses, heart-shaped pocket flaps, giant bows, logo-play, cartoon colours. He lifted vernacular references from the American South and Black culture and stitched them into runway clothes with Paris precision. The result felt humorous, seductive and politically charged at once. He played with stereotypes to neutralize them, sending out dresses with banana appliqués or Josephine Baker-style accents, but the fit and construction were serious, so the punchline stayed sharp.

Kelly also proved that an outsider could bend Paris's rules. He was self-funded, used friends as models, sent out press mailers with miniature Black baby dolls, and won over editors through sheer energy. His ready-to-wear sold fast because it was built on jersey and stretch fabrics that moved. His shows felt like parties, but his business sense was strict: clear deliveries, price points that brought young buyers in and a look that photographed itself.

Opposite: Patrick Kelly turned joy into a strategy long before it became a marketing trend, using humour as a Trojan horse for radical inclusivity on the Paris runway.

Before his untimely death in 1990 of AIDS-related illnesses, Patrick Kelly injected Black American culture into Paris, mixing it with its couture system to show that sheer exuberance and heritage can coexist. His legacy is a template for inclusivity, humour and speed that still influences how the city welcomes new voices.

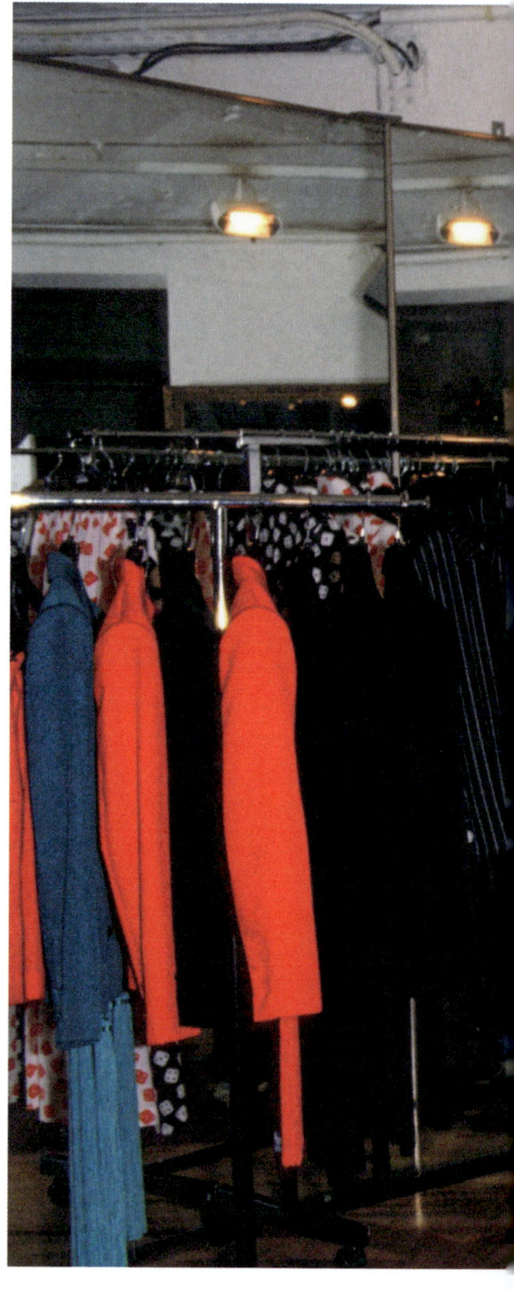

Right: Patrick Kelly in his Paris studio circa 1988.

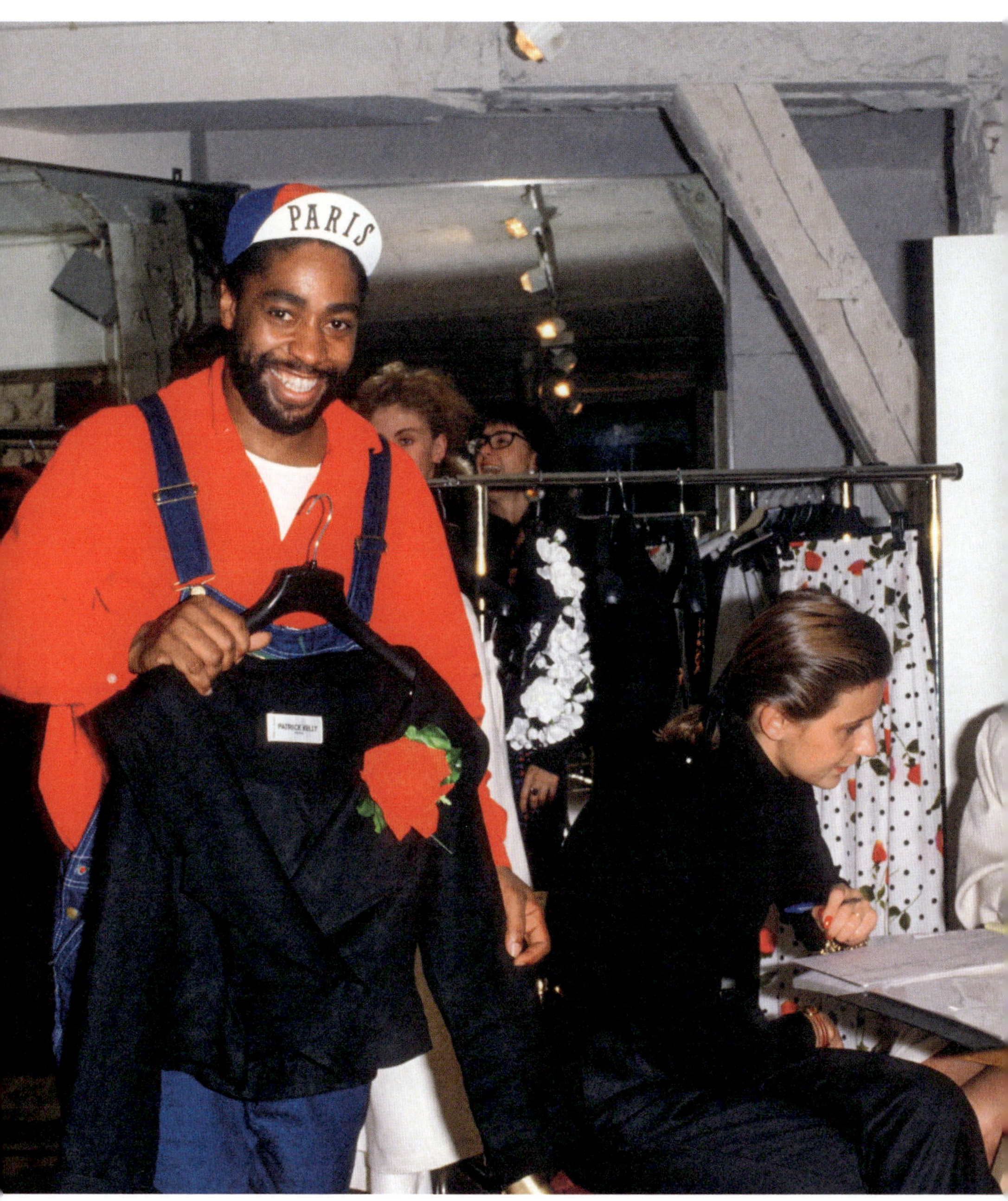
PARIS

Azzedine Alaïa

Azzedine Alaïa arrived in Paris from Tunisia in the late 1950s with a sculptor's training and a tailor's discipline. He worked quietly for Dior, Guy Laroche and Thierry Mugler, then began fitting private clients in a tiny apartment atelier. The word spread through models and editors: his fittings last hours, his precision is obsessive and the results feel like a second skin. By the early 1980s his own label was underway and the fashion world had a new benchmark for fit.

Alaïa's clothes were body-conscious but never careless. Stretch knits, zipped leathers, hoods and cut-outs read as sensual on the runway but held their line in motion. He built dresses on the body, not the table, pinning and sculpting until every seam supported posture. Models, stylists and celebrities grew loyal to him because the clothes empowered rather than displayed them. Grace Jones, Tina Turner, Naomi Campbell and Veronica Webb formed an unofficial Alaïa tribe, wearing his pieces on and off stage.

Azzedine Alaïa also rejected the Paris calendar entirely. Shows happened when he was ready, sometimes even at midnight and often in his own space. Editors and buyers waited because the clothes were worth it. That independence allowed him to self-fund, control production and maintain small, disciplined ateliers in-house. Alaïa perfumes and accessories arrived later but never drove the brand – the garment was always the main event. His impact on Paris was to prove that intimacy can outlast spectacle. He proved that a couture-level fit applied to ready-to-wear can create a global business and that a designer can set their own rhythm and still command the room. Today his name signals not just a look but a standard: precision as liberation.

Opposite: Azzedine Alaïa and model Frederique in 1986, walking the streets of Paris.

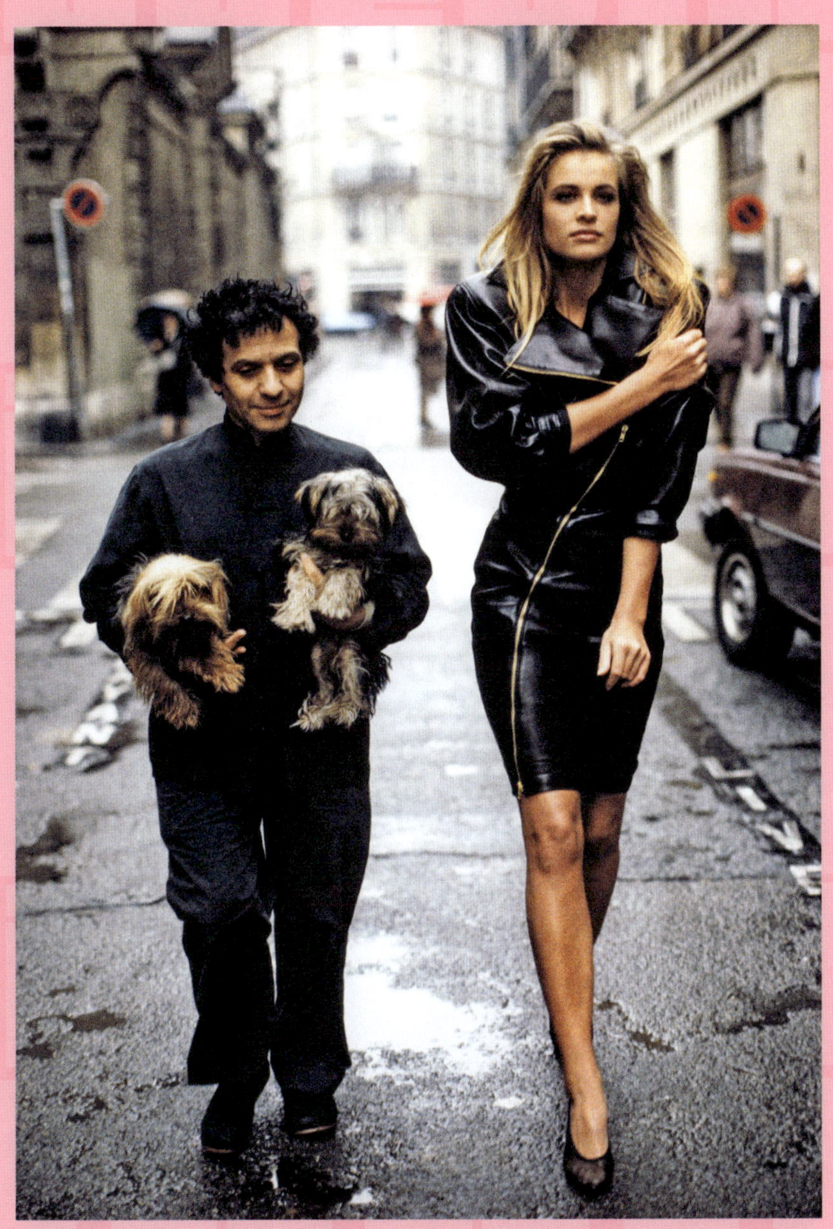

Right: Azzedine Alaïa and his muse, the singer Grace Jones.

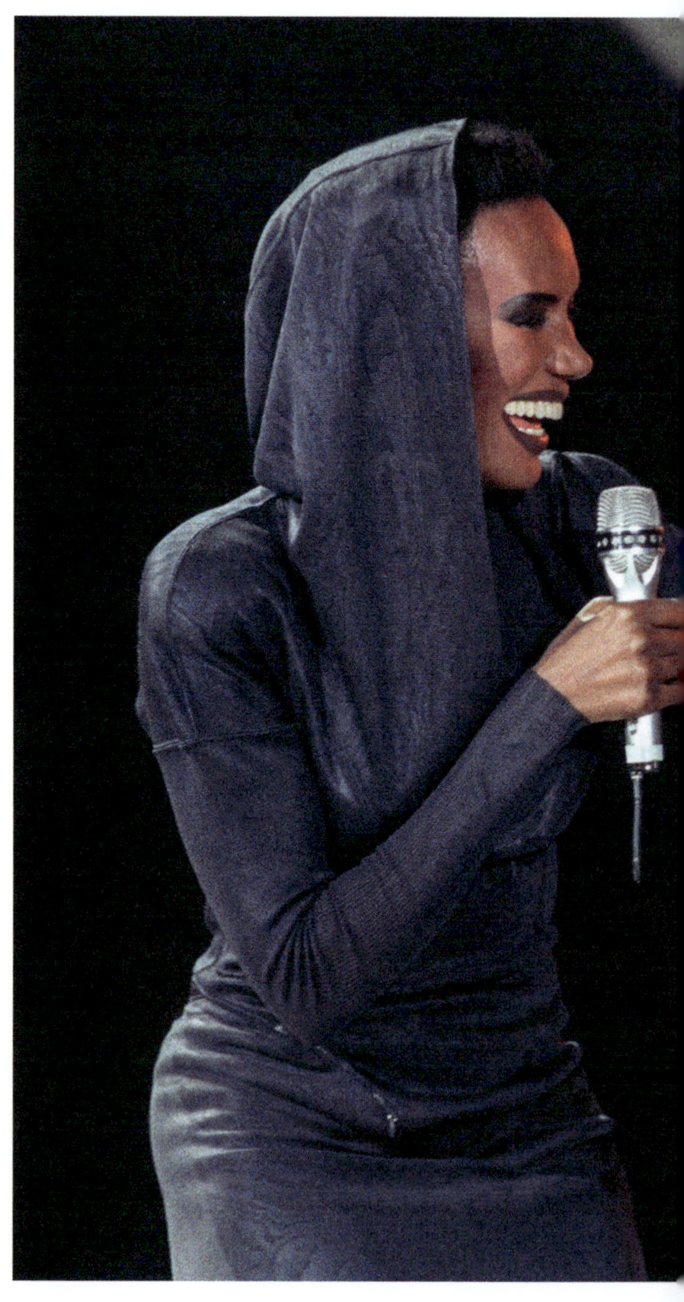

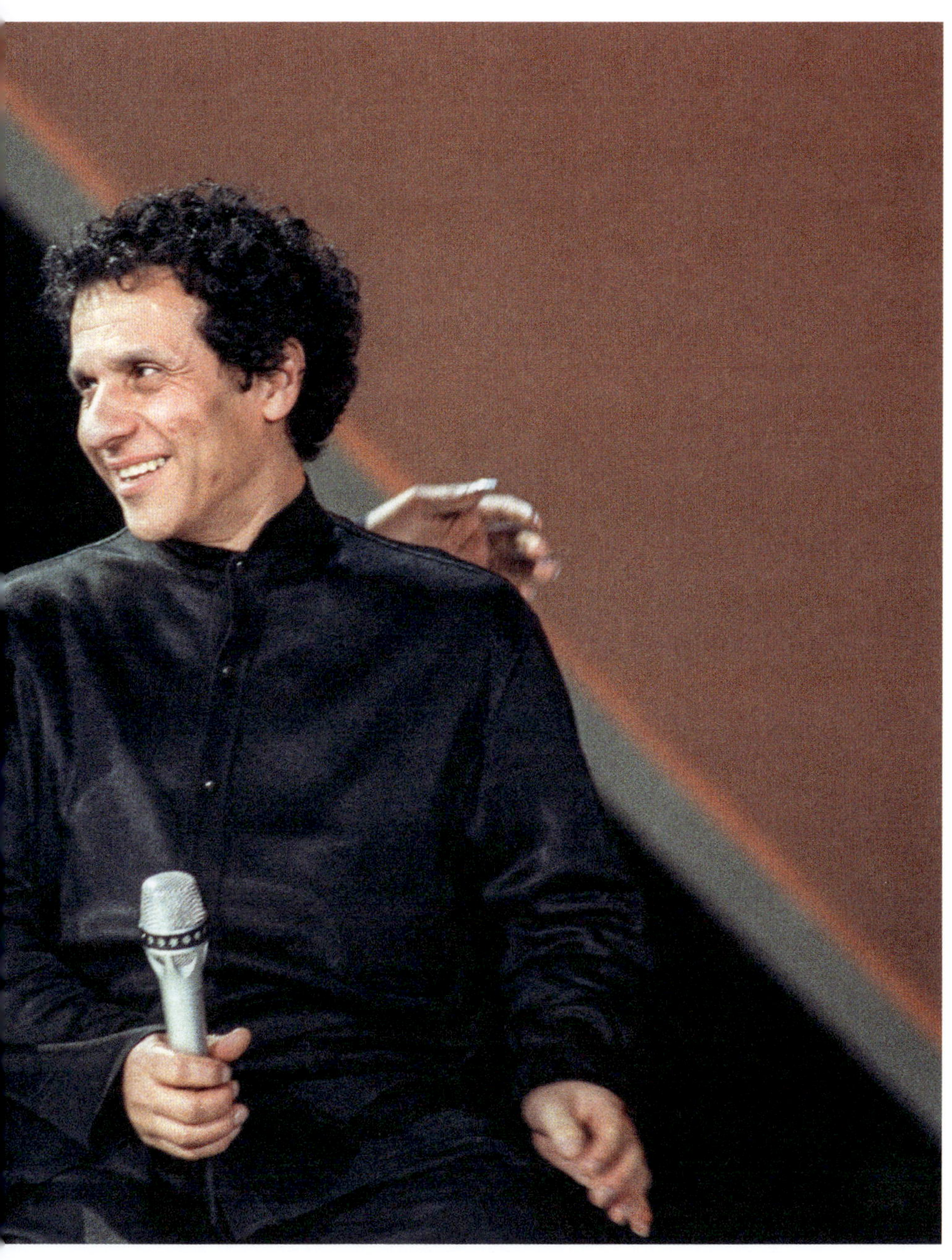

CHAPTER 3:

THE NEW GUARD OF DESIGNERS & CREATIVE DIRECTORS

Directorship today is choreography. Product, image, store, drop, feed, archive: everything must move in one rhythm across months and continents. In the twenty-first century, audiences expanded and codes hardened. Fashion shows turned into full environments: soundtracks, architecture, scent, digital screens. The challenge isn't scale; it's maintaining coherence.

The people in this chapter are the ones who can keep a single line audible in a crowded room. They inherit archives, global teams and constant scrutiny, yet still find a way to express a point of view. When they succeed, they don't just deliver a collection, they steer a system, turning heritage houses into living organisms, balancing commerce with experiment and keeping Paris at the centre of a world that no longer stops for a runway.

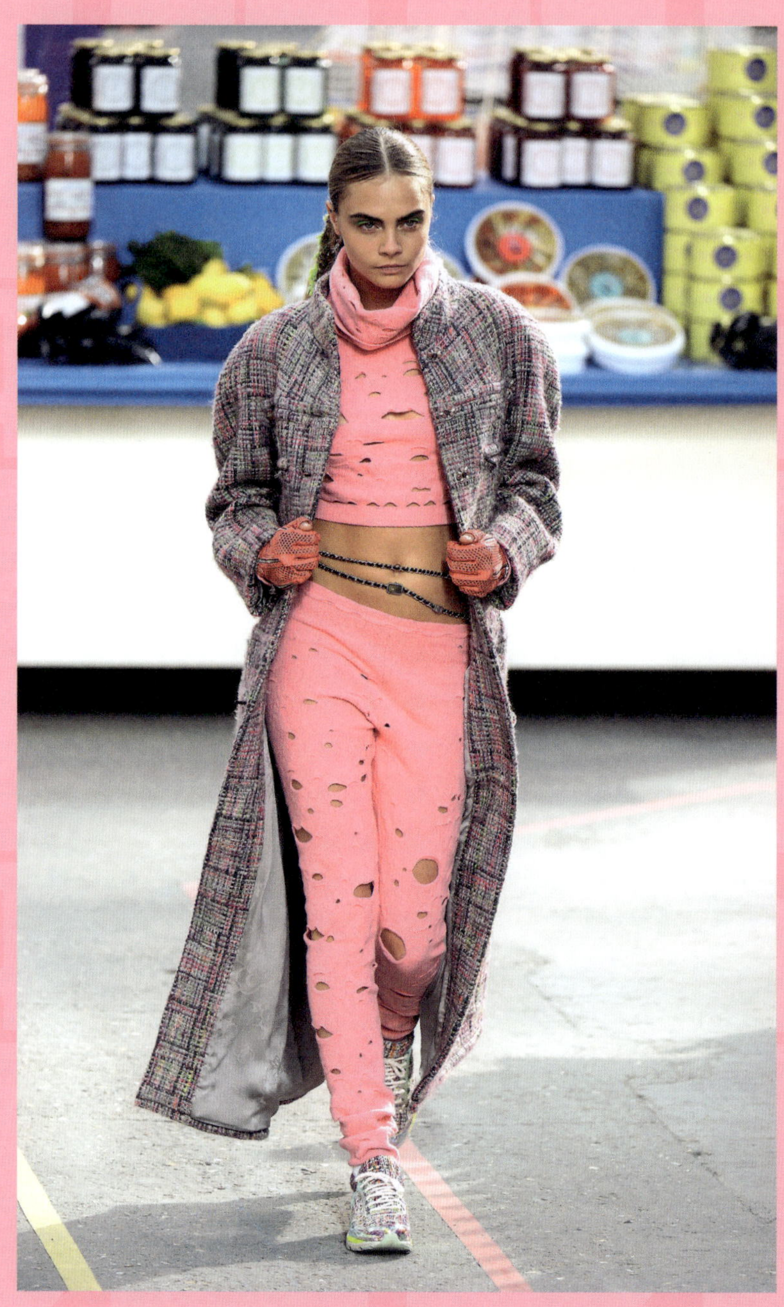

KARL LAGERFELD

Paris welcomed Karl Lagerfeld from Hamburg when he was a teenager. A design prize dropped him into Balmain's studio, where he learned fast: sketch, fit, deliver. He moved through houses, from Balmain to Patou, then built long habits at Chloé and Fendi. The lesson was simple and large: a designer can steer image, product and schedule at once if the studio rhythm is precise. In 1983 he took Chanel, then sleepy, and turned it into a living system – the living system we know today. In doing so, he did not freeze the archive; he edited it. Tweed became light. The jacket was shortened. Pearls mixed with denim. The logo learned to play in the street and still look grown-up.

Lagerfeld treated his shows as public chapters. The Grand Palais became a reliable stage: a beach, a rocket launch, a supermarket, a library. The set was generous; the clothes made to be sold the next morning. Boutiques expanded, beauty and fragrance scaled, and accessories carried the mood worldwide. The business grew because the handwriting stayed clear across every category. Lagerfeld kept drawing, kept shooting campaigns and kept reading the room. Six or more collections a year landed on time because the atelier discipline never softened. The designer also turned his own image into an instrument: white ponytail, black glasses, high collar, gloves. It read as a uniform and a promise that the line would remain steady.

Karl Lagerfeld's impact on Paris was immense and honest too. He proved a historic maison can feel current every season without trading away its core. He showed that a creative director can be archivist and futurist in the same hour. Under his gaze Chanel became a cultural engine again and the city kept the tempo he set.

Opposite: Cara Delevingne for Chanel by Karl Lagerfeld.

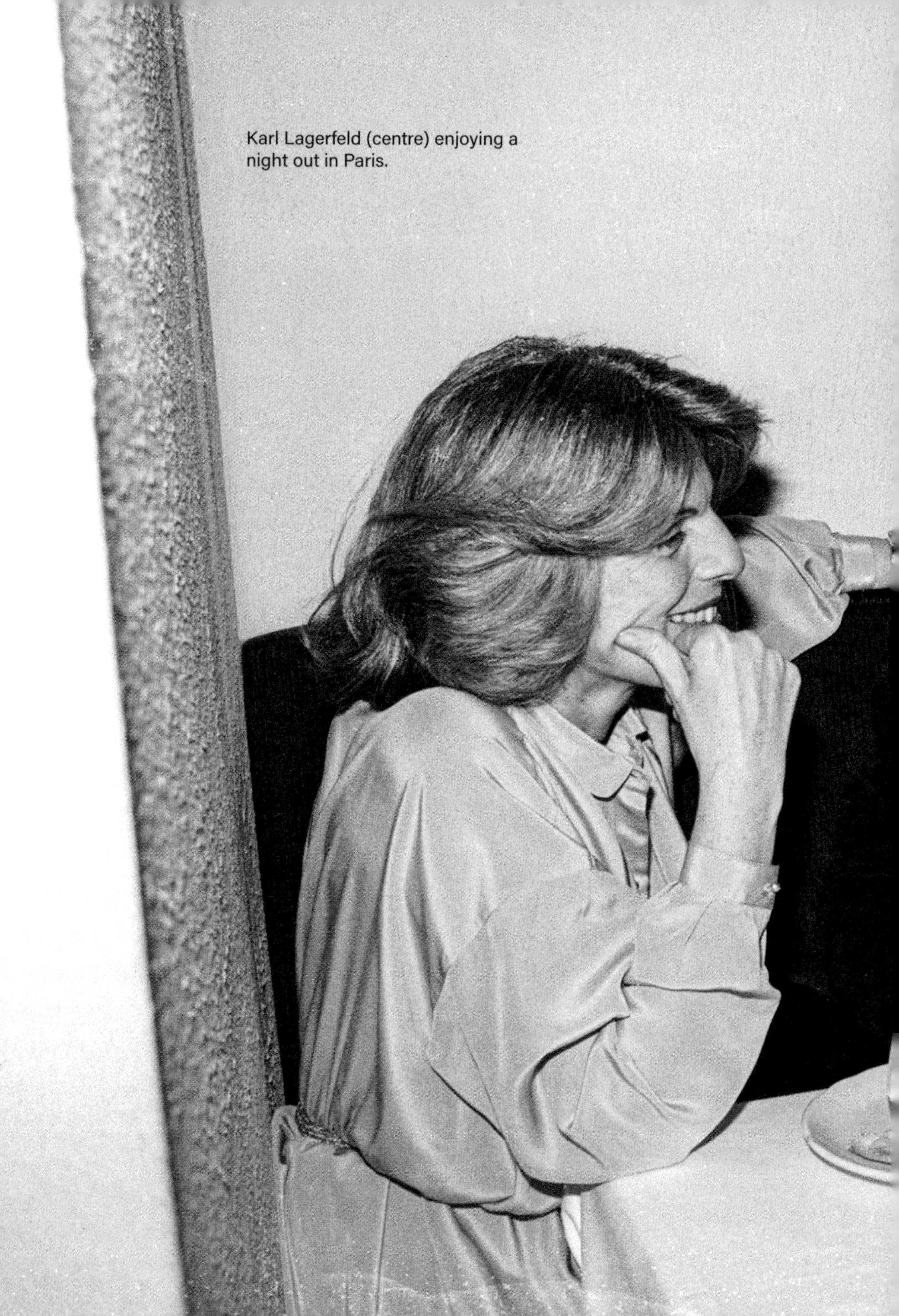

Karl Lagerfeld (centre) enjoying a night out in Paris.

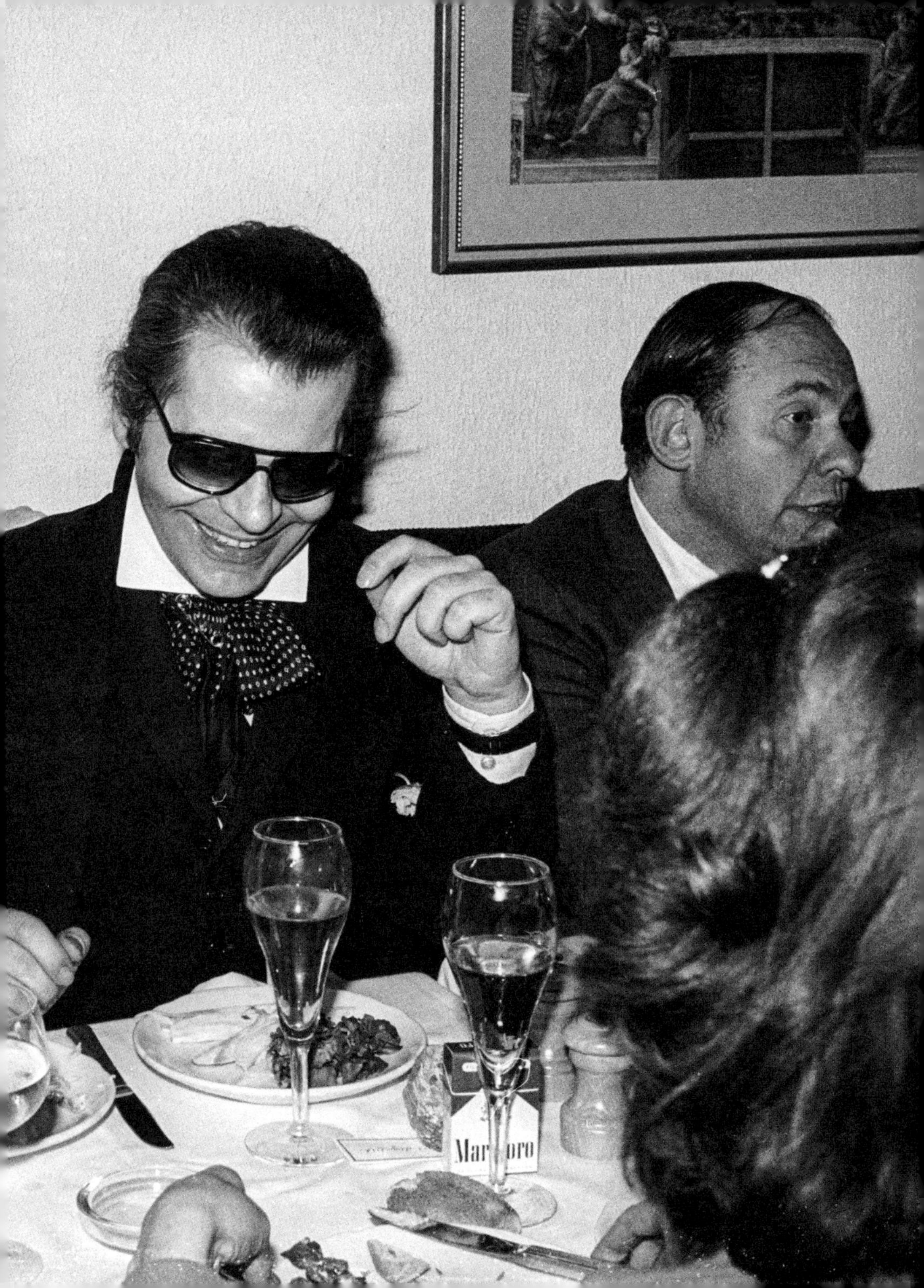

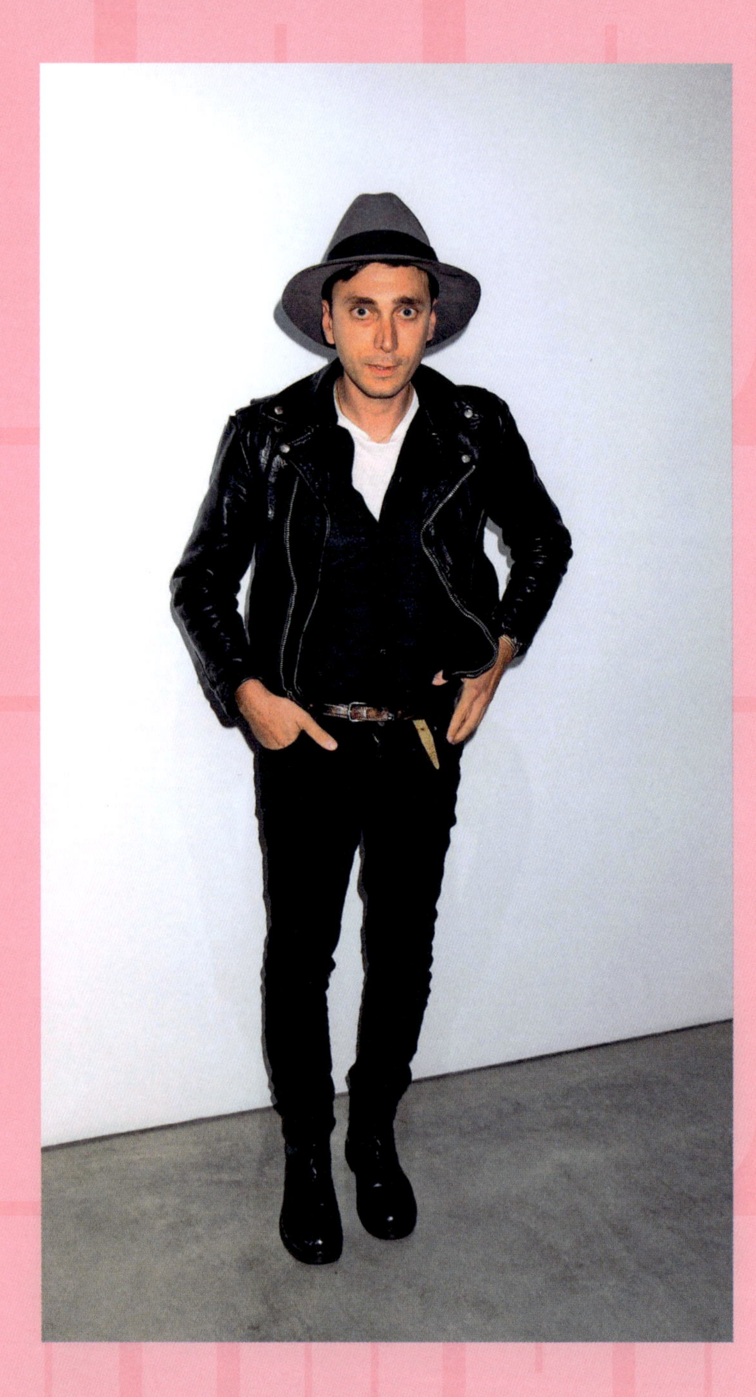

HEDI SLIMANE

Hedi Slimane started out as a studio assistant at Yves Saint Laurent and quickly became known for having a photographer's eye as much as a designer's hand. In 2000 Dior Homme handed him the menswear reins and he redrew the male silhouette: razor-sharp jackets, low-rise trousers, skinny lapels and a new attitude towards casting. Indie musicians, skaters and artists became his inspiration, muses and product placements. Editors called it a revolution. Sales proved it actually was. Dior Homme's skinny tailoring spilled onto every high street in the world and into women's wardrobes as well. The uniforms he created still live on today.

When Saint Laurent named him creative director in 2012 he applied the same method at scale. The house dropped "Yves" from its branding, amplified rock energy and tightened its ready-to-wear engine. Stores played live gigs, leather jackets sold like couture dresses once did and music culture returned to the heart of a Paris label. Slimane also shaped image control. Campaigns looked like his own photography. His move to Celine in 2018 repeated the cycle: archive plus youth culture equals global growth. It was more about the Hedi Slimane look and feel rather than the houses he was working at.

Hedi Slimane's impact on Paris is to show that music, image and classic tailoring can work as a single system. He creates a look that moves from runway to stage to street without losing status. The designer also sets a template for the creative director as image-maker who controls every frame, from store design to campaign. Paris learns a new way of doing things: leaner, faster, still luxury, but built for a generation raised on sound and early internet posts, the contemporary 2000s youth.

Opposite: You'll have to thank Hedi Slimane for popularizing skinny jeans in the 2010s.

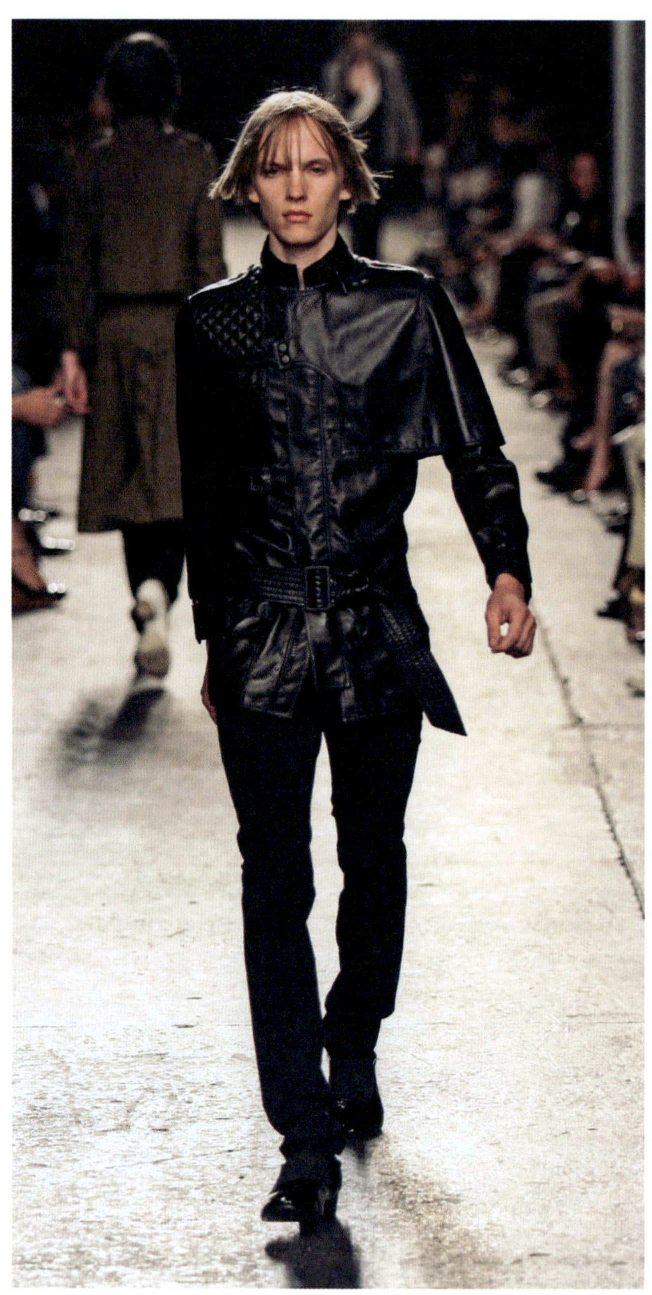

Left: A model on the runway in black leather at Dior Homme spring 2007.

Right: A model wears a Slimane suit jacket paired with a leather skirt at the Saint Laurent Spring/ Summer 2014 show, September 2013.

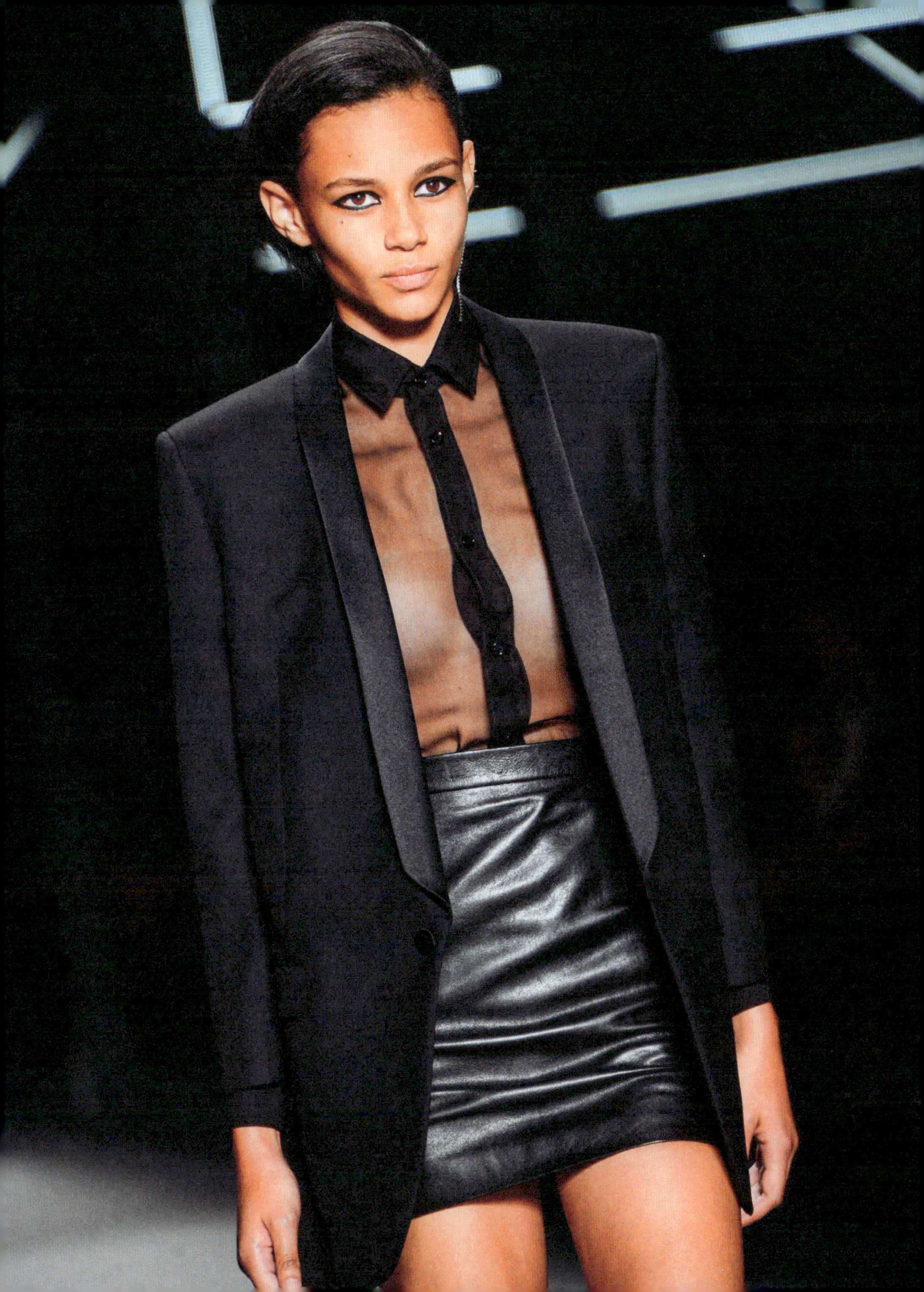

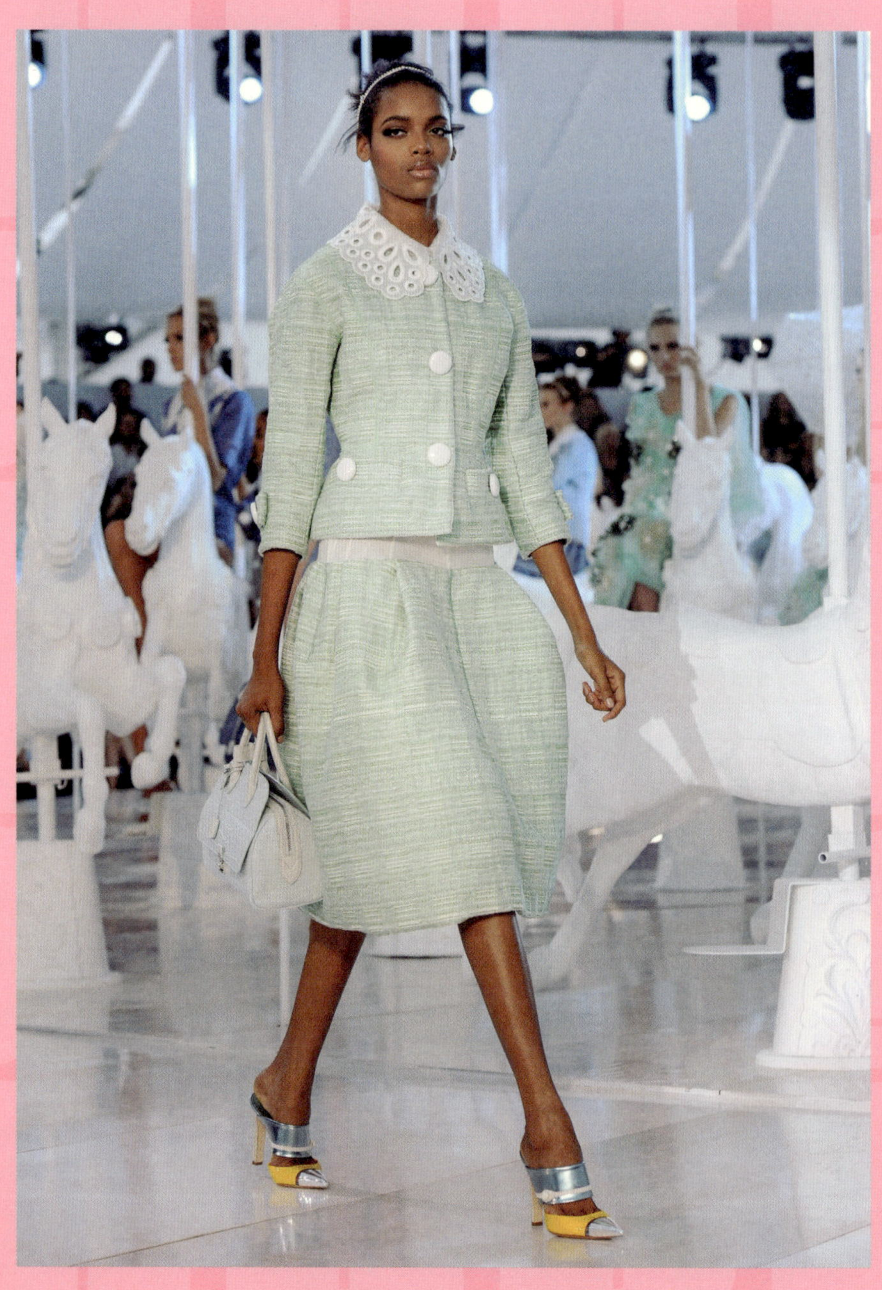

MARC JACOBS

Marc Jacobs made his name in New York, but his Paris chapter began when Louis Vuitton hired him in 1997 to create its first ready-to-wear line. At that point Vuitton was a luggage powerhouse with no clothing. Jacobs brought a downtown sensibility to the atelier and invented the modern luxury collaboration model. Artists such as Stephen Sprouse, Takashi Murakami and Yayoi Kusama entered the Vuitton orbit, their graphics on the LV monogram canvases travelling the globe.

Jacobs also expanded the show format. Vuitton runways became set pieces to rival those of Chanel. Trains pulled into stations, elevators rose, carousels span, yet the bags still shipped on time. Under Jacobs, the "Speedy", the "Alma" and the "Neverfull" got seasonal updates, and the artist collaborations created waiting lists around the block. The brand's turnover exploded, and Paris understood that a creative director can sit at the centre of a billion-euro supply chain while still taking risks.

Marc Jacobs' impact is to fuse American pop instinct with French luxury infrastructure. He shows that the right collaborations can refresh an archive and make a heritage brand feel young again. He also sets the stage for the designer-as-celebrity era: public persona, paparazzi and a clear point of view. His Vuitton years change how all major houses think about ready-to-wear, branding and spectacle. Paris gains a blueprint for the global luxury juggernaut that still defines the industry.

Opposite: From Louis Vuitton's Spring/Summer 2012, a collection where Marc Jacobs used pastel tweeds and carousel staging to soften Parisian polish into something weightless – luxury treated like a daydream rather than an emblem of power.

Overleaf: Louis Vuitton Spring 2008, where Jacobs lined up his "nurses" like a surreal chorus line – a wink to fetish and pop art with Warholian references.

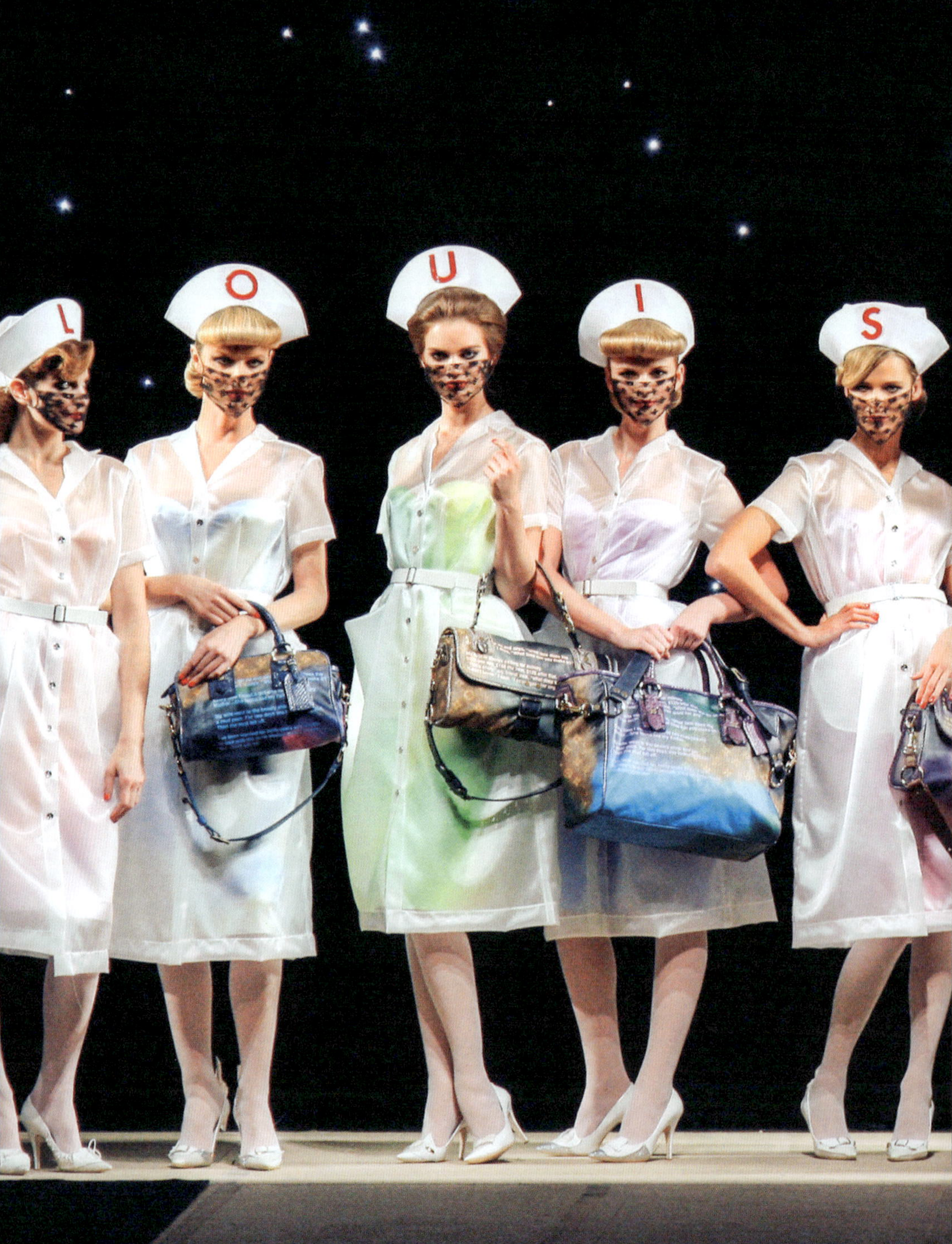
L
O
U
I
S

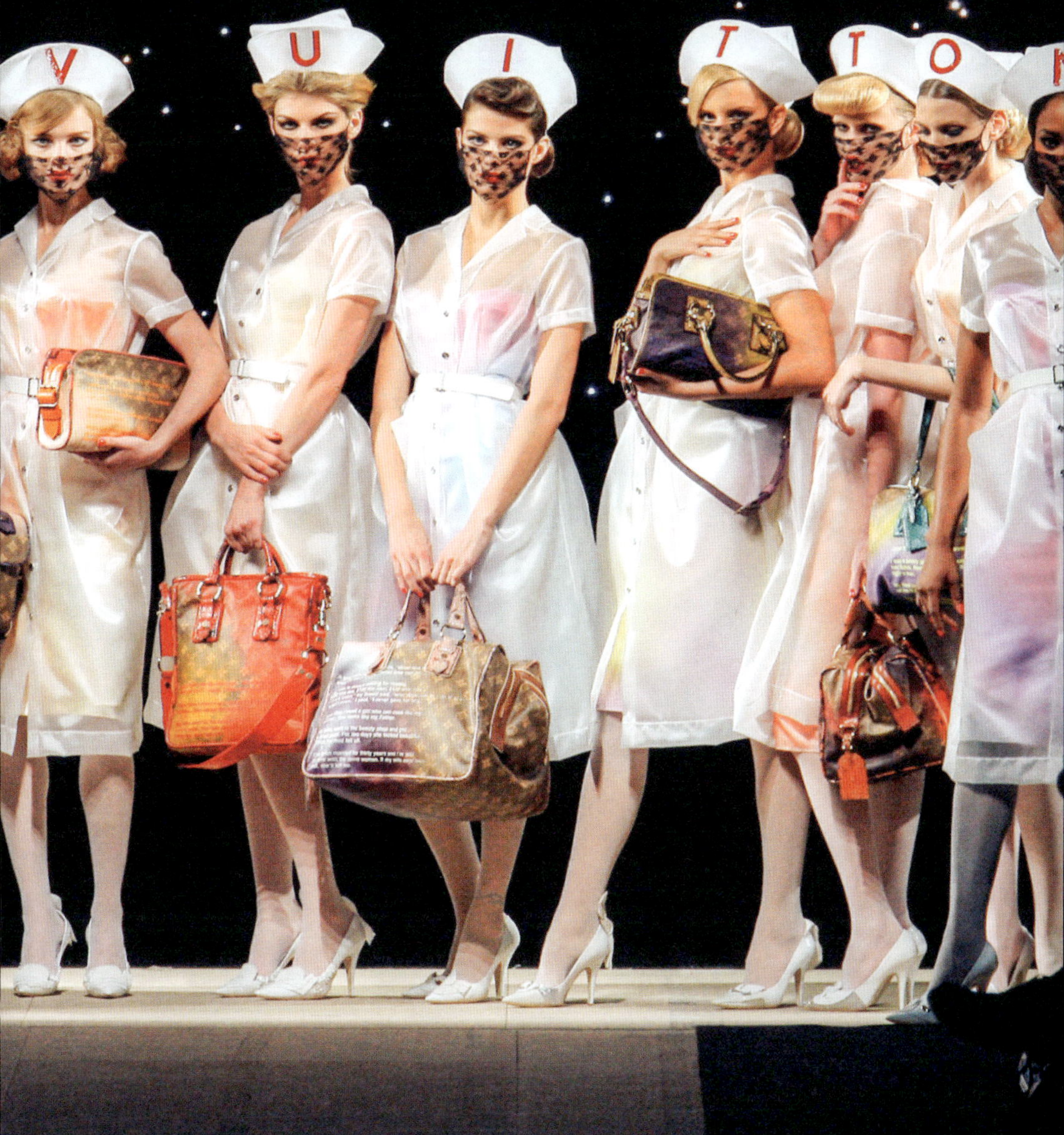
V
U
I
T
T
O

DEMNA GVASALIA

Demna Gvasalia arrived in Paris after training in Antwerp and working at Maison Margiela. In 2014 he launched Vetements with friends, showing in clubs, restaurants and parking garages. Hoodies, DHL T-shirts, cut-up jeans and oversized tailoring appeared on the runway like a live meme, but the pattern cutting was precise. Within two years buyers were rewriting orders, editors rewriting vocabulary. Paris suddenly had a new outsider inside the system.

Balenciaga hired him as creative director in 2015. He kept the subversion but scaled it to a couture archive. Streetwear proportions became luxury; ugly XXL dad sneakers became billion-euro products; the model casting looked like a cross-section of the metro fauna. Balenciaga's sales multiplied and its influence radiated outwards through memes, collaborations and resale markets. At the same time the designer was experimenting with show formats: stadiums, mud pits, news feeds, avatars. Each one read like a comment on culture as much as a product launch.

Demna Gvasalia's impact is to prove that disruption can be disciplined. He translates Margiela-style deconstruction into mass desirability, brings a post-Soviet eye to French luxury and rewrites how houses handle communication. Buyers now expect hot drops, social media activation and products that can live as both viral image and durable object. He expanded what Balenciaga could be and set a new playbook for the next generation of creative directors, and is now cementing his legacy at Gucci.

Opposite: A model walks at Paris Fashion Week in a bright pink piece designed by Demna Gvasalia for Balenciaga Spring/ Summer 2017.

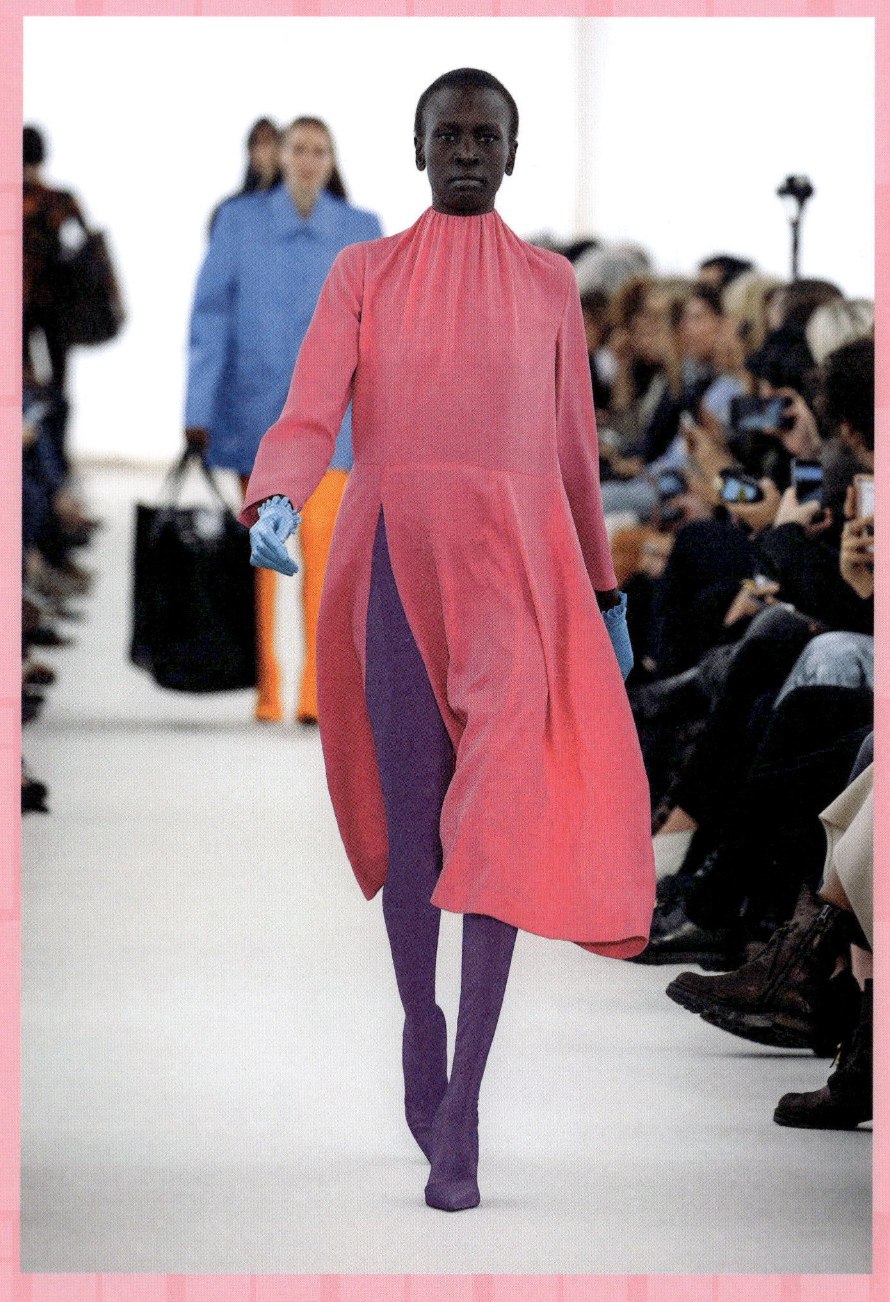

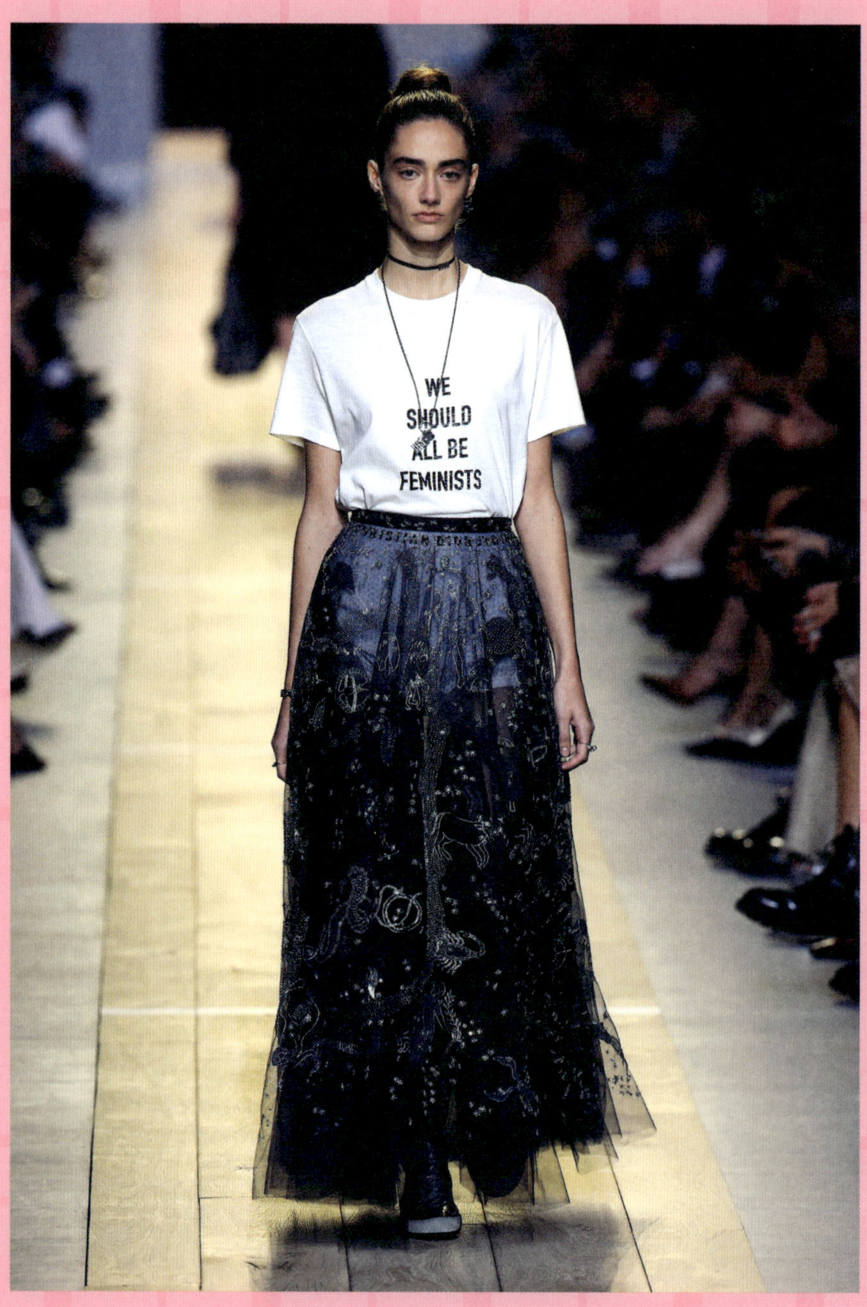
WE
SHOULD
ALL BE
FEMINISTS

MARIA GRAZIA CHIURI

Maria Grazia Chiuri arrived at Dior in 2016 from Valentino and immediately began rewriting what a French couture house could look like in the twenty-first century. She was the first woman to lead Dior and brought with her both Italian atelier discipline and an interest in the social role of clothes. Her debut T-shirt, "We Should All Be Feminists", pulled a slogan from Chimamanda Ngozi Adichie and put it on a Paris runway, signalling a shift from muse to citizen. Dior's ateliers translated her vision into pleated tulle, flat sandals, Bar jackets softened for daily wear and embroidery that quoted female artists instead of heraldry.

Chiuri also refocused the business. She multiplied ready-to-wear, accessories and travel-friendly pieces without losing couture craft. Her shows took place in gardens, palaces and temporary structures filled with feminist art installations. She opened up the casting, worked with choreographers and dancers, and treated Dior as a platform for women across fields, not just models and celebrities. Sales responded really well and Dior became one of LVMH's fastest-growing fashion houses under her watch.

Chiuri's goal was to show that activism and commerce can coexist if the making is serious. Maria Grazia changed the conversation around what "heritage" can include and built a wardrobe that let a global audience live in Dior day to day. The legacy so far is not a single garment but a new posture: Dior as a community of women rather than a pedestal for one.

Opposite: My favourite collection of Maria Grazia's at Dior, Spring/Summer 2017 – it was also her first collection.

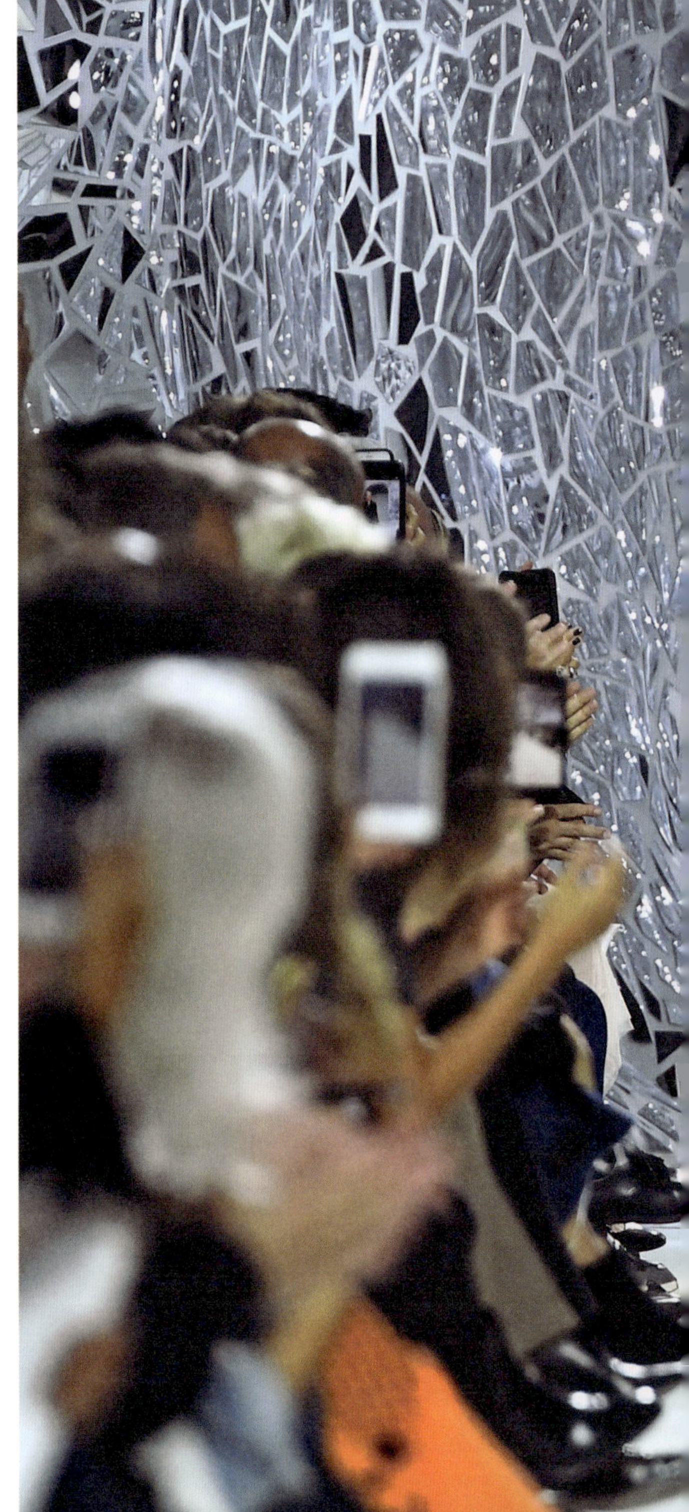

Right: Maria Grazia Chiuri coming out after the Dior show to say "Hi"!

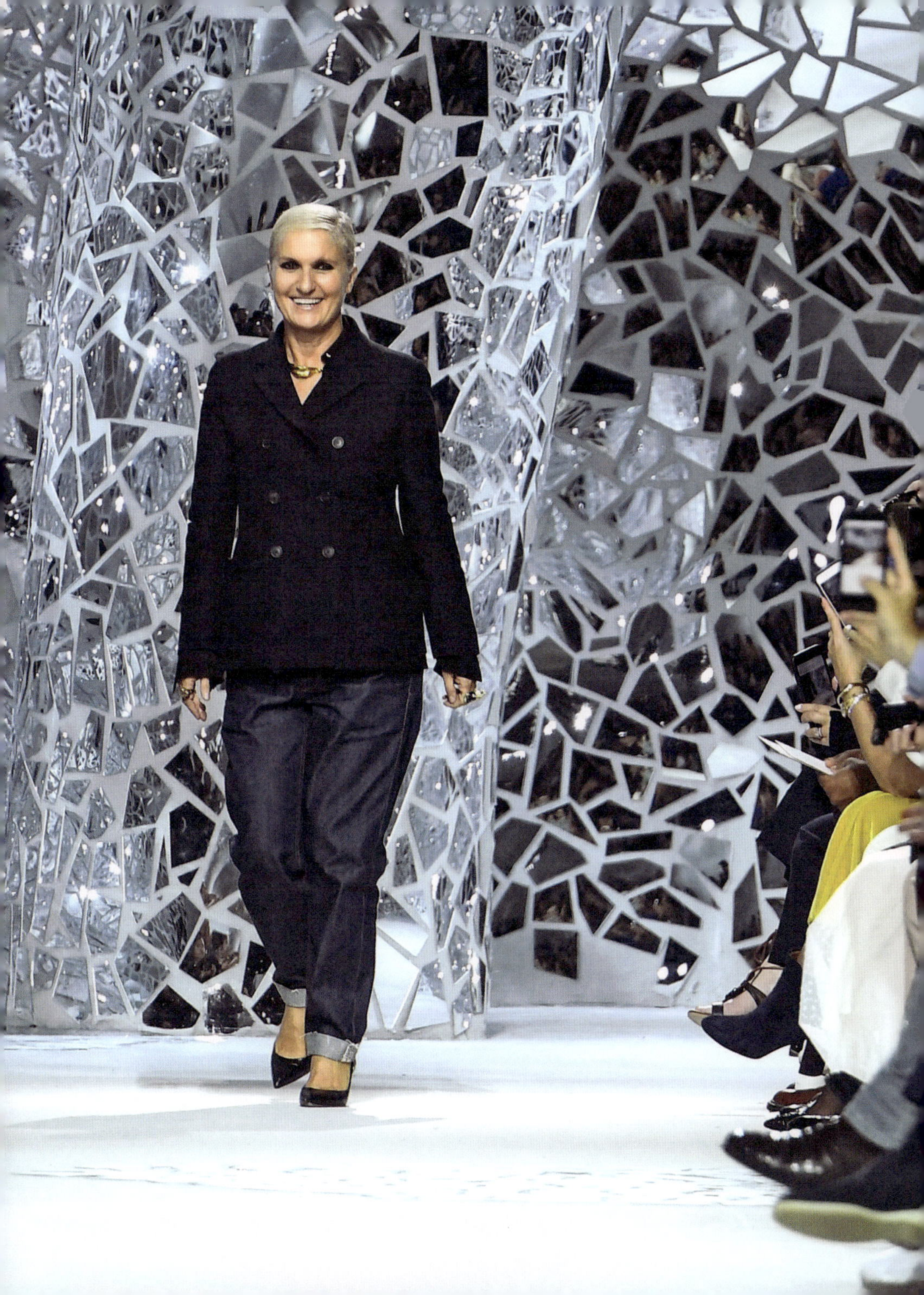

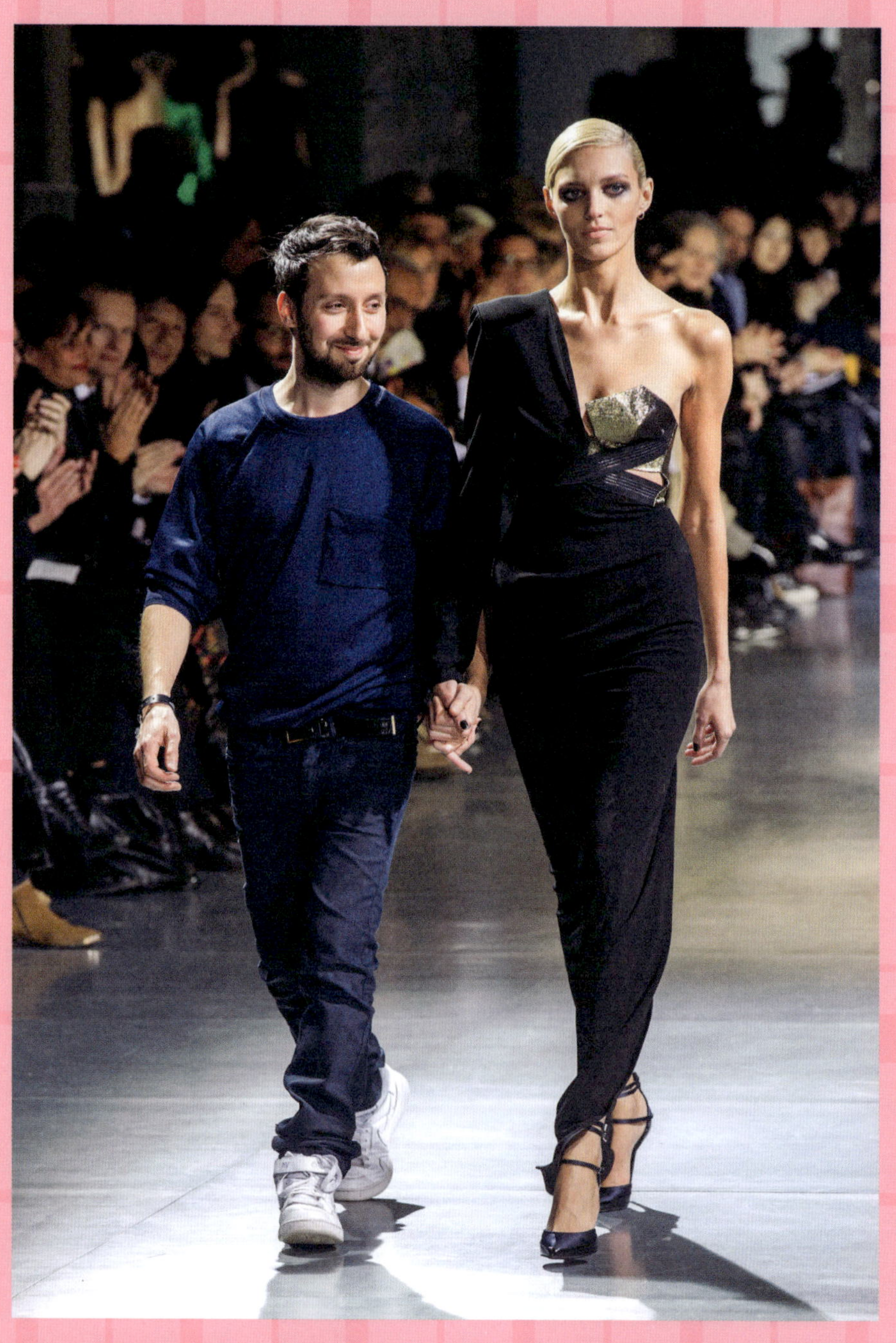

Anthony Vaccarello

Anthony Vaccarello took over at Saint Laurent in 2016 after building a reputation at Versus and his own line. He inherited the house from Hedi Slimane and chose continuity over rupture: sharp tailoring, black leather, smoking jackets and short dresses, but stripped of nostalgia. He kept the music high, the lighting low and the silhouettes close to the body. Under his watch Saint Laurent's shows moved to dramatic outdoor settings – the Eiffel Tower, beaches, desert runways – that turned Paris into a cinematic backdrop.

Vaccarello's real shift was to modernize Saint Laurent's business engine without dulling its edge. He accelerated ready-to-wear, accessories and menswear, building clear seasonal drops and reintroducing couture as a limited but potent halo. He leaned on the house codes ("Le Smoking", the little black dress, rock attitude) but retooled them for a social-media era where an image needs to travel globally in a matter of seconds.

Vaccarello's impact on the city is to prove that heritage can stay sharp and consistency can still feel fresh. He keeps Saint Laurent's black-and-gold universe intact but speeds up its rhythm for a new generation. Accessories, boots and leather goods scale to fund the spectacle, while the shows keep Saint Laurent at the centre of Paris Fashion Week's conversation. The result is a house that looks steady, modern and still unmistakably Parisian, carrying Yves' legacy of liberation into a new century with nightclub precision.

Opposite: Anthony Vaccarello walks the runway during his Fall/Winter 2012 show at Paris Fashion Week.

PHOEBE PHILO

Phoebe Philo grew up in London but built her legend in Paris. She joined Chloé in the late 1990s under Stella McCartney and took over as creative director in 2001. In that role she cleared away fuss, sharpened tailoring and gave the house its cool-girl streak. Her Chloé bags, most of them but especially the "Paddington", created waiting lists that helped define the It-bag era. Then she stepped back, took time off, but returned in 2008 to lead Celine.

At Celine she reshaped the conversation about women's clothes. Minimalist lines, real pockets, architectural coats and clean leather bags felt like a relief after a decade of hyper-embellishment. She cast women who look like her audience, showed at quiet hours and avoided celebrity overload. Celine became a working woman's luxury: understated, modern, almost private in tone. Editors called it "intellectual chic", but the business story was even stronger. Leather goods exploded, ready-to-wear became a uniform and a generation of women recalibrated their wardrobe around her vision.

Phoebe Philo's heritage was to centre female experience in a way that felt lived in rather than aspirational. She proved a brand can be quiet and still drive global sales, that subtlety can move as much product as spectacle. Her Celine years became the template for a new kind of luxury brand image: intelligent, edited and consistent. Even after she left in 2017, the audience she built remained loyal to that "old Celine", as fashion commentators love to call it today.

Opposite: Phoebe Philo is applauded on the runway following the Celine Spring/Summer 2017 show at Paris Fashion Week.

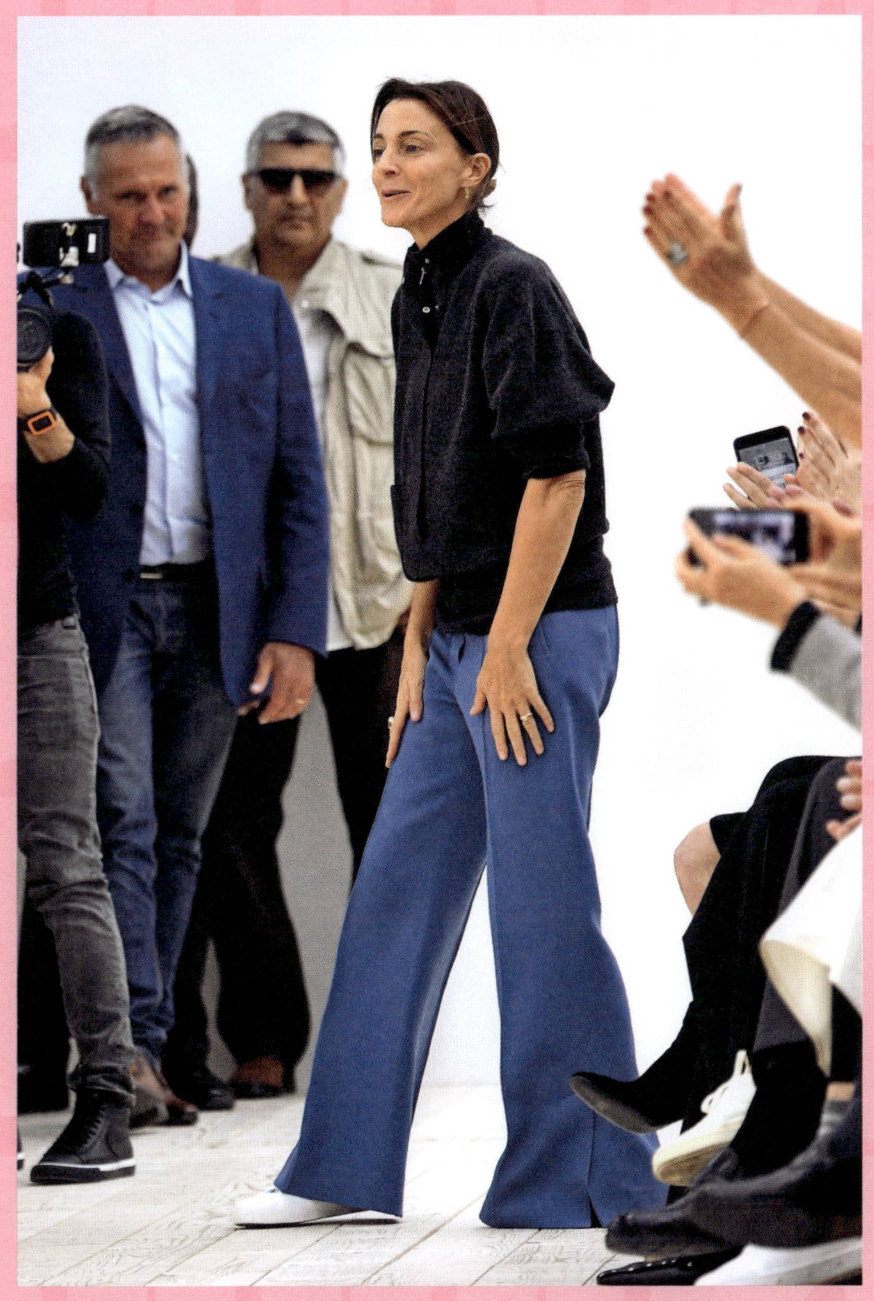

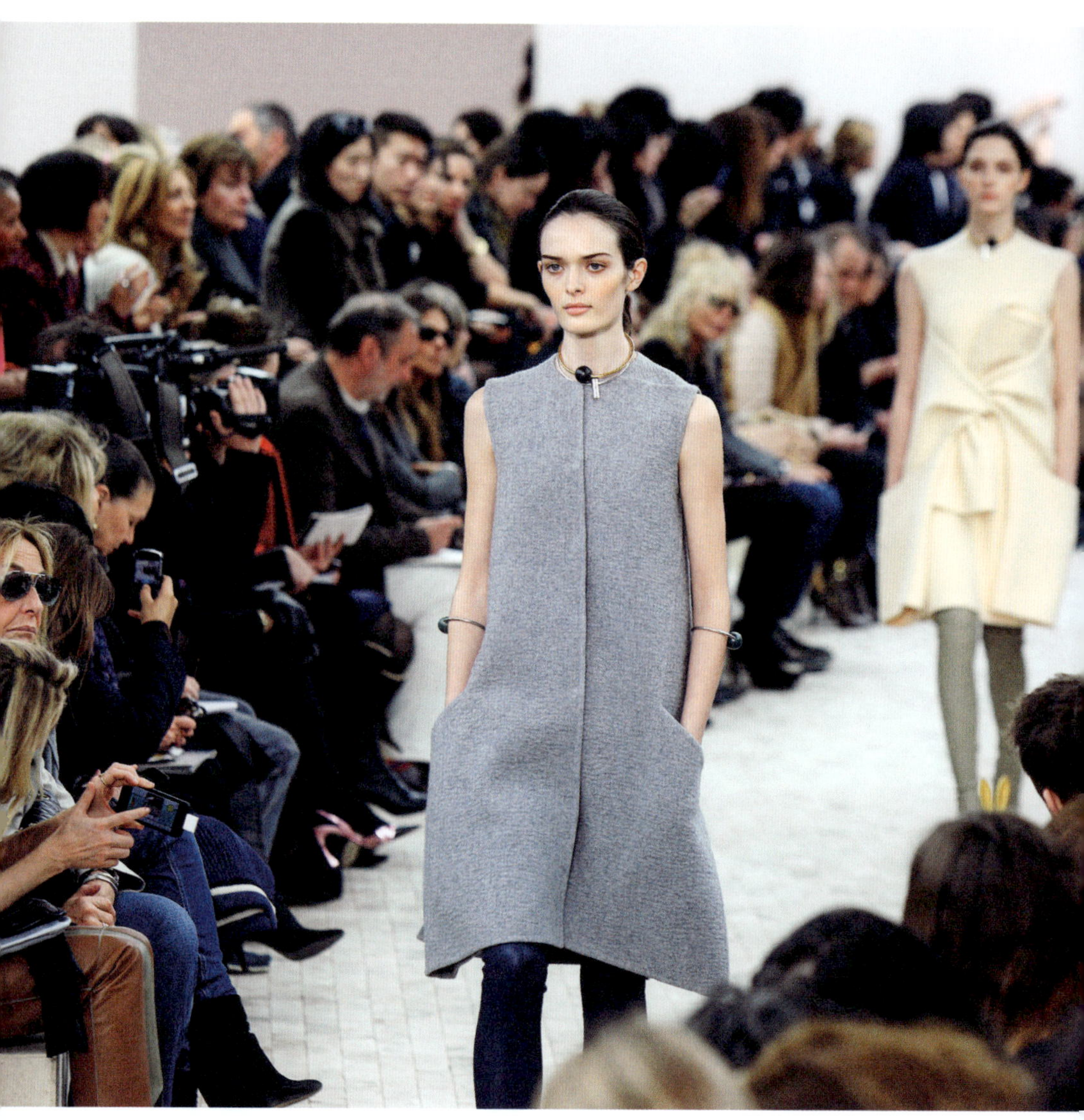

Above: Phoebe Philo is that rare designer who made restraint feel like power, teaching a generation that quiet clothes can hold the loudest authority.

Opposite: One of the most impactful shows of Phoebe at Chloé, especially from the bag's point of view.

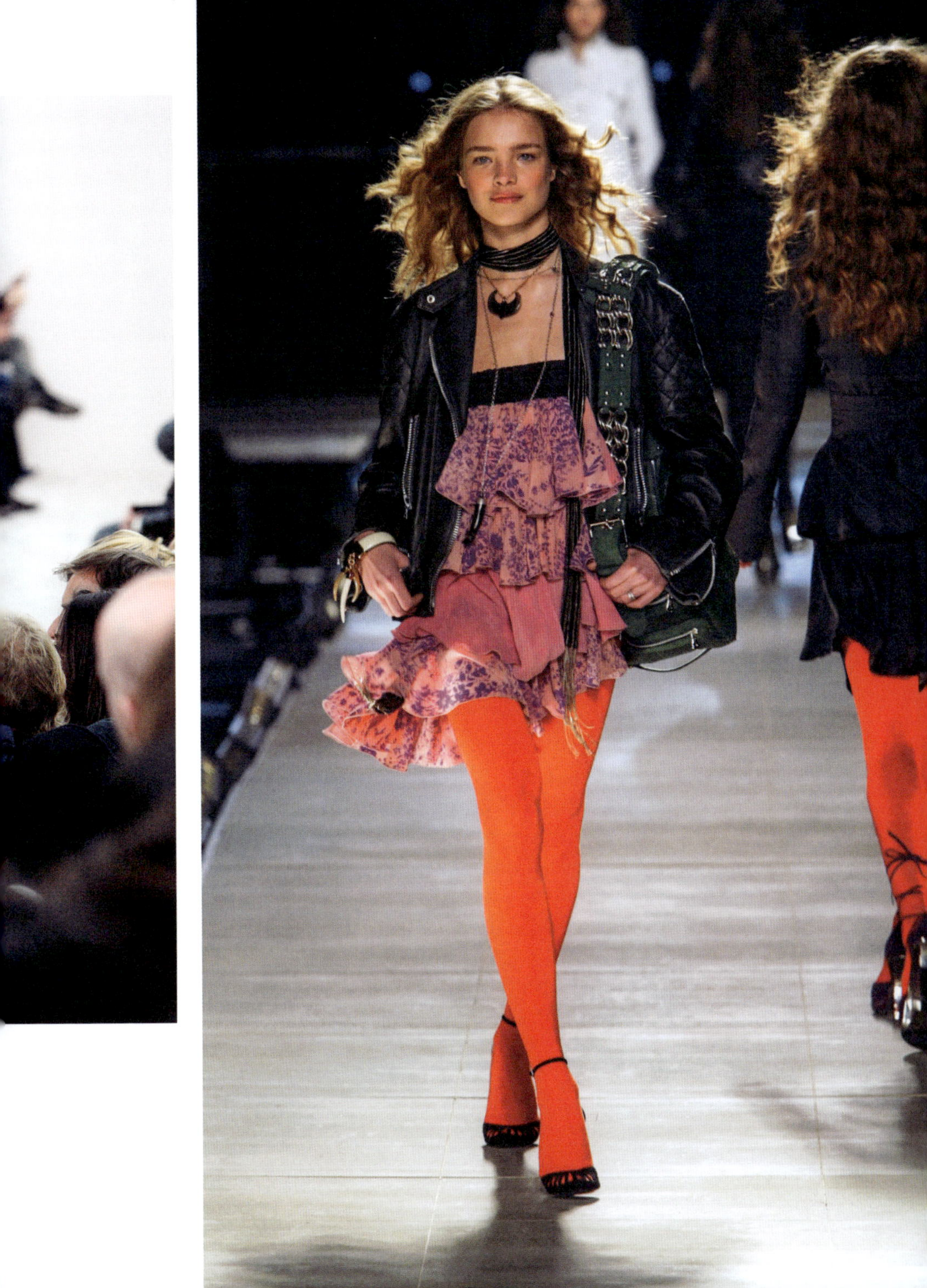

ISABEL MARANT

Isabel Marant built her world in Paris from the 1990s onwards, starting with a jewellery line and small shows before expanding into a full label. Her aesthetic emerges as an unforced mix of bohemian ease, sporty attitude and French street sense. Long before the phrase "high-low" became a cliché, she showed how a silk blouse can live next to a parka and cowboy boots can walk the rue Saint-Honoré.

In the late 2000s Marant made a decisive business move with the wedge sneaker. The shoe looks like a trainer but adds height and it was instantly copied worldwide and worn by celebrities, stylists and off-duty models. This one product funded Marant's global expansion and turned her into the go-to name for relaxed, wearable Paris cool. Stores opened from New York to Tokyo, but the centre remains on the Right Bank, where Marant's boutiques feel like lived-in apartments rather than temples of fashion.

Marant's goal is to democratize the idea of the "Parisienne" wardrobe without draining its credibility. She shows that real-life clothes can still have an edge, boho can be disciplined and accessories can turn a small label into a global powerhouse. Editors credit her with making daywear a Paris headline again and young designers watch how she balances the market with easy entry pieces, a signature shoe and seasonal updates that never feel forced. She gives the city a model for modern casual luxury that still carries the authority of its esteemed couture heritage.

Opposite: Isabel Marant, Fall/Winter 2025.

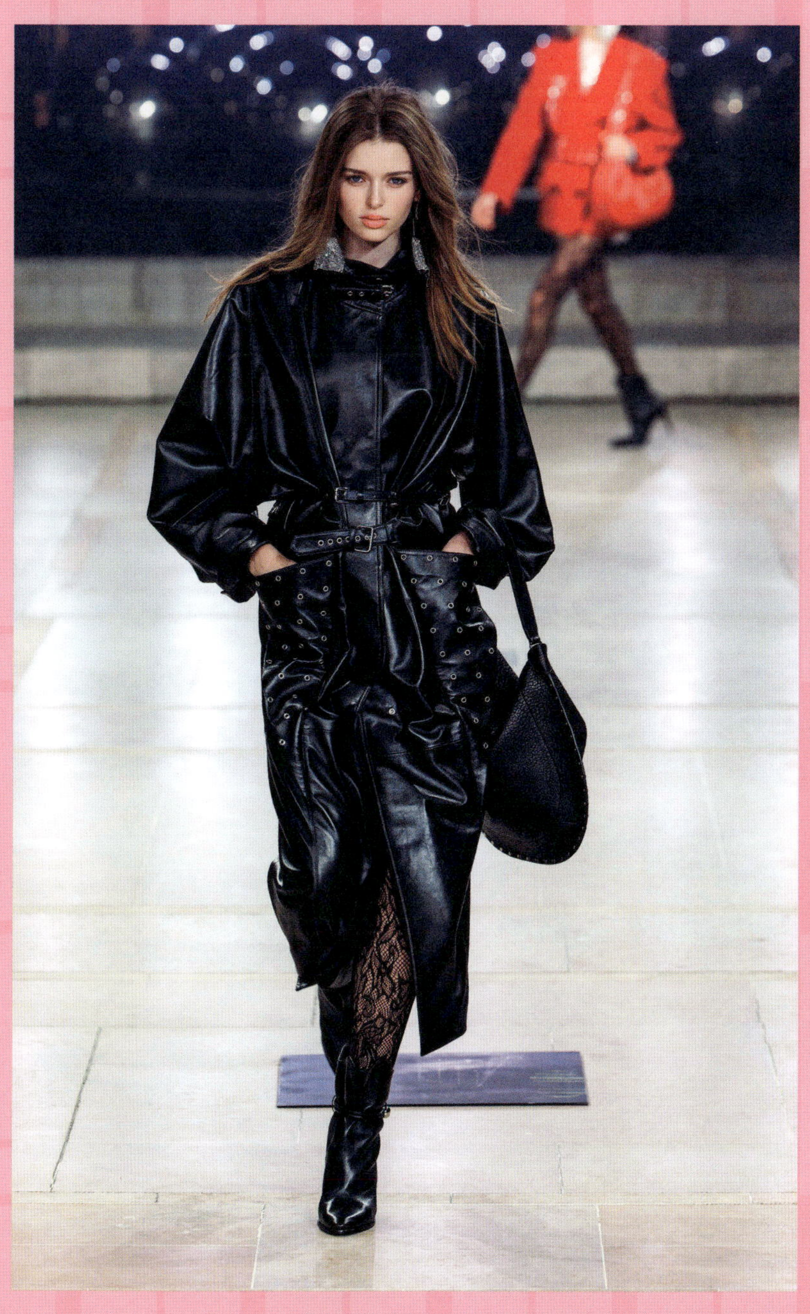

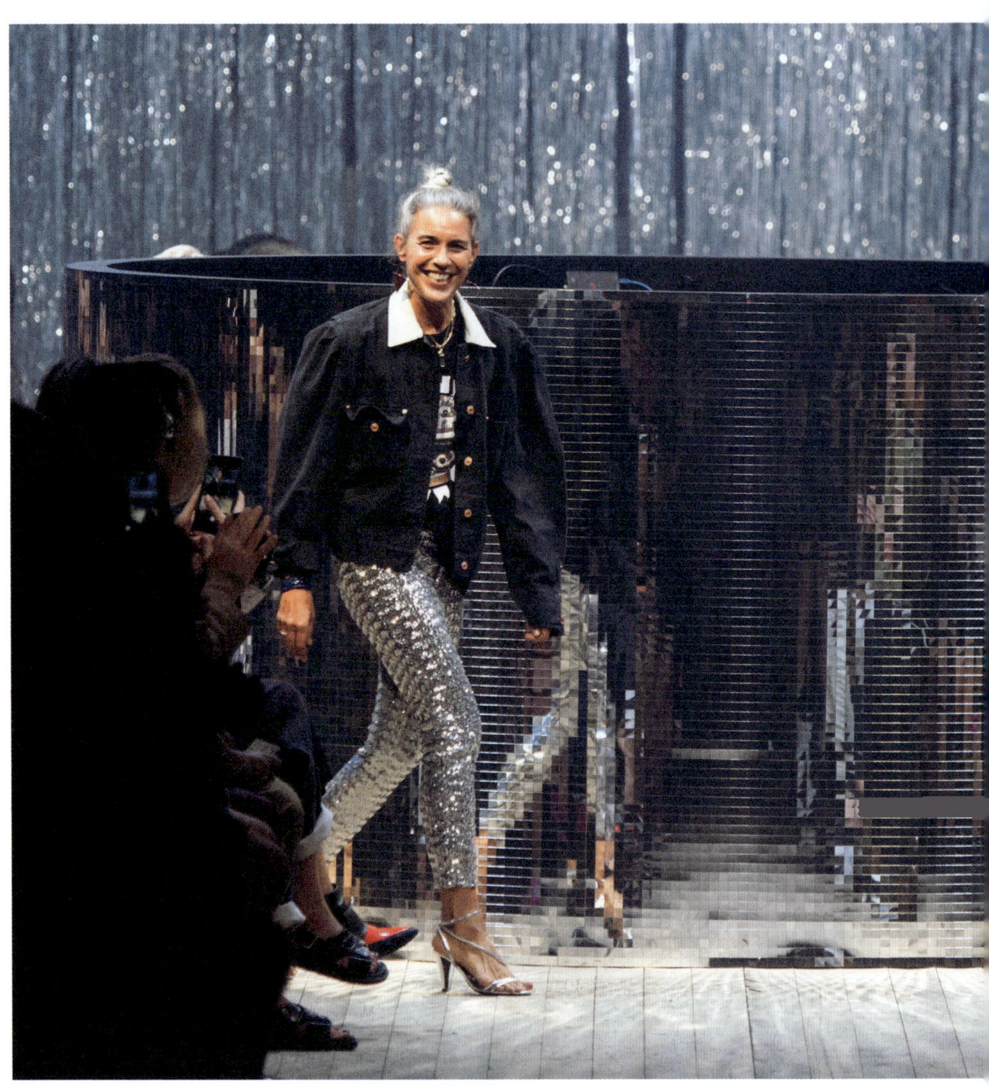

Above: Isabel Marant understands how to turn ease into structure in a way that feels almost effortless.

Opposite: The style is a mix of bohemian ease and Parisian grit held together by silhouettes that move.

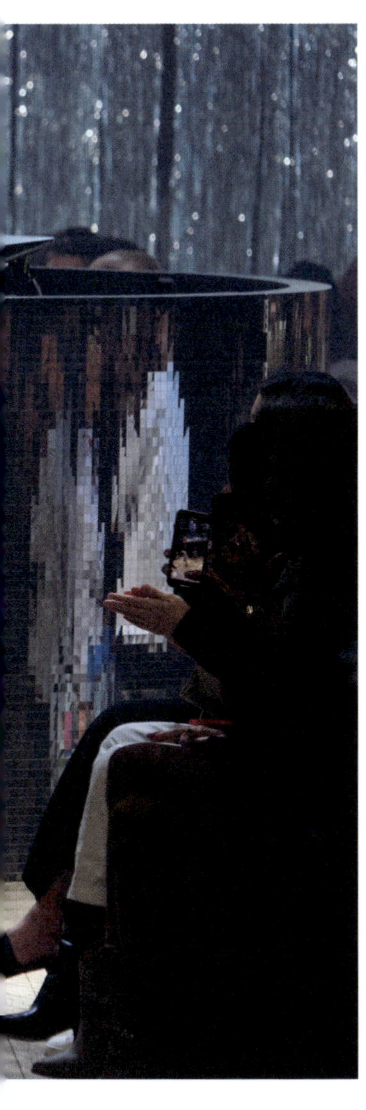

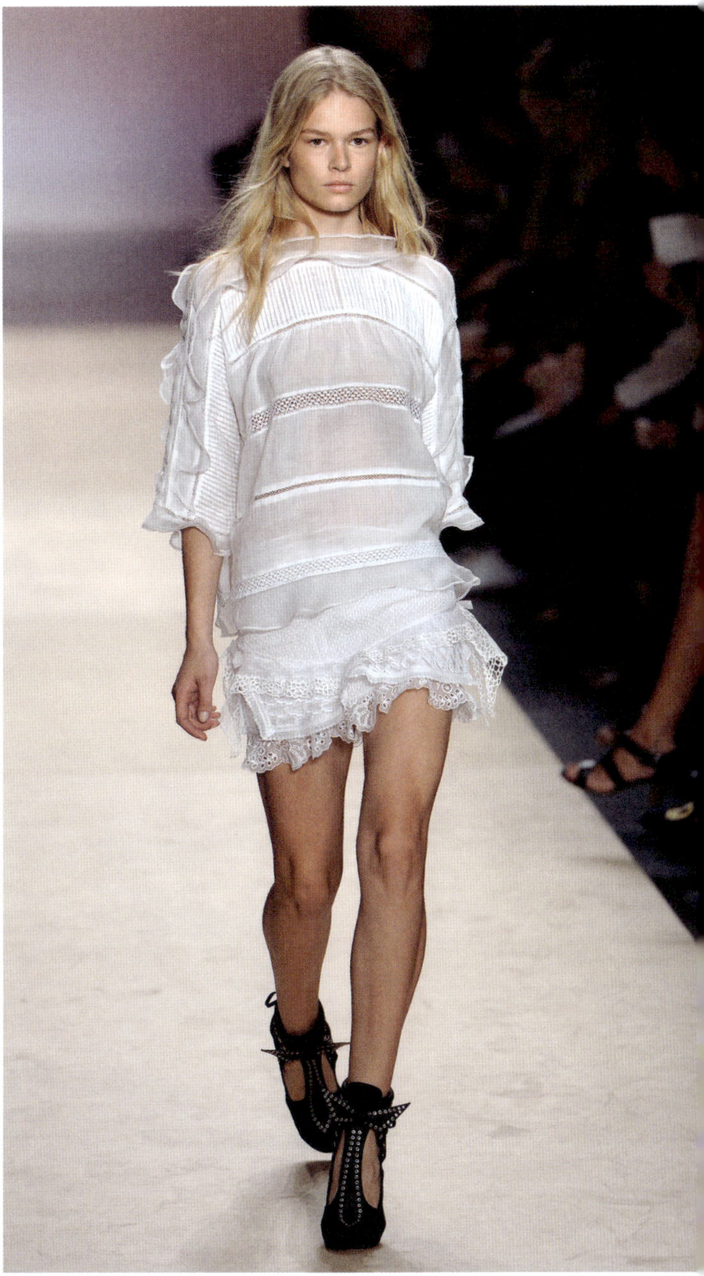

JACQUEMUS

Simon Porte Jacquemus grew up in the South of France and arrived in Paris aged 19 with no backers and a small collection. He staged early shows off-schedule, using friends as models and Instagram as a press office. The clothes are simple at first glance, but the vision is already clear: sun-drenched tailoring, naive cut-outs, a mix of Provençal memory and Paris discipline. Editors call it charming. Buyers see it moving fast. Social media pushes it exponentially.

Within a decade Jacquemus turned that charm into an industrial rhythm. He scaled accessories first: the tiny "Chiquito" bag became a viral object and funded the studio. His shows became open-air installations in lavender fields, salt flats or Versailles gardens, streamed to millions but still rooted in hand-finished clothes and exact casting. He stayed independent, reinvested profit and kept his headquarters in Paris, while producing in Europe.

Jacquemus's impact on the city is to show that a designer born after the digital revolution can build a global house on personal narrative, disciplined product and spectacle timed for social media, all of it independently. He treats geography, casting and scale as part of design itself. The result is a new model for the city: a young label acting like a heritage house in terms of quality but using a pop-star stagecraft to sell summer ease. Paris gains a blueprint for how to grow a new luxury player from nothing in the 2010s.

Opposite: Gigi Hadid walking for Jacquemus.

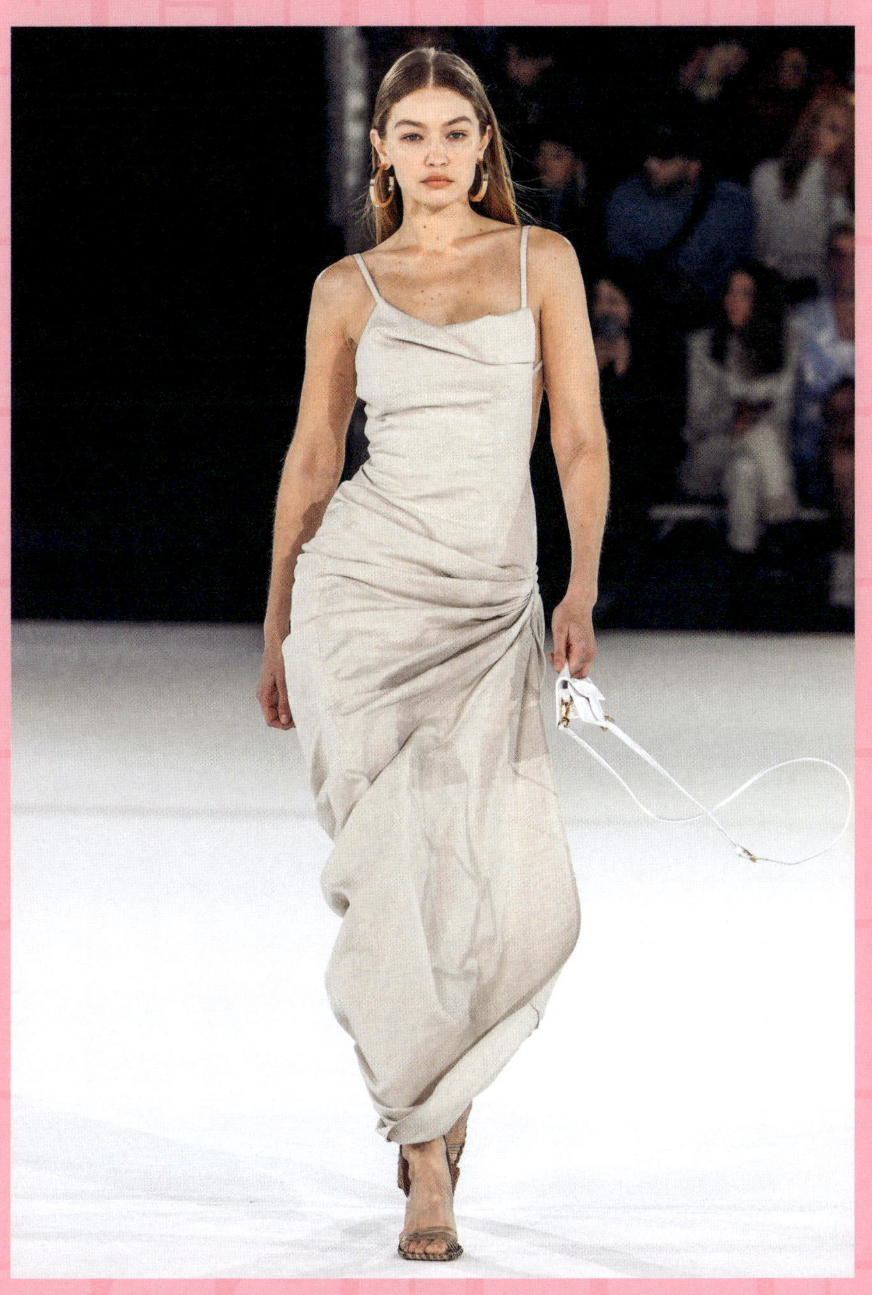

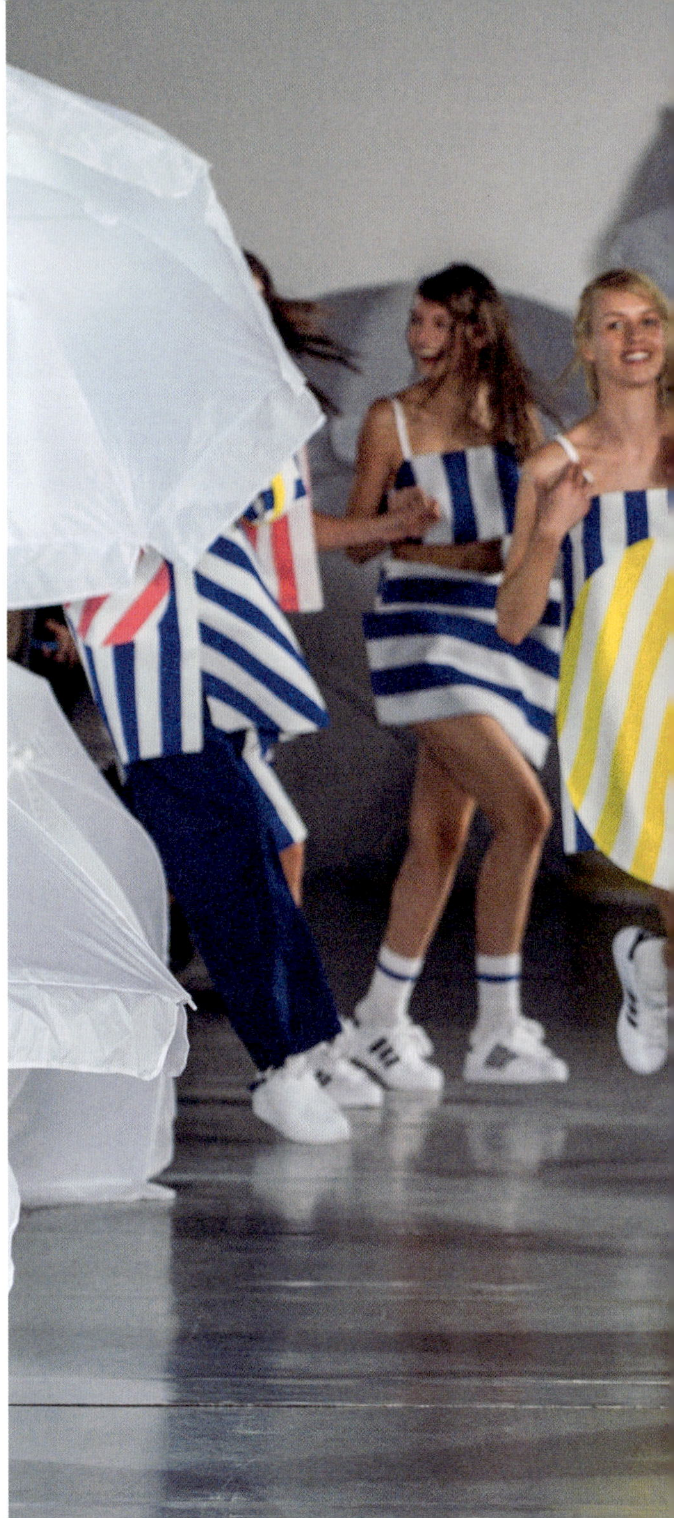

Right: Jacquemus's Spring/
Summer 2015.

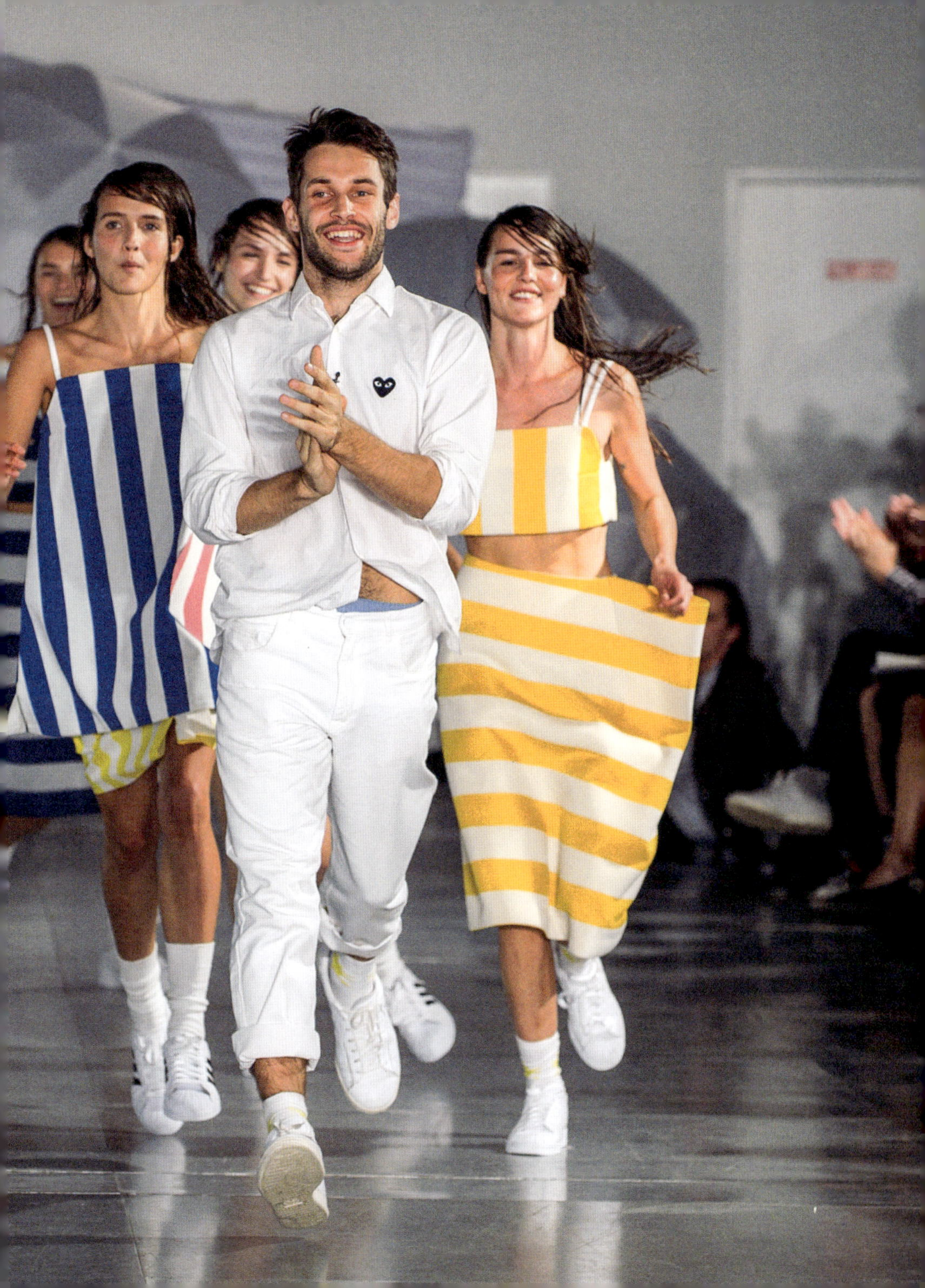

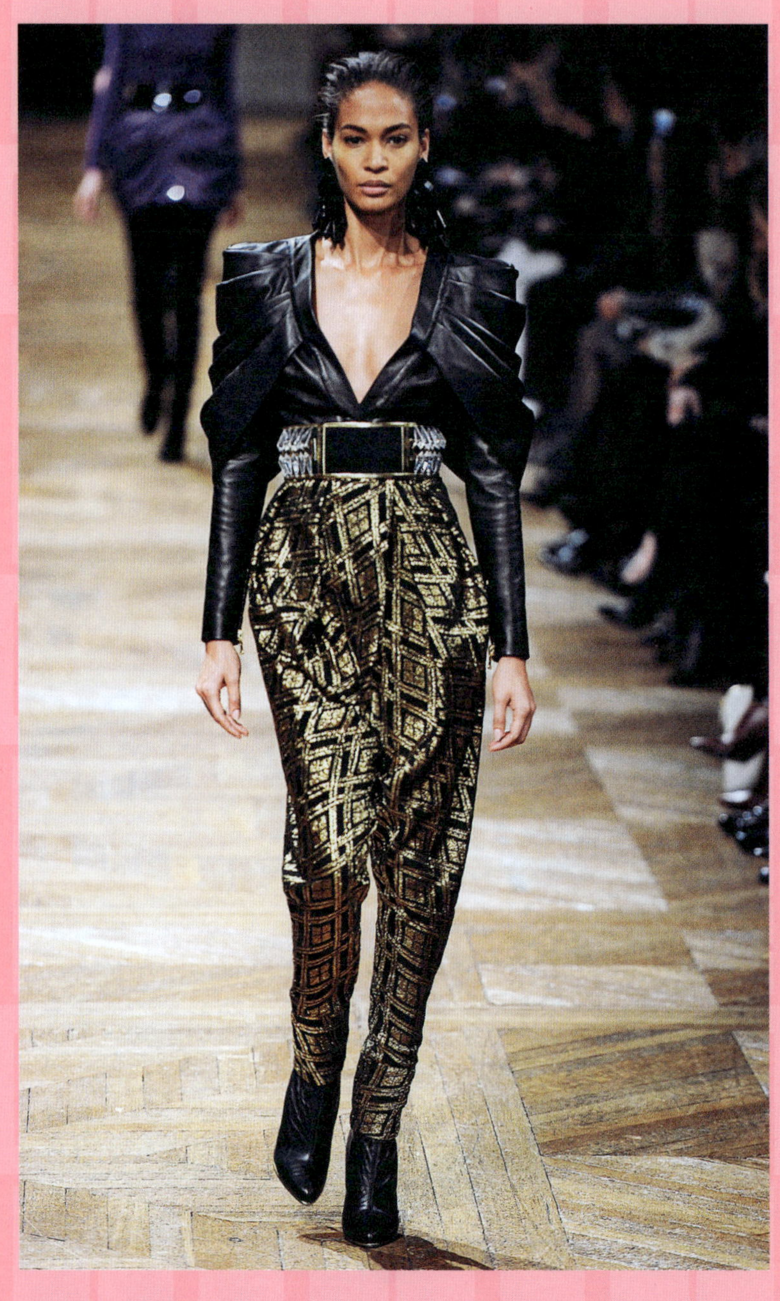

Olivier Rousteing

In 2009 Olivier Rousteing joined Balmain and became creative director at 25, one of the youngest in the industry. The house had been known for structured, opulent tailoring. He updated that DNA with sharp shoulders, body-conscious dresses and military details but pushed the casting, celebrity access and social media to an unprecedented level. By 2011 he had rebuilt Balmain as a pop-culture label.

Rousteing's real innovation is to treat social media as a runway extension. He uses Instagram to cast models, preview collections and show the work of the atelier, creating what the press calls the "Balmain Army". Beyoncé, Rihanna, Kim Kardashian and a rotating cast of supermodels became his public ambassadors, turning Paris Fashion Week into a global feed event.

Rousteing also tightened the business. Balmain launched accessories, menswear and a steady ready-to-wear stream to match the headline dresses. Prices remained high but the visibility broadened. He revived the idea of a house built on disciplined atelier work, yet carried by mass attention.

Olivier Rousteing's impact revolves around fusing couture craft with digital reach, showing that a centuries-old maison can speak the language of youth culture without losing its structure. He makes inclusivity and celebrity part of the Paris vocabulary and sets a template for how a creative director can behave as both designer and digital producer.

Opposite: Olivier Rousteing for Balmain, Fall/Winter 2013 ready-to-wear.

Overleaf: Olivier Rousteing made Balmain part of pop culture, turning the house into a place where craft, celebrity and spectacle all lived on the same wavelength.

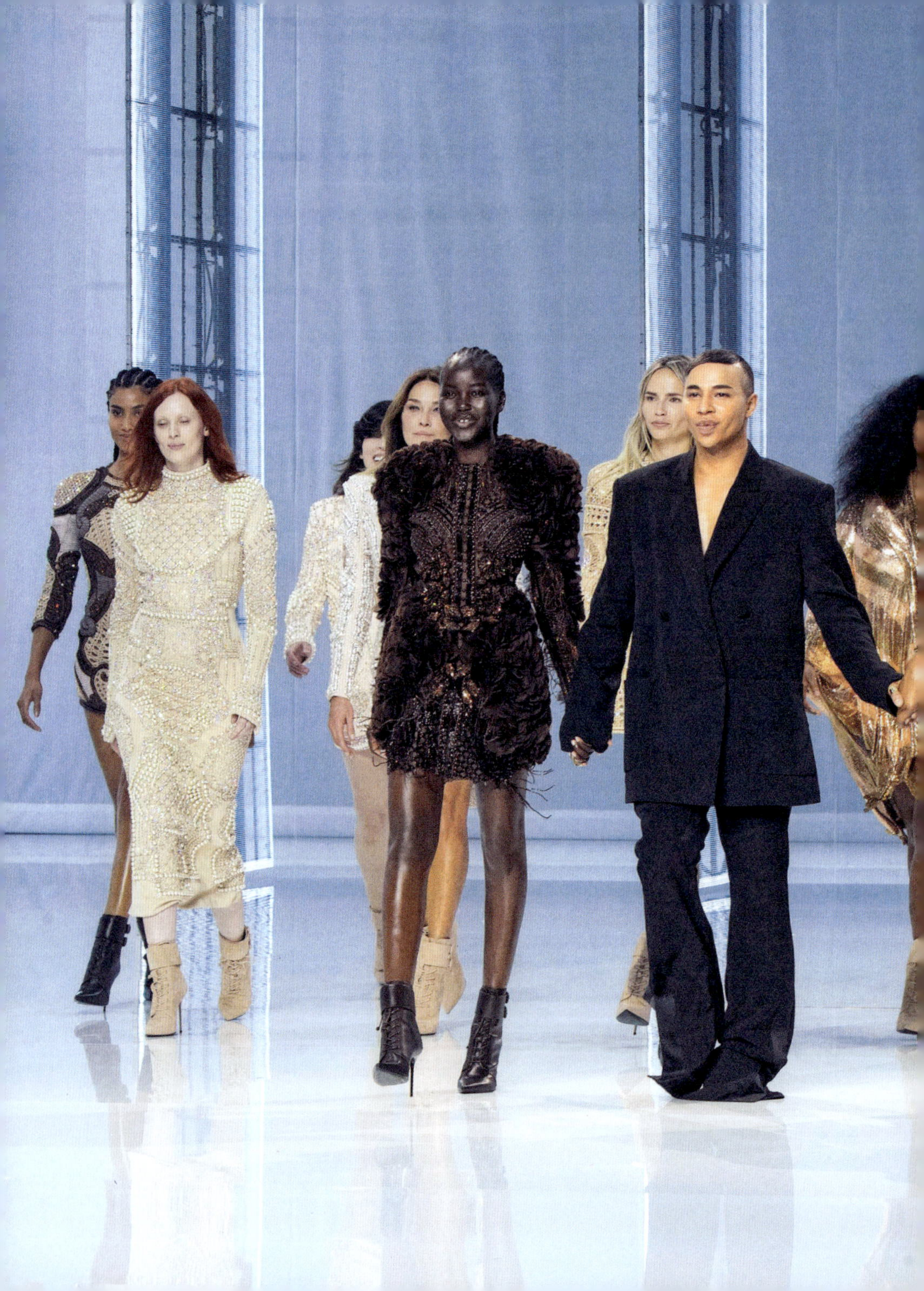

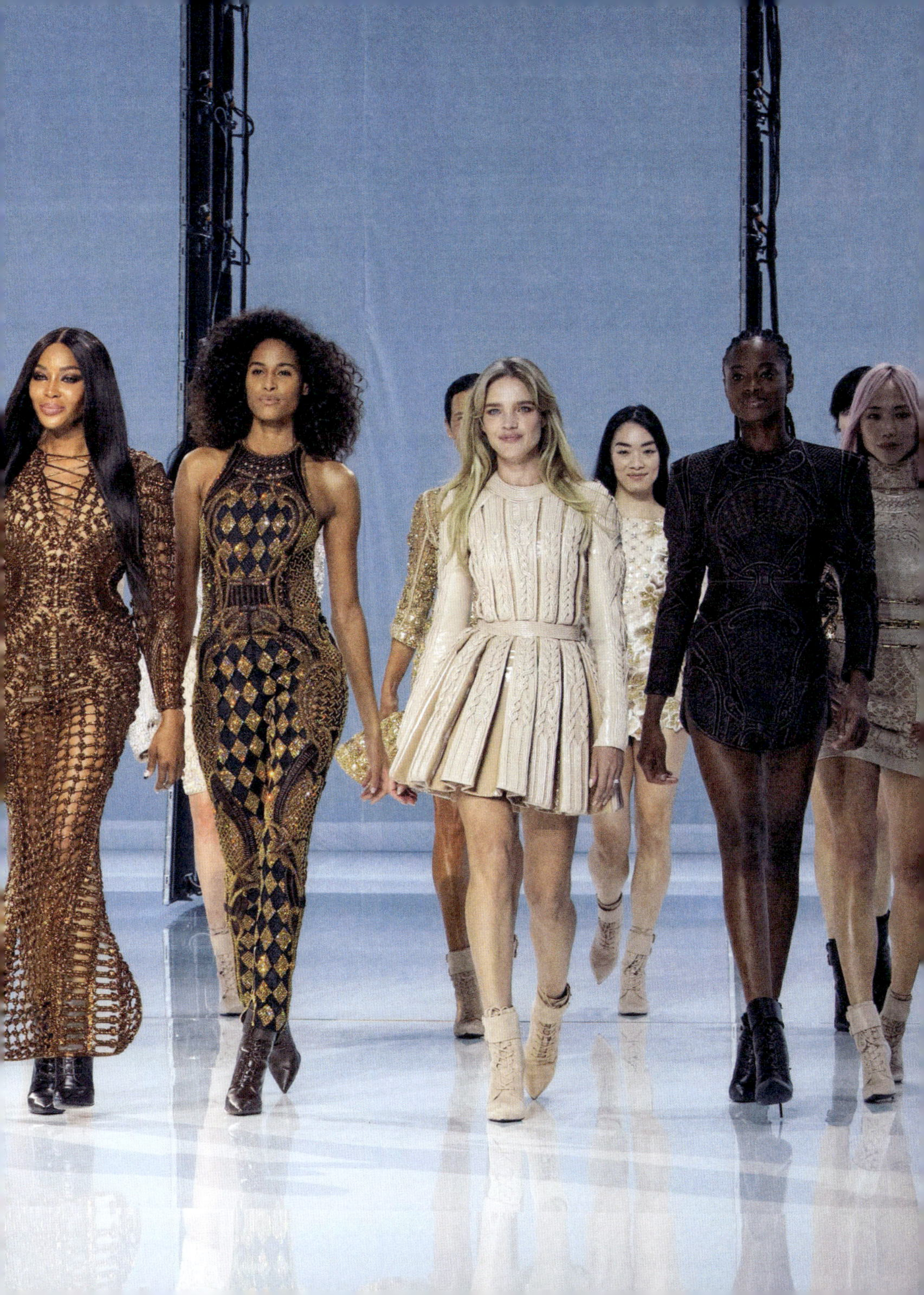

CHAPTER 4:

MUSES & PLACES

Clothes gain speed on the right person. A cut on a hanger is an idea; on a muse it becomes a signal that travels through photos, clubs, sidewalks and then the world. Repetition turns into reference. A muse is not just a model but a translator, someone whose posture explains the line, whose life makes the garment believable.

When it works, designers don't need long campaigns or slogans. The muse carries the tone of the house without speaking. They appear in editorials, street shots and everyday life, making a new silhouette readable long before the stores deliver it. In Paris this link between atelier and muse is a tradition as old as couture but keeps renewing with each generation.

This chapter looks at the faces who made the codes visible – the women and men who turned private fittings into public language and who gave designers the feedback loop every great house needs.

JANE BIRKIN

Jane Birkin landed in Paris in the late 1960s, an English actress and singer who never quite left. Her arrival coincided with a shift in the city's mood: fewer couture salons, more Left Bank cafés, more rock and cinema. Her personal style – men's shirts over bare legs, wicker baskets instead of handbags, T-shirts tucked into flared trousers – reads like an anti-uniform at first. Yet photographers and designers notice she is not rebelling against chic so much as relaxing it.

Through her relationship with Serge Gainsbourg and her constant public presence, Birkin gave Paris an image of undone glamour. She showed that sensuality can come from simplicity, that you can wear a slip dress to the market and a basket bag to dinner, and still look unforgettable. When Hermès named a bag after her in 1984 – the "Birkin" – this was not just a marketing move. It was a recognition that she had changed the way women treat luxury accessories: soft, capacious, lived-in rather than perched and pristine.

Birkin's impact on the culture of the city was to turn casual gestures into aspirational codes. She helped move French style from rulebook to rumour, something you copy without knowing exactly why. Decades later, every "effortless" mood board still traces back to Jane Birkin's nonchalance – she proves that a muse can shift an entire market simply by being herself in public.

Opposite: Name a more iconic JB look – I'll wait!

Overleaf: Legendary couple Birkin and Serge Gainsbourg.

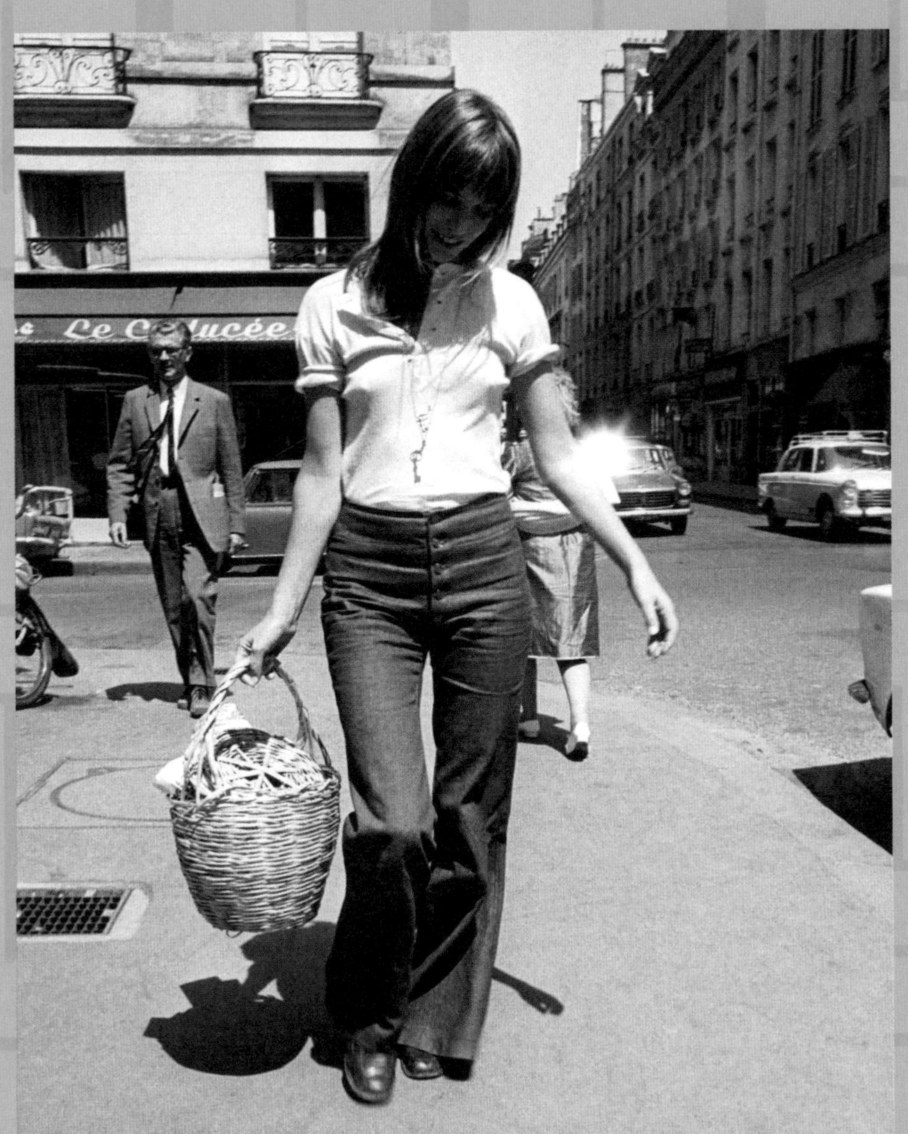

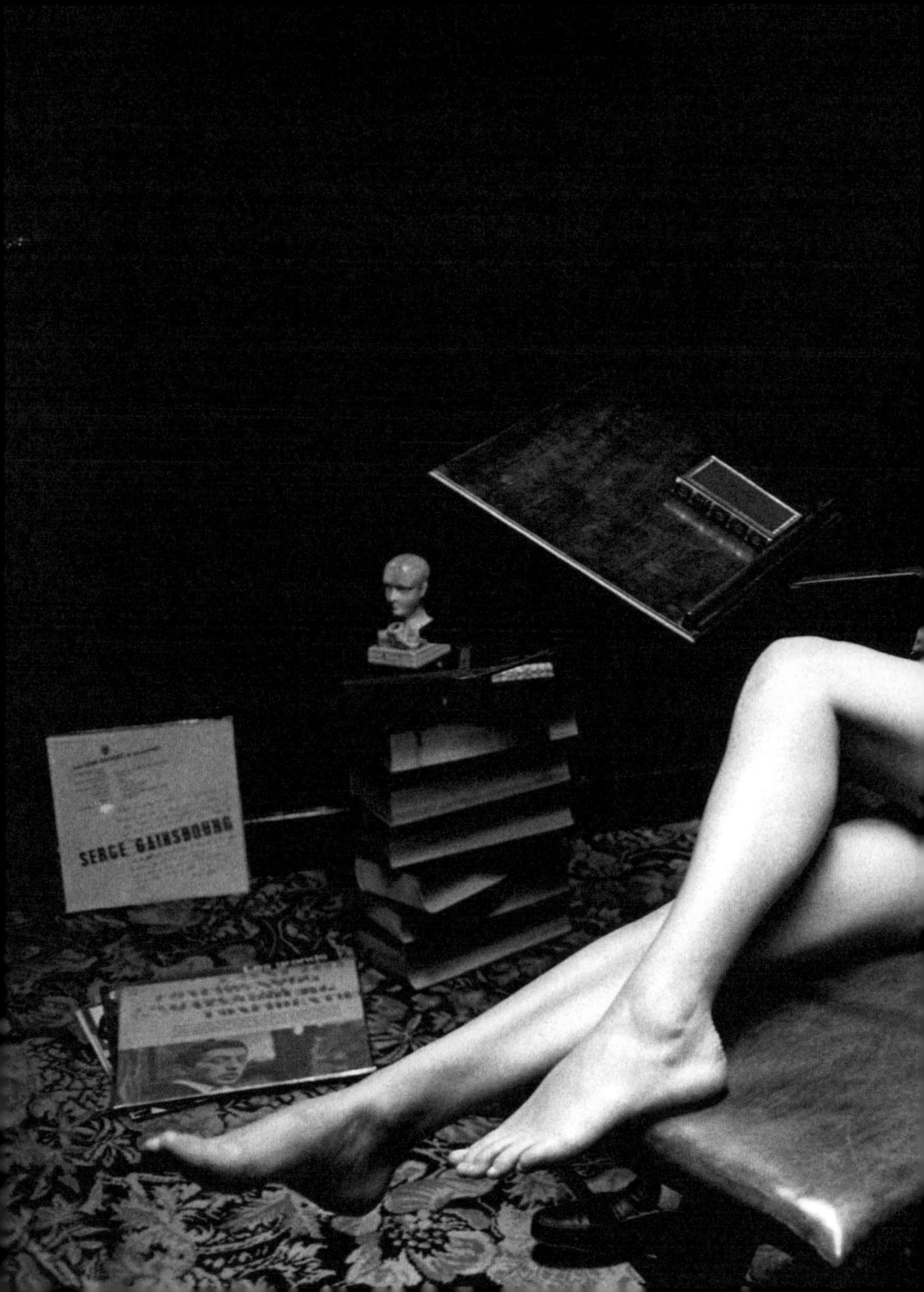
SERGE GAINSBOURG

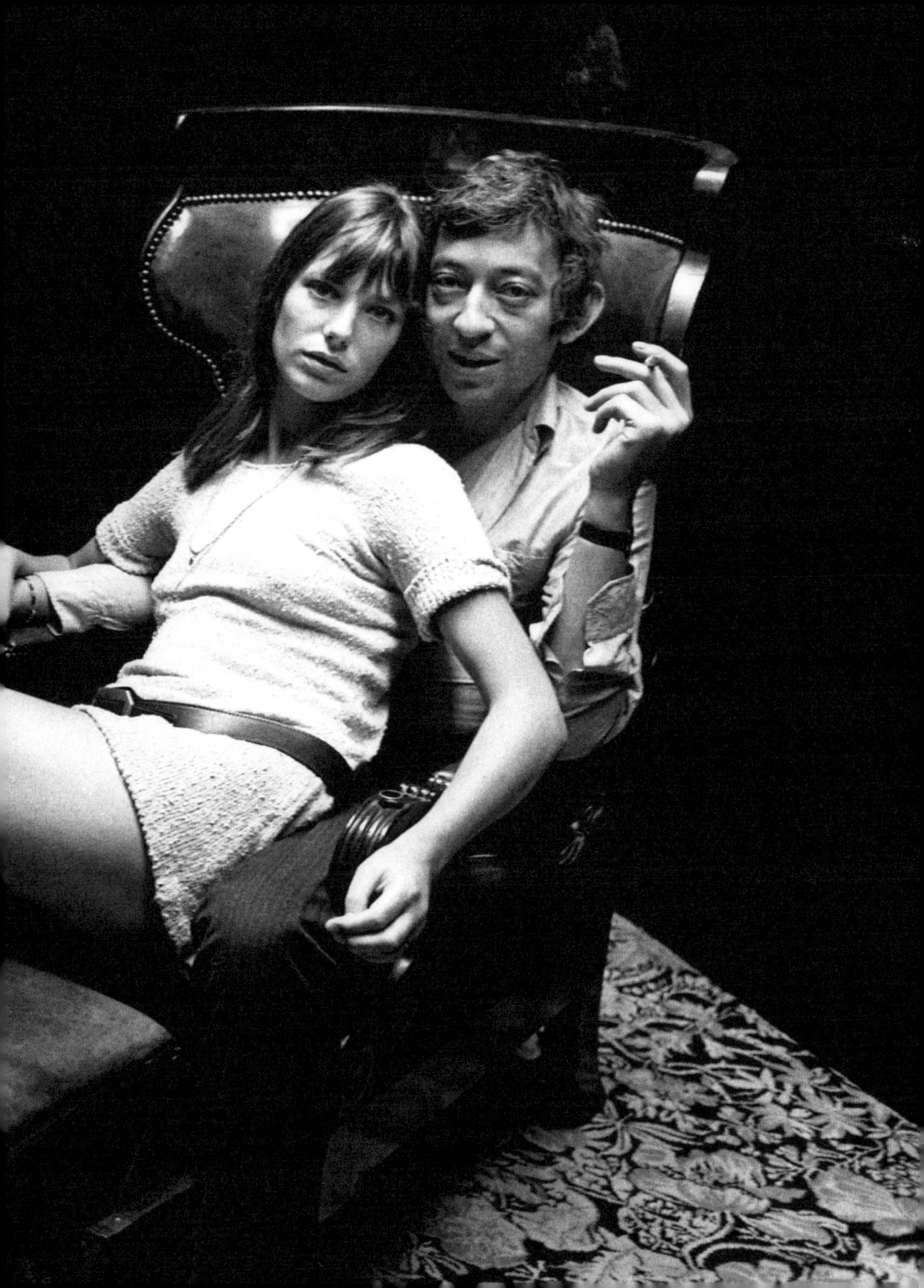

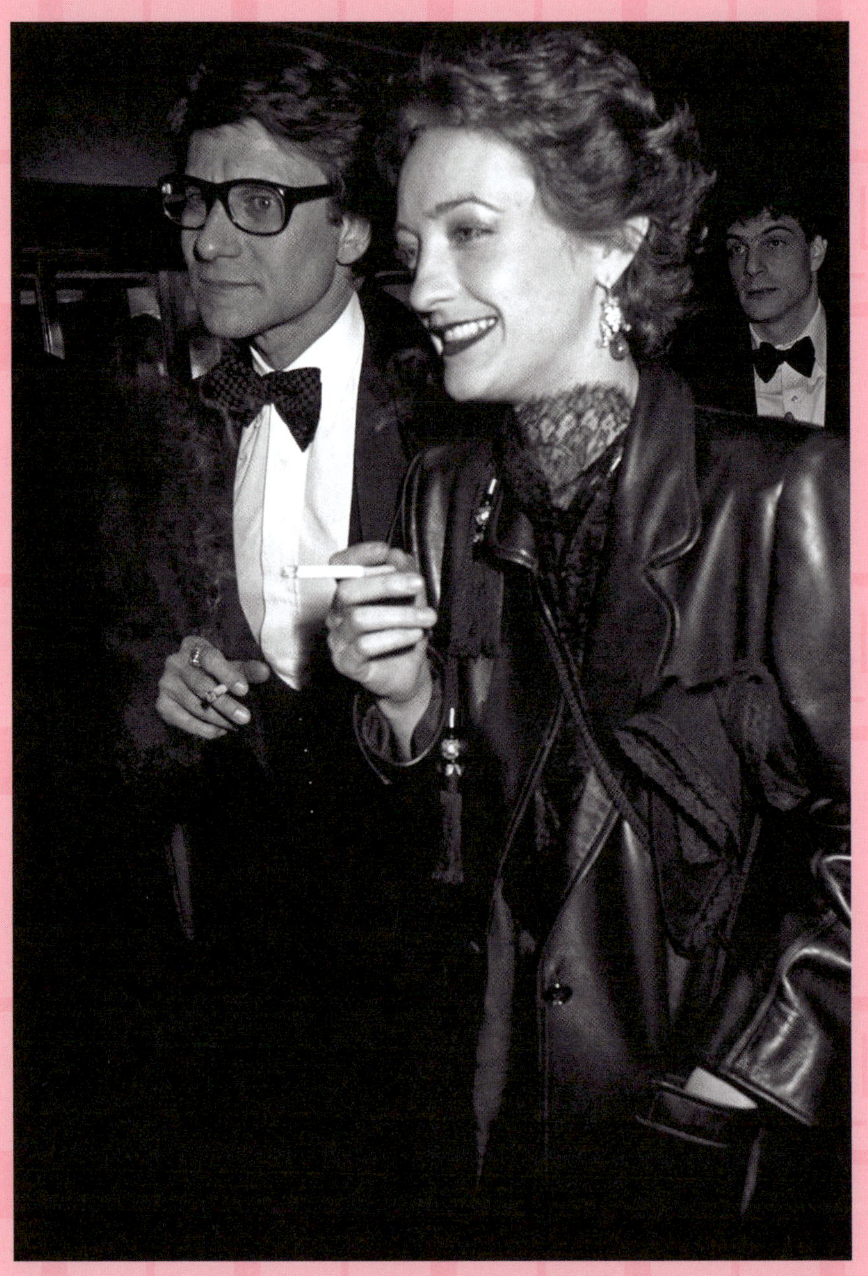

Loulou de la Falaise

Loulou de la Falaise entered Yves Saint Laurent's orbit in the early 1970s and quickly became more than a stylist or jewellery designer. She was the energy around his fittings, the co-pilot for his risks, the person who turned references into living outfits on the studio floor. She brought English irreverence to French couture, mixing Saint Laurent's tuxedos with turbans, stacks of bangles and vintage finds.

Unlike a model who wears looks after the fact, de la Falaise helped invent them. She sketched, sourced fabric, built accessories and then wore the results out to dinner the same night. Her presence reassured Saint Laurent when collections pushed further into fantasy. She embodied the Rive Gauche woman: intelligent, bohemian, capable of crossing an embassy party and a club in the same outfit.

De la Falaise's impact on the fashion movement of the city was to show how a muse can also be a maker. Loulou de la Falaise's jewellery and styling became part of the Saint Laurent vocabulary and her public life spread the code onto the street. She blurred the line between atelier and nightlife, between couture and the real city. Decades later, her name still signals a way of dressing that is fearless but grounded – enduring proof that the right collaborator can make a designer's vision walk on its own.

Opposite: Loulou de la Falaise's real power was her instinct. She could turn a bolt of fabric or a flea-market trinket into a Saint Laurent idea within minutes. Shown here with the designer himself.

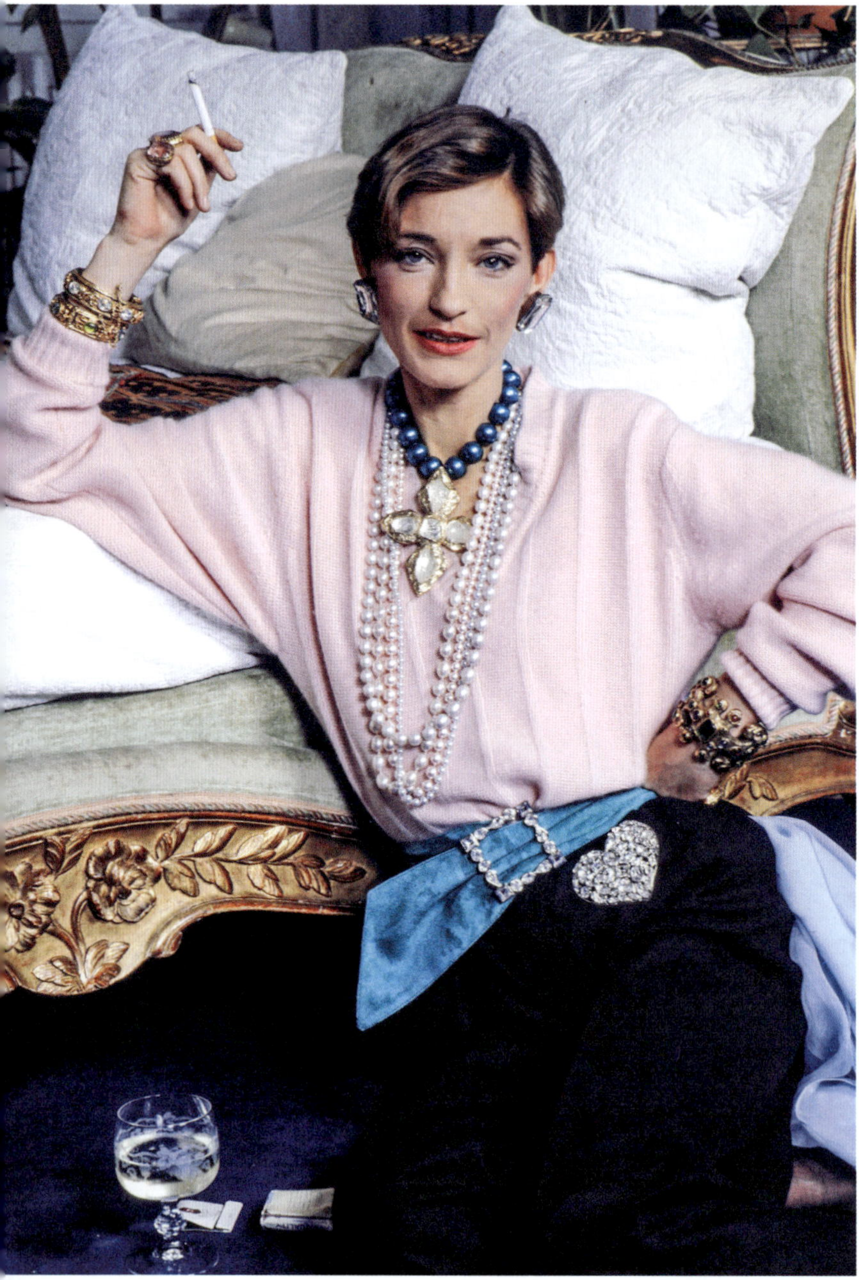

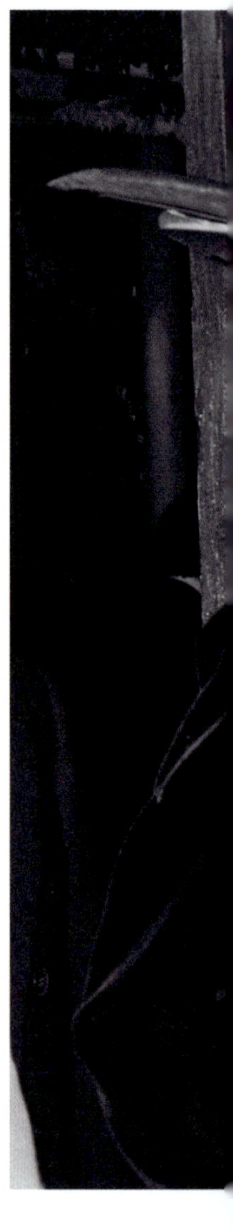

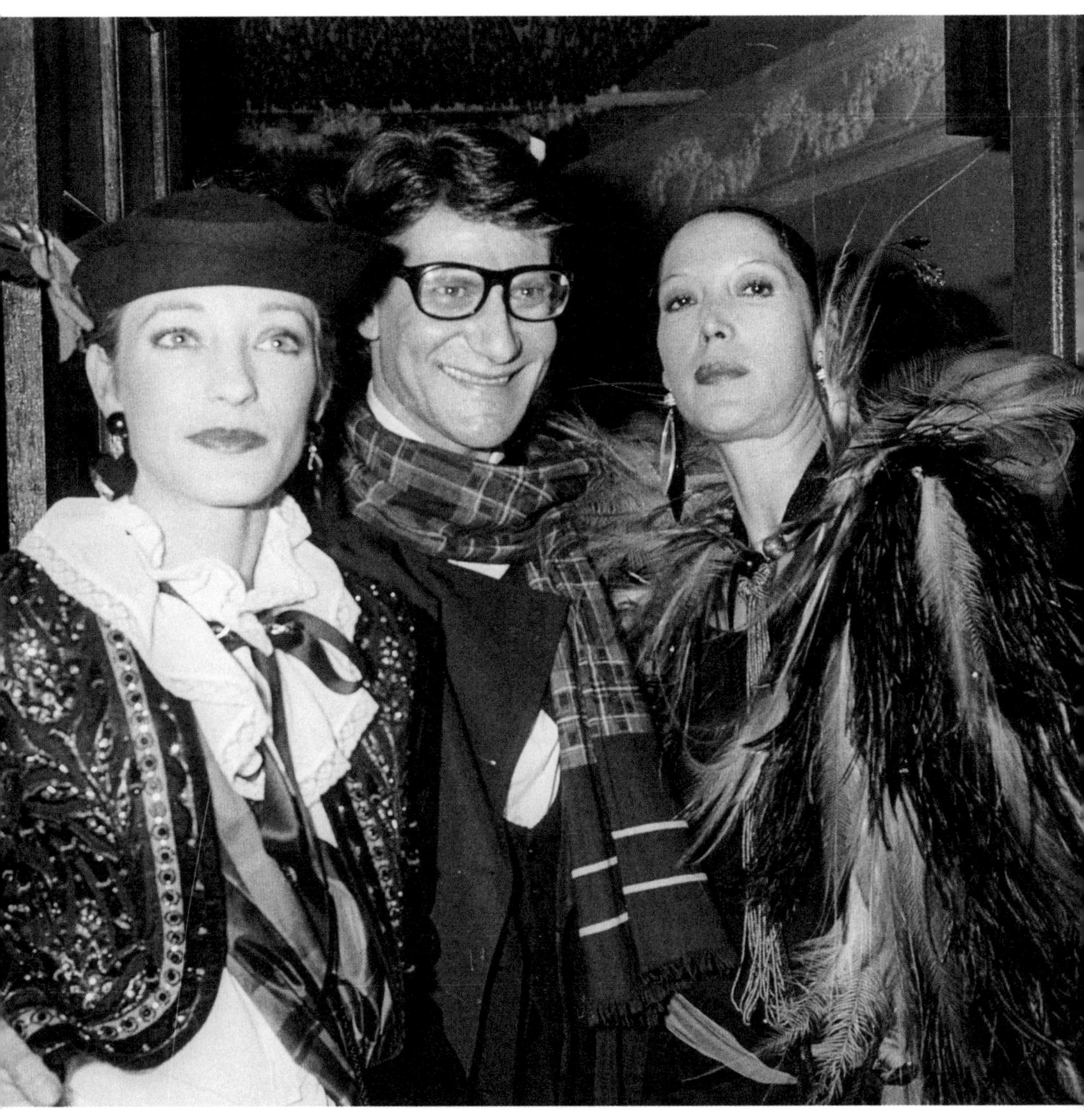

Above: De la Falaise's style taught Paris that eccentricity can be elegant when it's lived, not performed.

Opposite: De la Falaise wasn't a muse in the passive sense; she edited Yves' world as much as she inspired it.

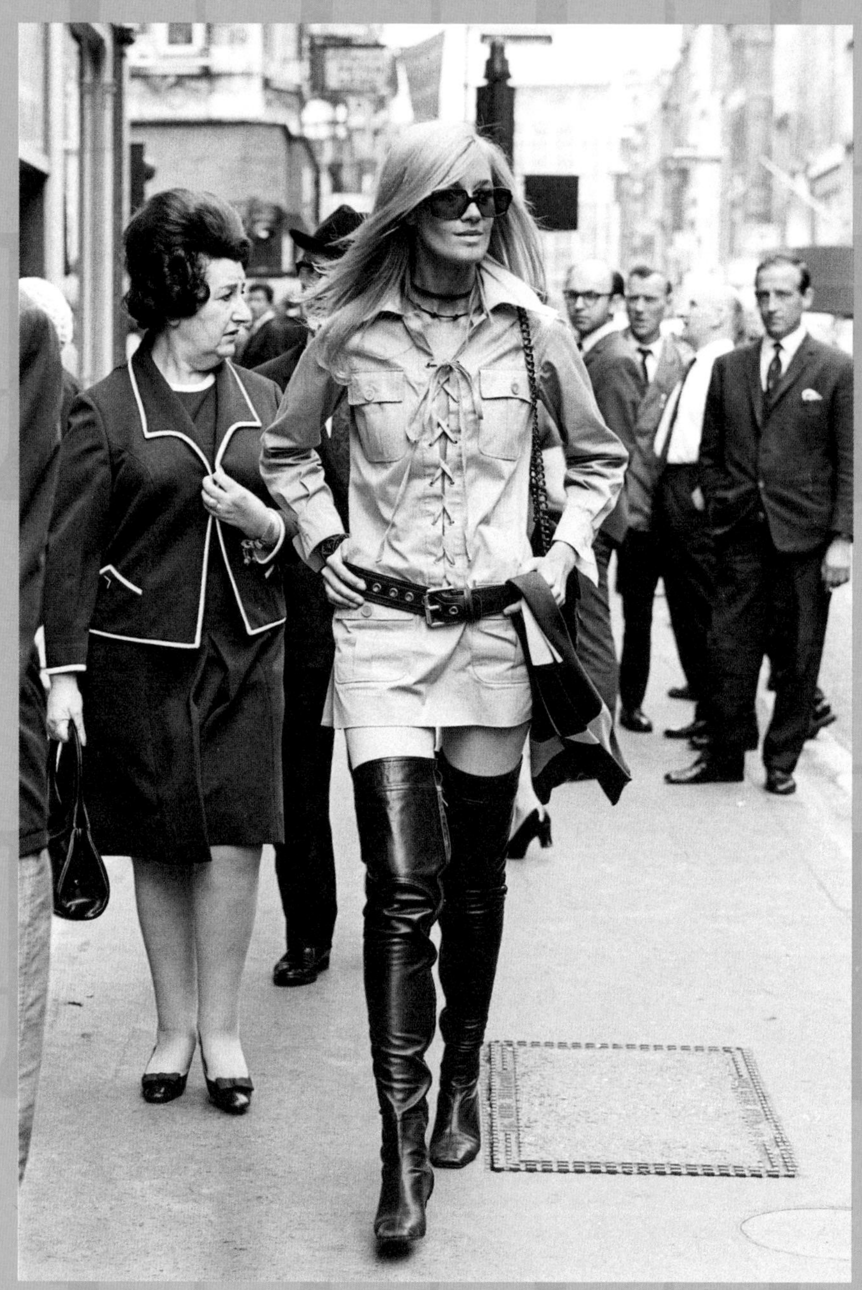

Betty Catroux

Betty Catroux met Yves Saint Laurent at a Paris nightclub in the mid-1960s and instantly became his mirror image: long, pale, androgynous, a cigarette always in hand. She was not a model by trade but a fashion insider by instinct, moving between studios, nightclubs and photo shoots as if they were the same room. Saint Laurent called her his twin and presented her with "Le Smoking", safari jackets and tuxedo shirts before anyone else. She wore them without compromise, hair straight, make-up 24 hours a day.

Catroux became proof of concept for Saint Laurent. When editors saw her at a club in the same pieces that walked the runway, they understood how the clothes worked away from the catwalk. She also shaped casting, styling and the designer's social world. Her presence around him steadied his mood and reinforced the house's identity as a place where gender rules dissolve.

Catroux's impact on Paris is to embody the masculine-feminine style at street level and to make it aspirational worldwide. Betty Catroux shows that a muse can be a partner in defining a movement rather than just wearing it. Today, every brand that leans into androgyny or nightlife owes a quiet debt to her image, which still reads as the template for Yves Saint Laurent's urban woman.

Opposite: Betty Catroux moved through the world of Paris with the cool of someone untouched by trend or expectation, which made people study her before they even understood why.

Overleaf: Betty showed that androgyny lives in attitude more than in styling, a kind of ease that made Paris look at women differently.

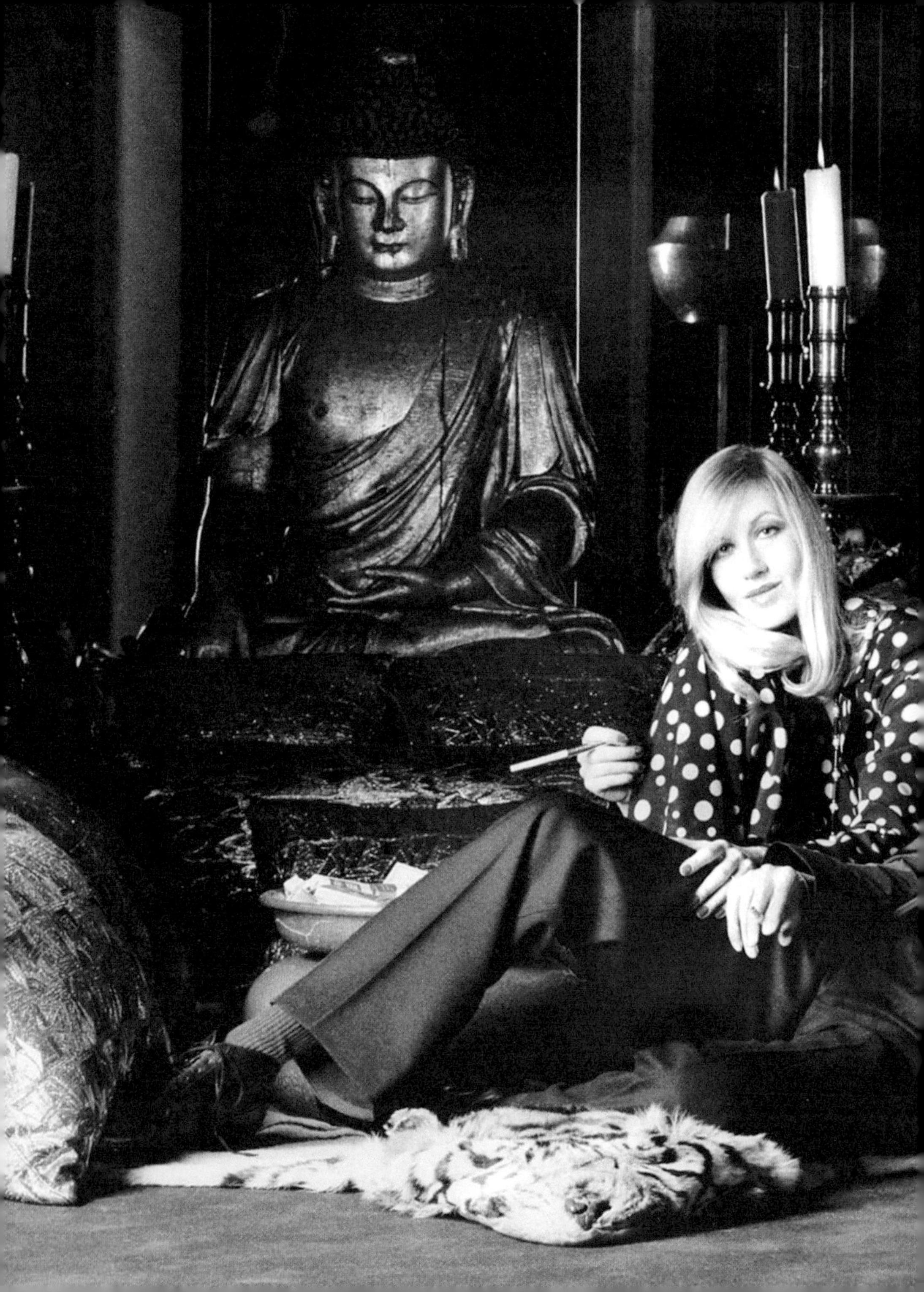

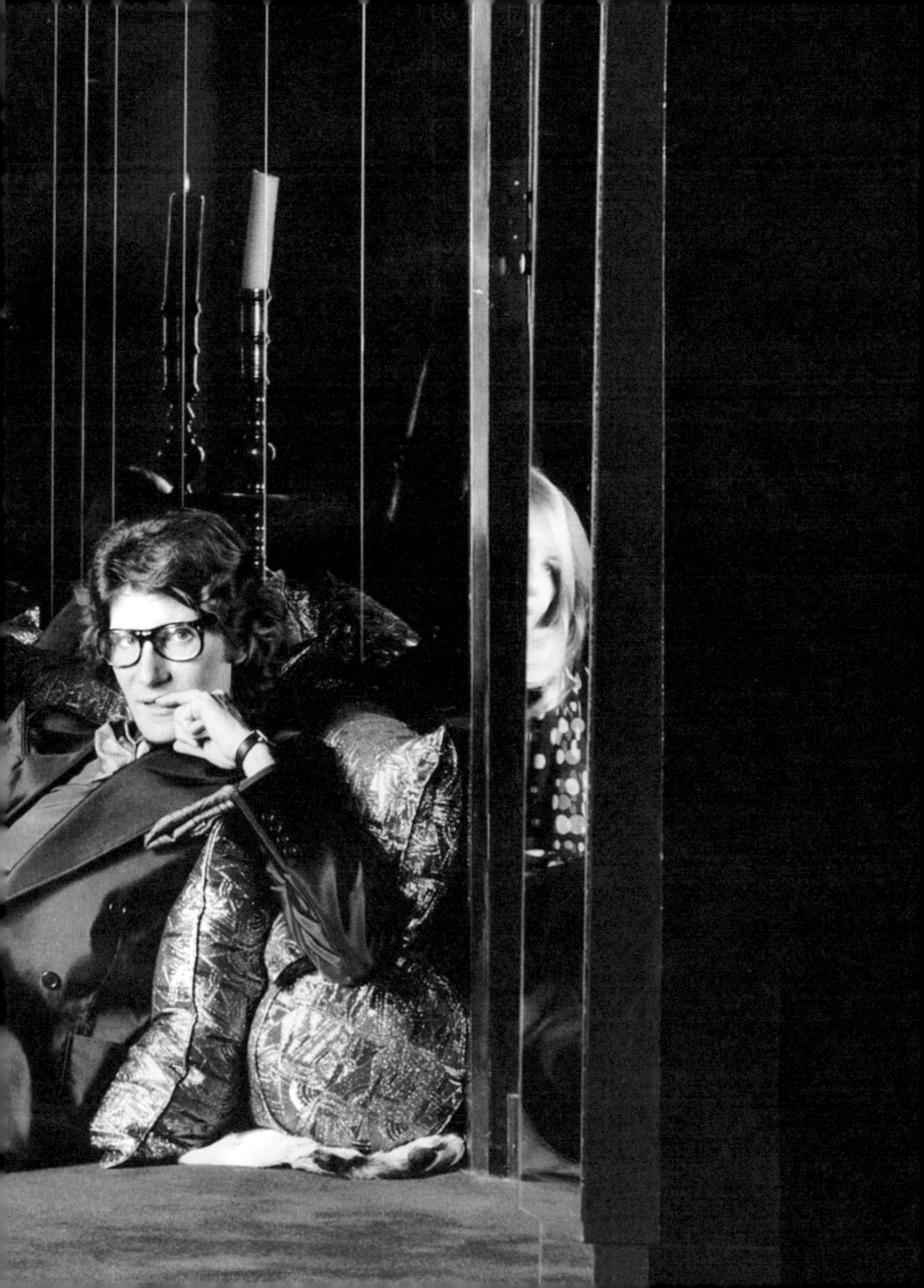

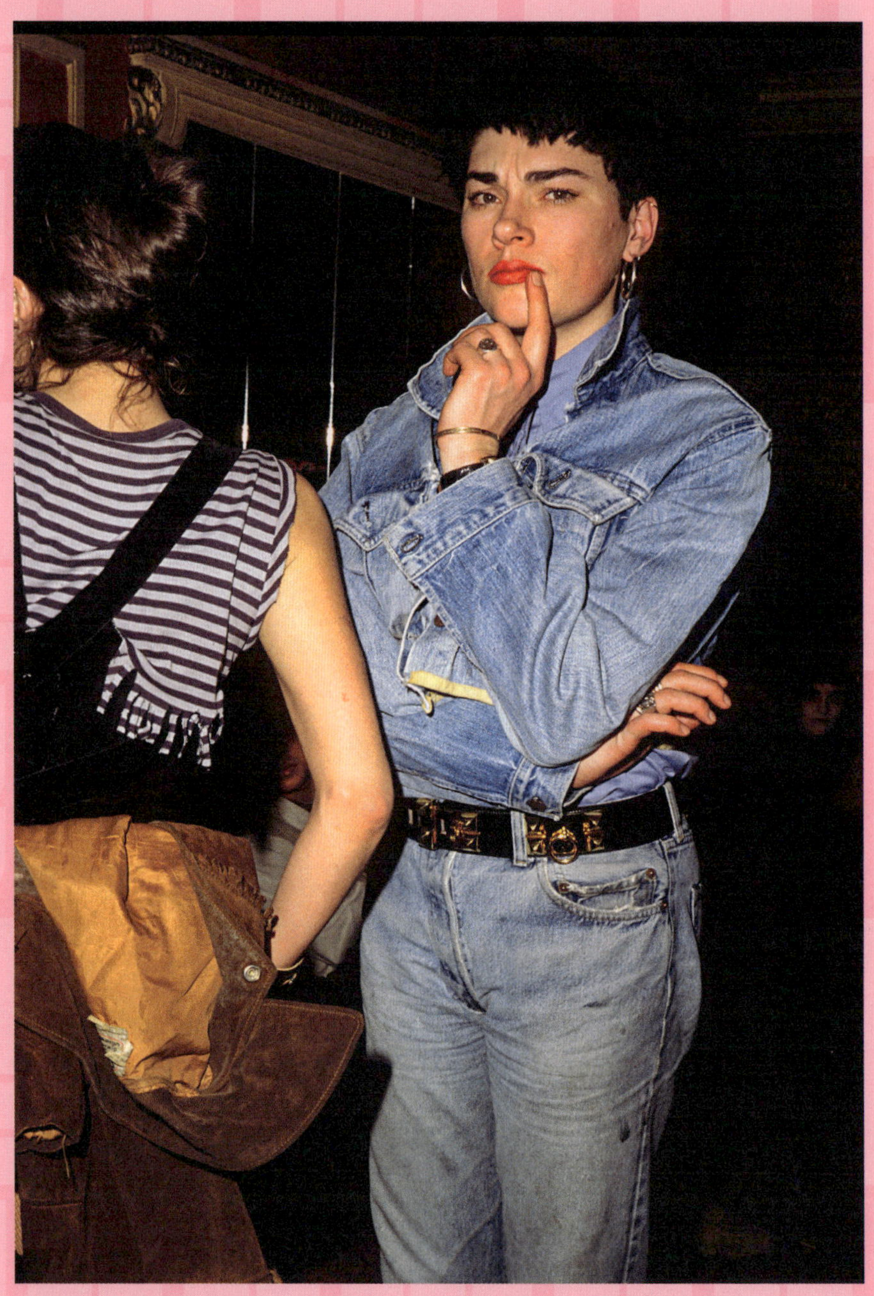

EDWIGE BELMORE

Edwige Belmore rose from Paris's punk scene in the late 1970s and early 1980s, and was crowned "the queen of punks" at Le Palace, the hottest nightclub in town. She was not a couture client but a door girl, DJ and provocateur, standing at the entrance to the city's most famous club, while wearing clothes in ways no stylist could plan. Her platinum buzz cut, ripped T-shirts, men's jackets and heavy boots became shorthand for a new kind of Paris nightlife: aristocratic in poise, anarchic in practice.

Designers and photographers flocked to her because she bridged underground energy with couture discipline. She modelled for Thierry Mugler, Jean Paul Gaultier and others, who saw in her the embodiment of controlled chaos. Belmore showed that nightlife style can migrate to runway casting, that street kids can set the tone for elite houses, and that self-styling can be as potent as a campaign.

Edwige Belmore's impact on Paris was to make the club door a stage equal to the runway. She turned her own look into a city landmark and gave designers permission to recruit directly from nightlife rather than waiting for agencies. This broke the former hierarchy between muse, model and civilian and set up the more porous casting culture we take for granted today. Her legend still explains why Paris remains a laboratory for hybrid identities.

Opposite: Edwige Belmore had that rare ability to make the most ordinary and common pieces into the most desirable looks.

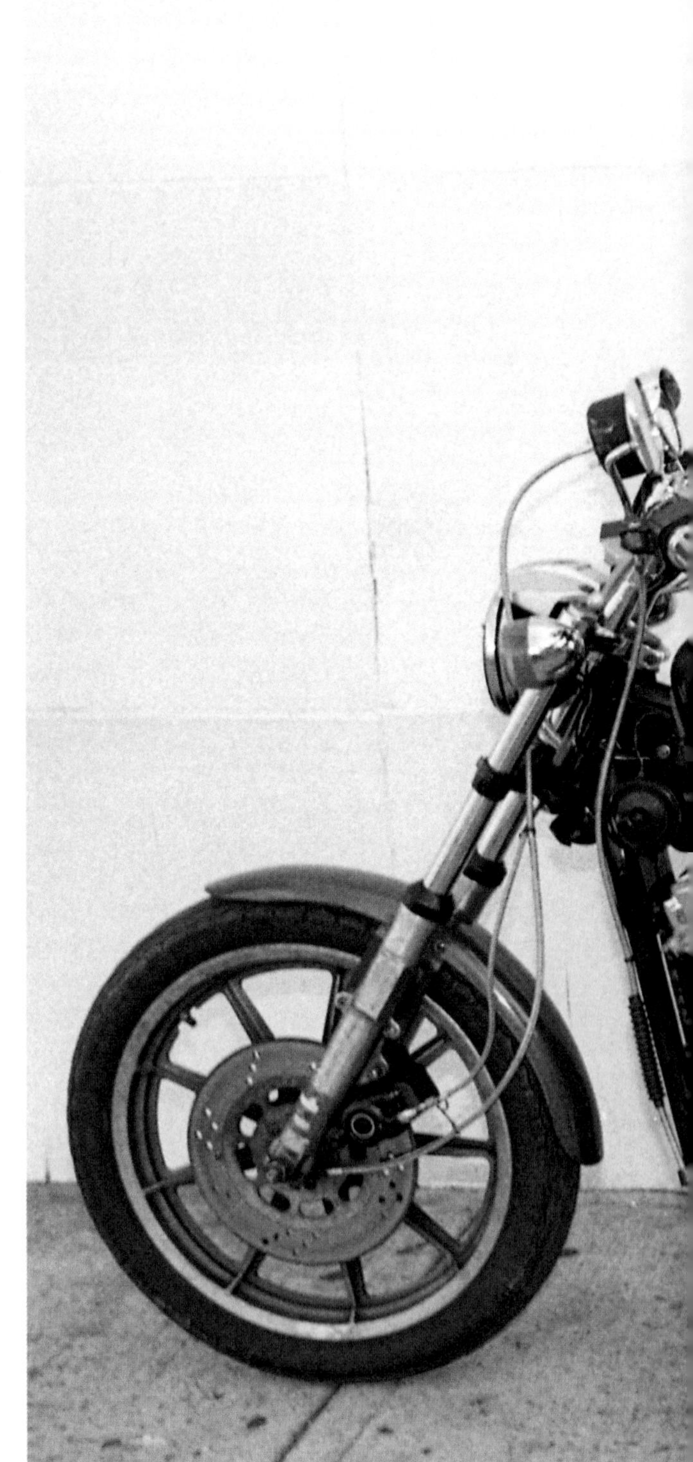

Right: Edwige on a Harley – the kind of cool you just can't manufacture.

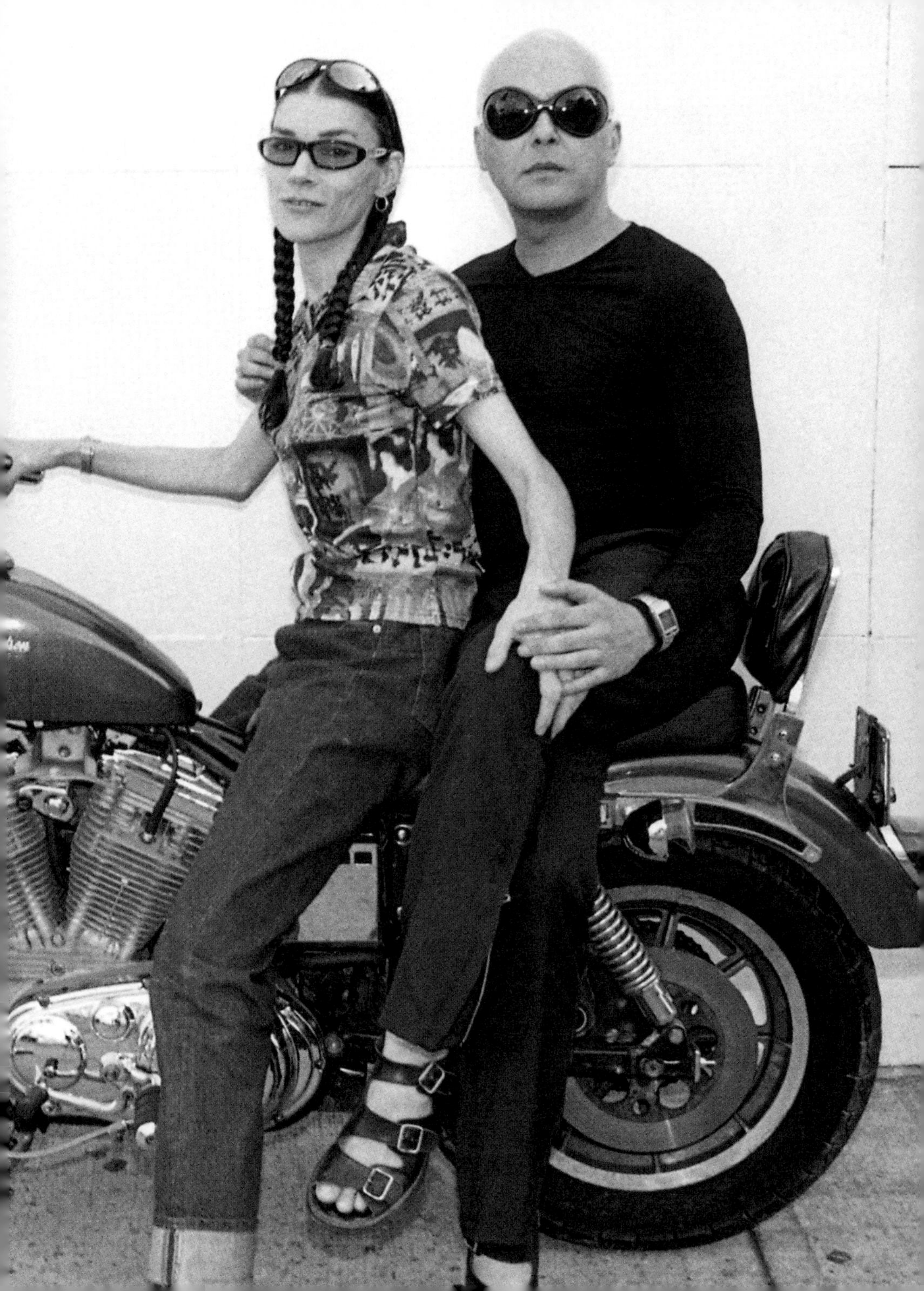

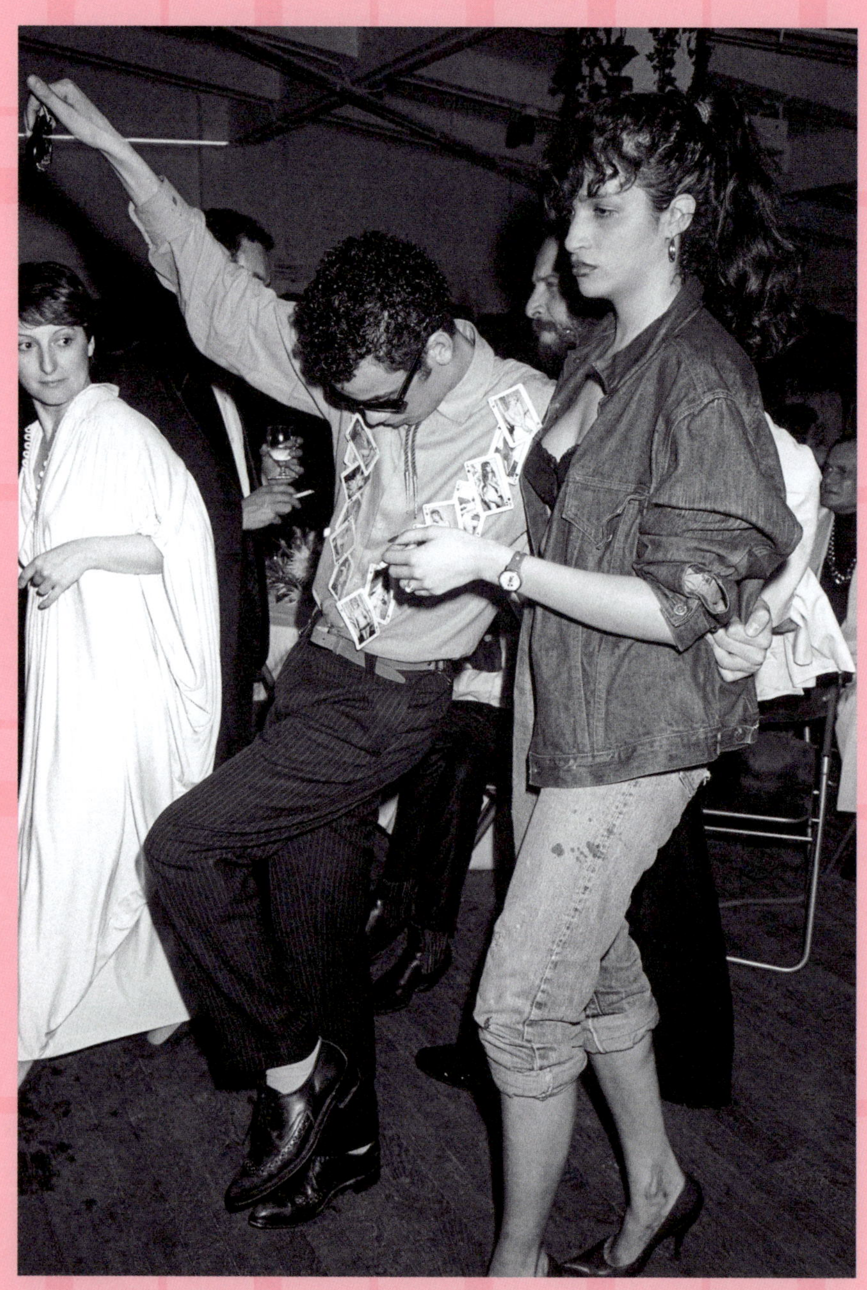

FARIDA KHELFA

Farida Khelfa grew up in Lyon and arrived in Paris as a teenager in the late 1970s, drawn to the clubs and the possibilities of the capital. She worked at Le Palace, met Jean Paul Gaultier, Azzedine Alaïa and Thierry Mugler, and quickly became part of the inner circle. Tall, striking and Algerian-French, she broke the model template of the time and brought a new elegance to designers hungry for change.

But Khelfa was more than a runway presence. She became a friend, confidante and stylistic partner to Alaïa in particular, walking his shows and helping fit his famously precise garments. She embodied the sculpted knit dresses, zipped leathers and hooded gowns, giving them ease and authority at once. She also appeared in campaigns, films and editorials that exported a new image of Paris beauty: multicultural, confident, direct.

Khelfa's presence helped expand who can represent French fashion at the highest level. She helped bring diversity to casting decades before it became a policy. Her journey from club girl to muse to documentary filmmaker mapped out a different career path entirely, one that links creative communities instead of siloing them. By living the clothes day and night she proved to designers that their ideas can survive real life. The legacy she leaves is a model of collaboration and representation: Paris as a meeting point of cultures, a place where a teenager from Lyon can redefine what glamour looks like on the global stage.

Opposite: Farida Khelfa at a party, Paris Fashion Week 1979.

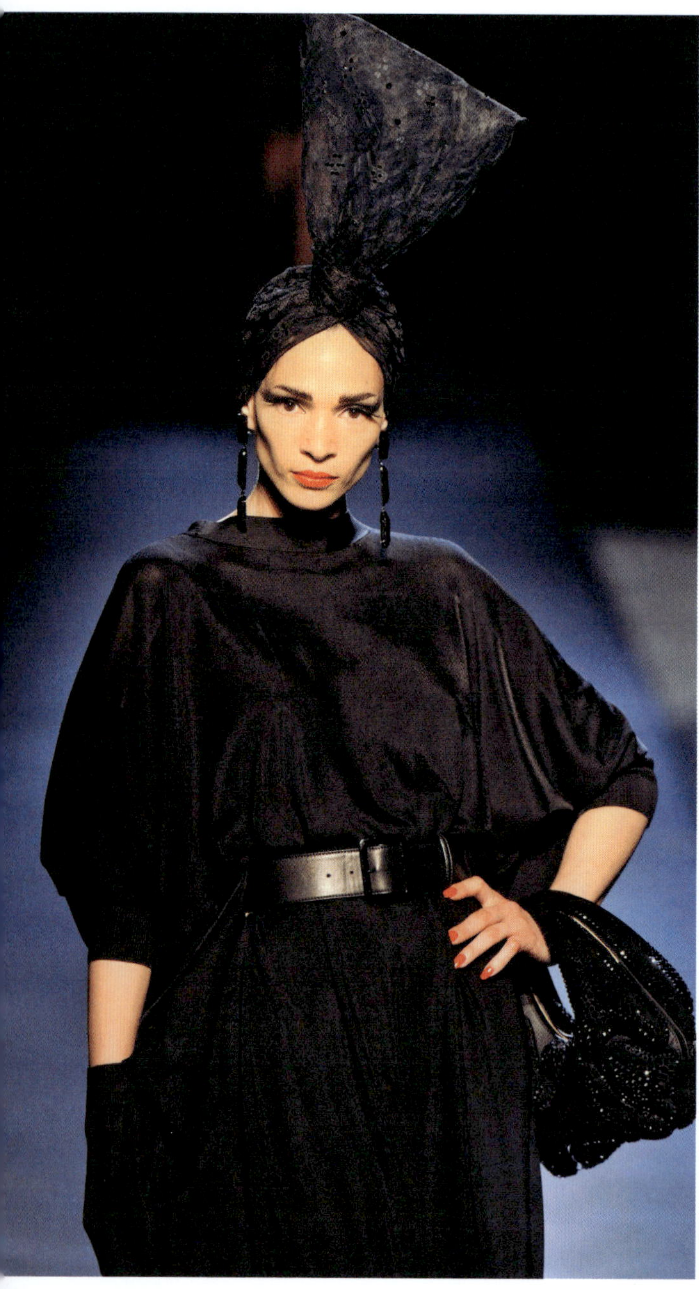

Left: Farida Khelfa wears an entirely black Jean-Paul Gaultier creation from the Fall/Winter 2011 collection.

Opposite: Farida poses in a denim dress with Azzedine Alaïa by her side.

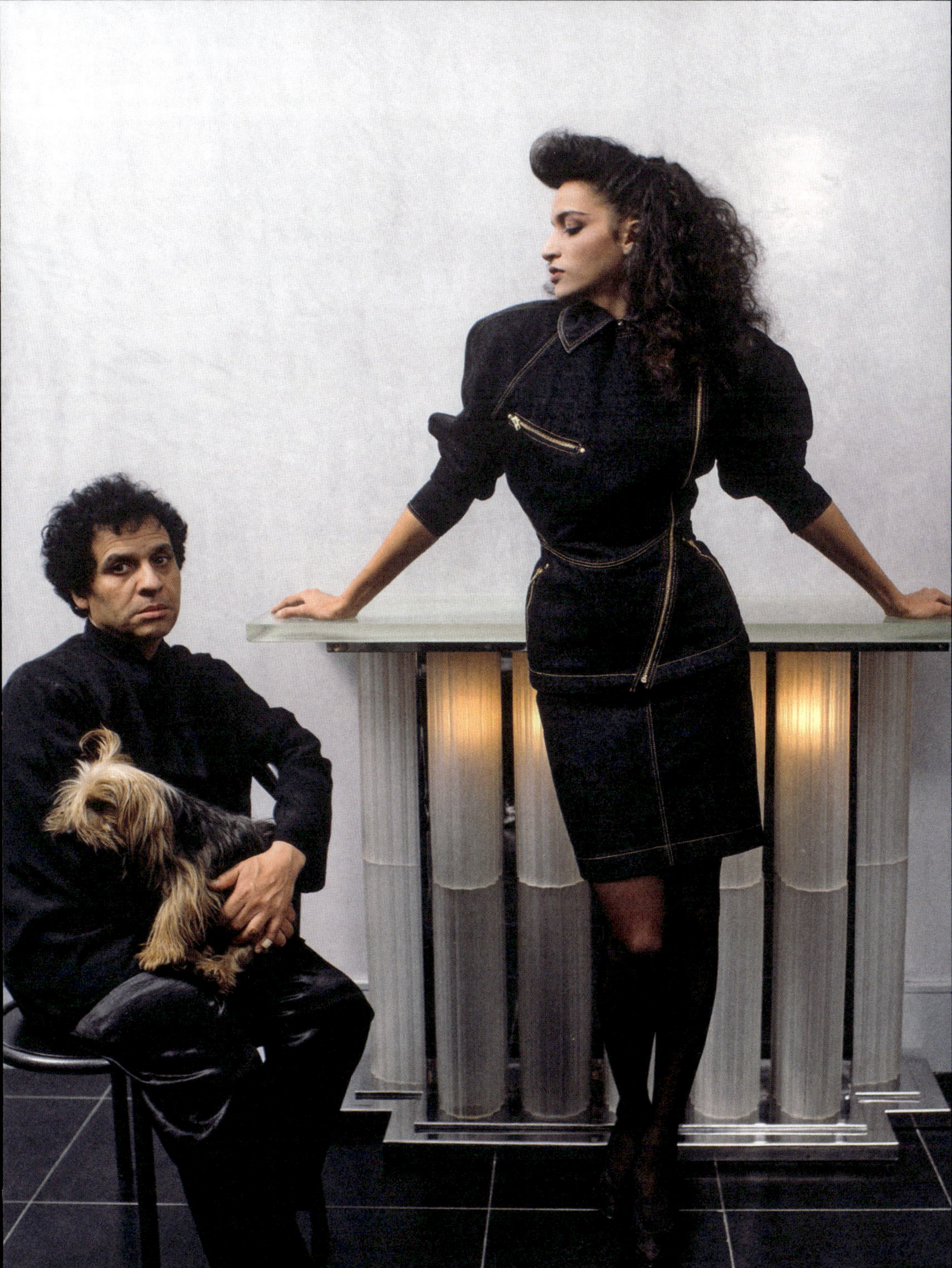

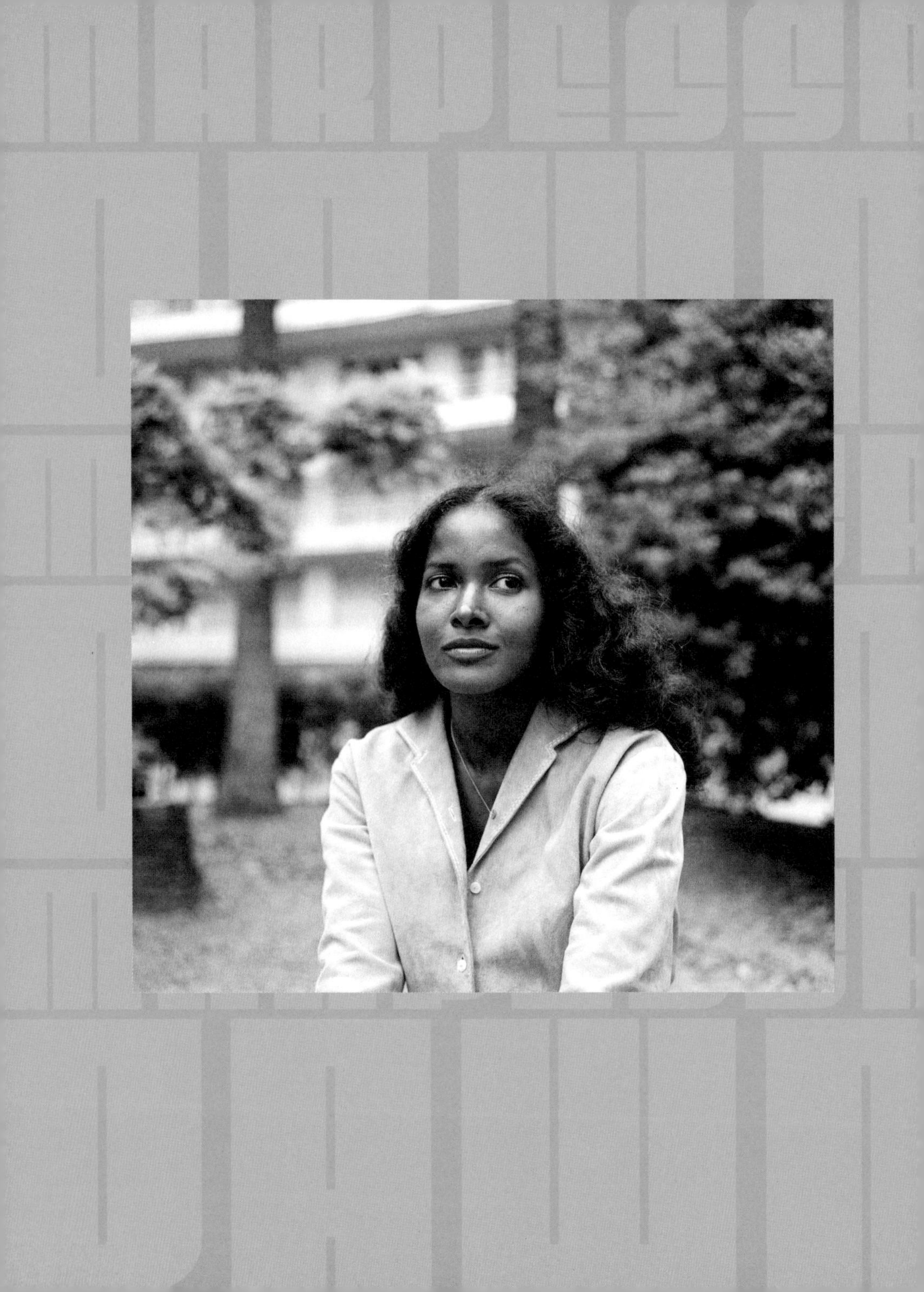

MARPESSA DAWN

Marpessa Dawn arrived in Paris in the 1950s from the United States and found work on stage and screen. In 1959 she became the face of *Black Orpheus*, a film that won at Cannes and moved through the world like a new postcard of the city. Her presence is light and assured, her American ease and Filipino heritage feeling fresh in a capital still shedding old glamour. She was not a couture mannequin, nor a chanson diva, but an actress who carried modern Paris in her posture.

Designers and photographers noticed. Off-screen she kept things simple and lively, with cotton dresses, clean lines, hair that framed the face rather than hiding it. She bought from small Montparnasse shops, borrowed from friends and let young designers test ideas on her figure. Editors shot her in cafés and on bridges because the camera loved how she moved. It looked like everyday life with focus and that's what fashion needs.

Marpessa Dawn's impact was quiet and wide. She widened the city's image of beauty and helped open space for Black and mixed-race women in French media. She offered a way to show joy without excess and elegance without stiffness. Designers learned they can reference Brazil and Paris in one look and still stay coherent. Students keep her on mood boards because the balance is right, with natural light, honest shape and a confidence that does not beg. One performance becomes a long reference and Paris keeps it close.

Opposite: Marpessa Dawn at the Cannes Film Festival in 1960 for *Black Orpheus*.

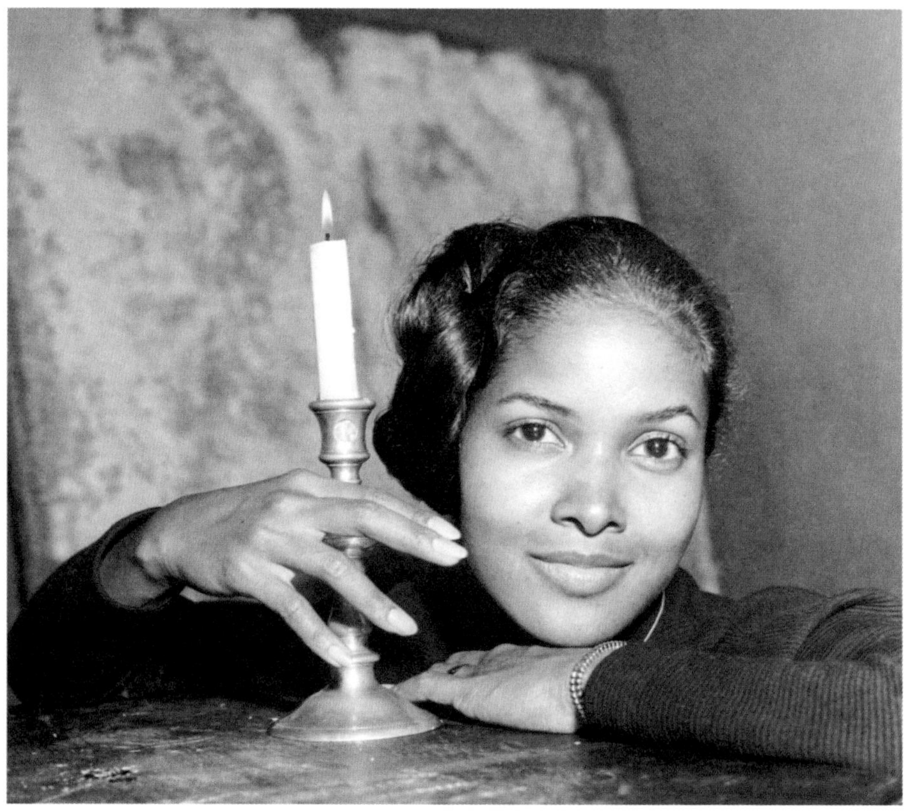

Above: Marpessa Dawn poses with a candle.

Opposite: Marpessa Dawn radiant in a white dress.

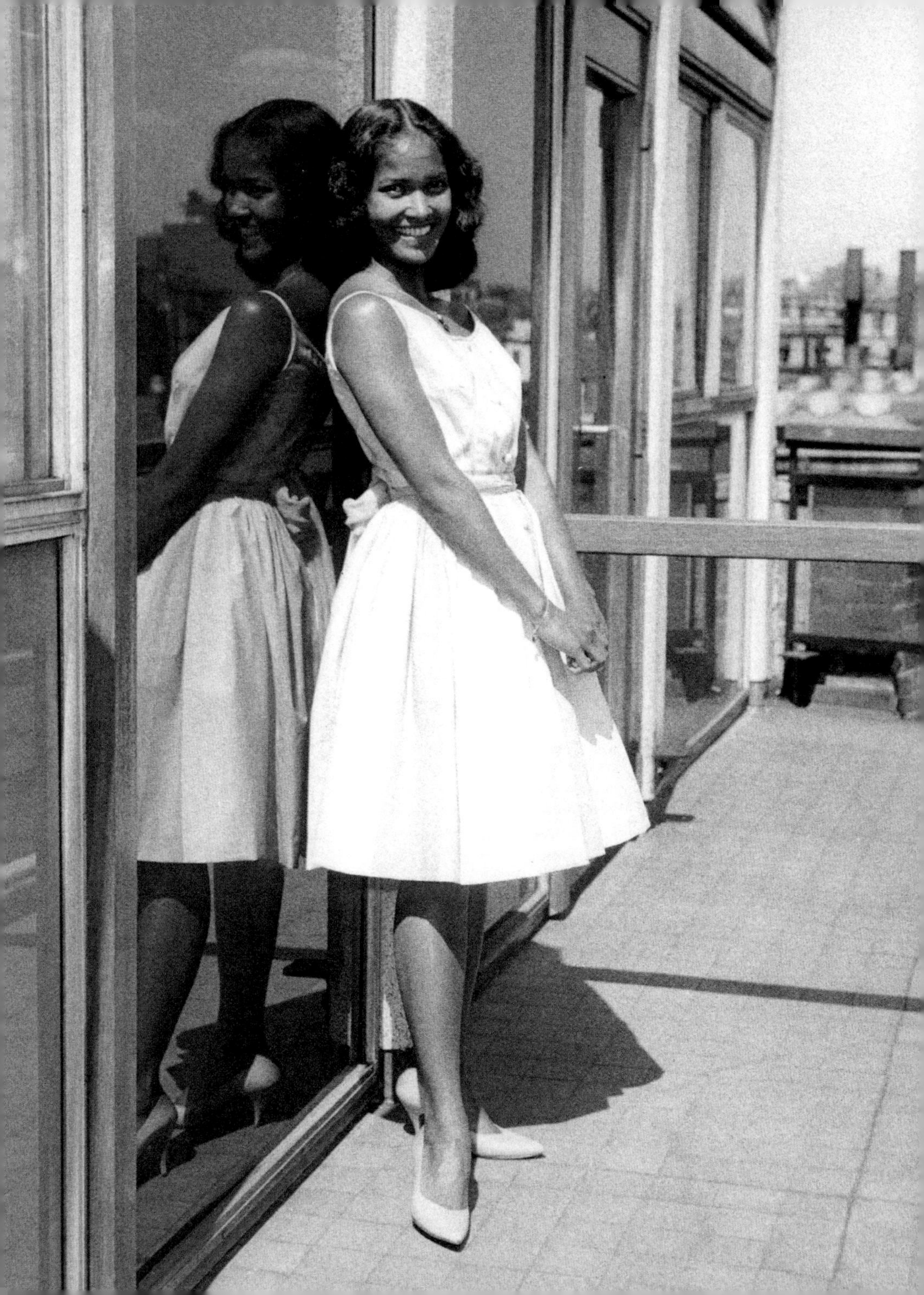

VANESSA PARADIS

In 1987 Vanessa Paradis arrived as a teenager with the single "Joe le Taxi" and quickly became part of Paris culture. Within two years she was front row next to Karl Lagerfeld and soon became the face of the house. She carried a new kind of youth image into couture. Small, direct, self-possessed, she wore tweed and pearls like band T-shirts. The brand saw that she could translate the codes for a generation raised on music videos, not salon shows.

Lagerfeld cast her in campaigns throughout the 1990s. The Coco ad where she swings inside a birdcage makes the point clearly: playful pictures, strict making. She sang at events, appeared in films and walked in shows. But the partnership was not a stunt – it was a conversation that allowed Chanel to look youthful without chasing trend noise. Stores saw it in sales, leather goods, beauty and ready-to-wear that moved with a younger clientele who wanted craft.

Vanessa Paradis also models a modern muse role. She works, raises a family, acts and returns to music, while keeping a steady link to the house of Chanel. The image matures without breaking. For young artists she is proof indeed that a pop career and high fashion can support each other without one consuming the other. Paradis makes celebrity ambassadorship feel credible. She shows that a singer can carry couture codes across decades and formats. The result is a template that others follow. Chanel keeps the posture, Paris keeps the lesson.

Opposite: Vanessa Paradis at the 1990 Victoires de la Musique awards.

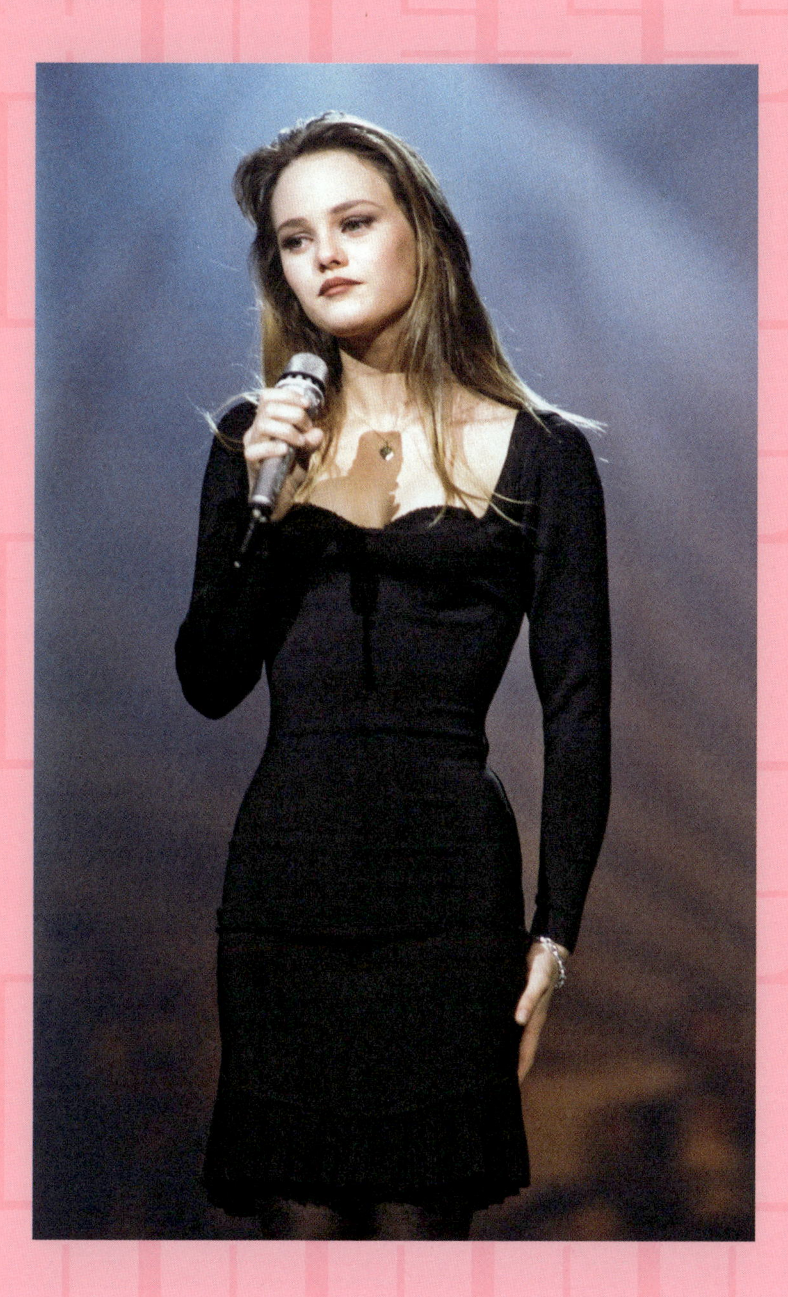

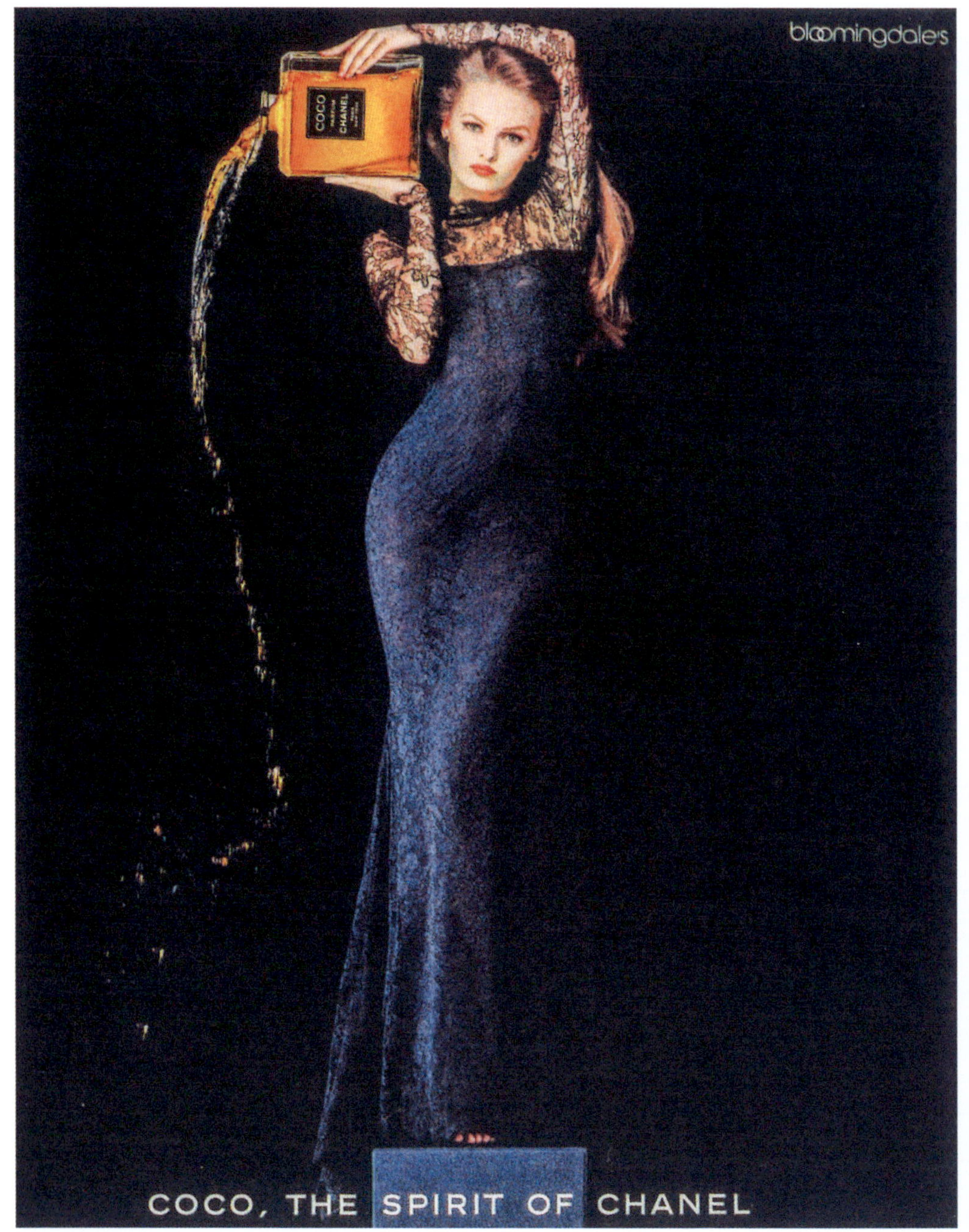
bloomingdale's
COCO
CHANEL
COCO, THE SPIRIT OF CHANEL

Right: Vanessa Paradis at the Chanel show during Paris Fashion Week, Spring/Summer 2011.

Opposite: *Coco, The Spirit of Chanel* perfume ad with Vanessa Paradis in 1994.

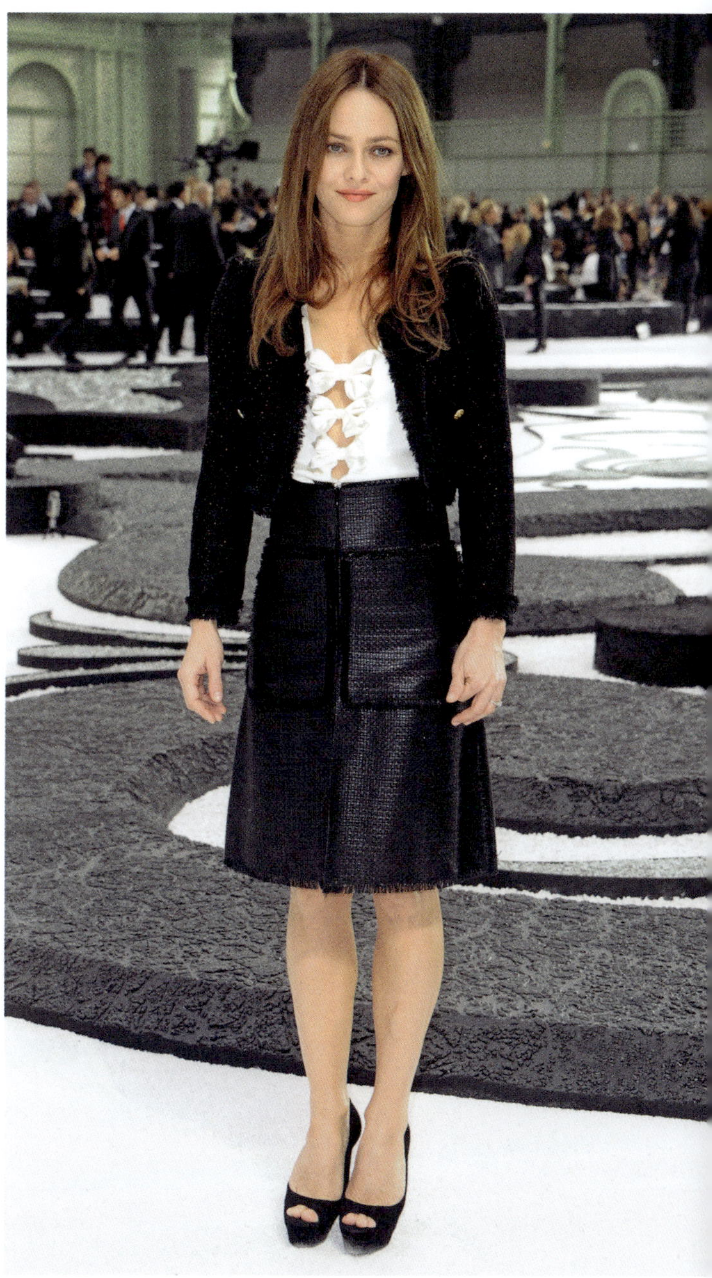

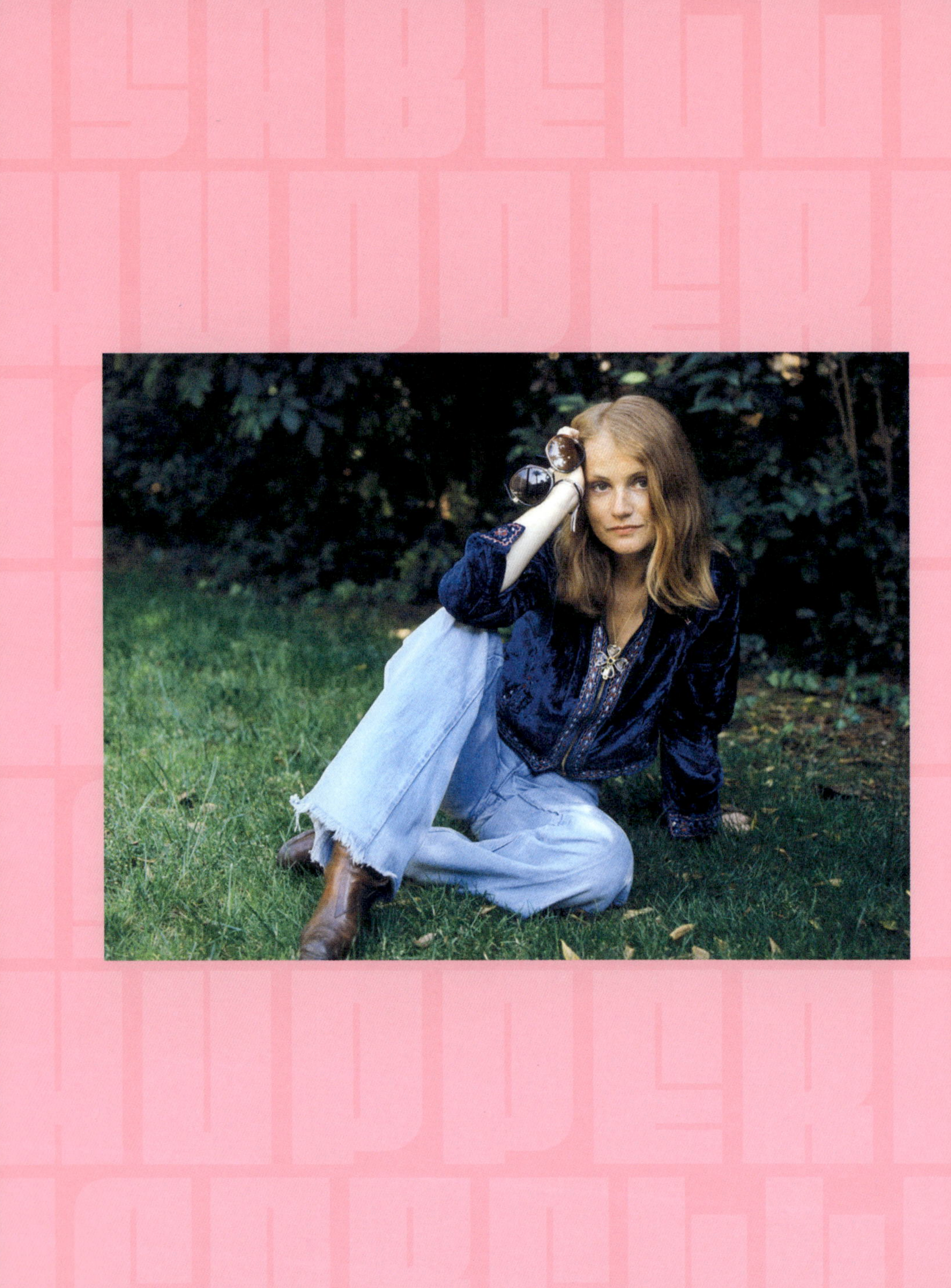

Isabelle Huppert

Isabelle Huppert grew up in Paris, studied at the Conservatoire and made her film debut in the early 1970s. By the time she won Best Actress at Cannes for *Violette Nozière* in 1978 she had become the city's most intriguing screen presence. Her characters are often complex, restrained or even dangerous, and her off-screen style reflects the same quiet intensity. She favours tailored coats, precise blouses, dark colours and a studied stillness that photographs beautifully. Paris sees in her a way of dressing and moving that matches its own self-image: intelligent, private and exact.

Designers responded early. Yves Saint Laurent, Balenciaga under Nicolas Ghesquière, and later Balenciaga under Demna Gvasalia invited her to do their shows and campaigns. She appeared in shoots by Guy Bourdin, Juergen Teller and Inez & Vinoodh, translating difficult clothes into legible images. She does not play muse as decoration; she brings gravitas to looks that might otherwise read experimentally. Her face can hold a headline dress without shrinking it and her discipline made her a natural fit for couture fittings.

Isabelle Huppert's impact on fashion was to provide a grown-up template in an industry obsessed with youth. She showed that the city's clothes can belong to a woman with a career, with depth, with a point of view. Huppert has walked runways, sat front row and lent her name to campaigns without ever surrendering to celebrity style churn. She makes Paris look serious in the best way. The legacy is a bridge between cinema and fashion, where intelligence itself becomes aspirational and restraint reads as power.

Opposite: Isabelle Huppert sits and poses on the grass, circa 1970.

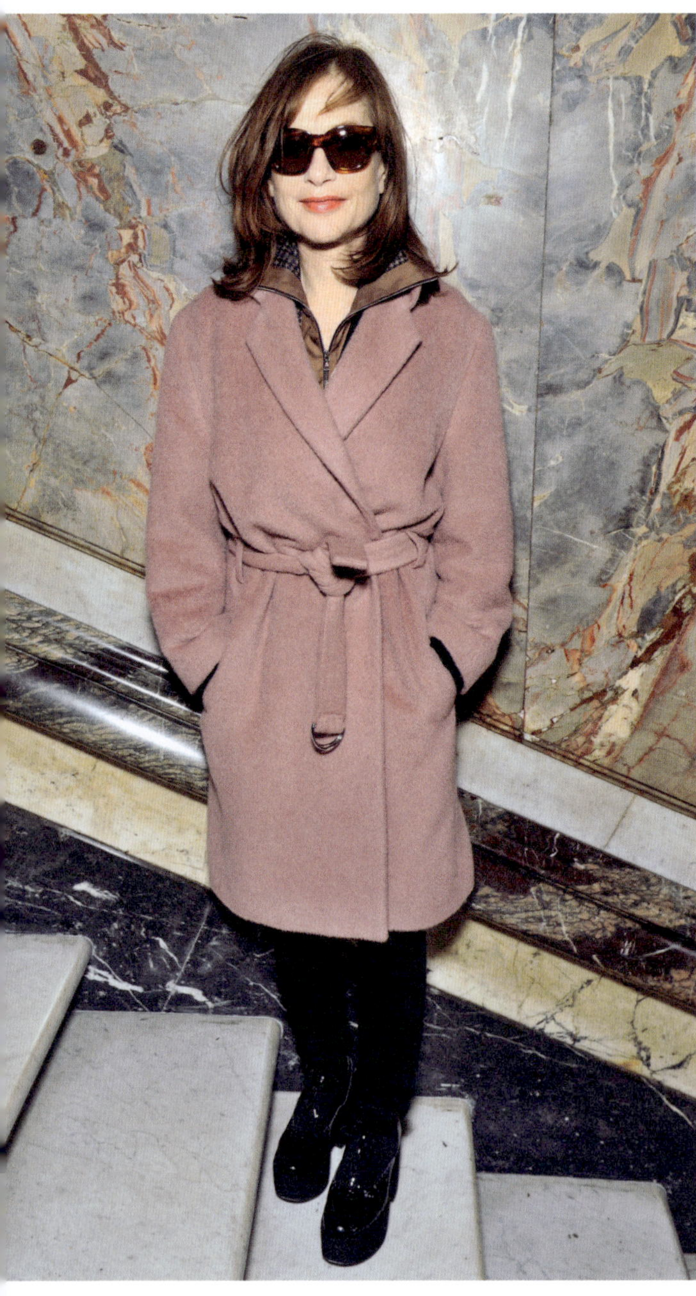

Left: Isabelle Huppert at an Autumn/Winter 2016 Paris Fashion Week show.

Opposite: Isabelle Huppert at the Balenciaga Spring/Summer 2026 show.

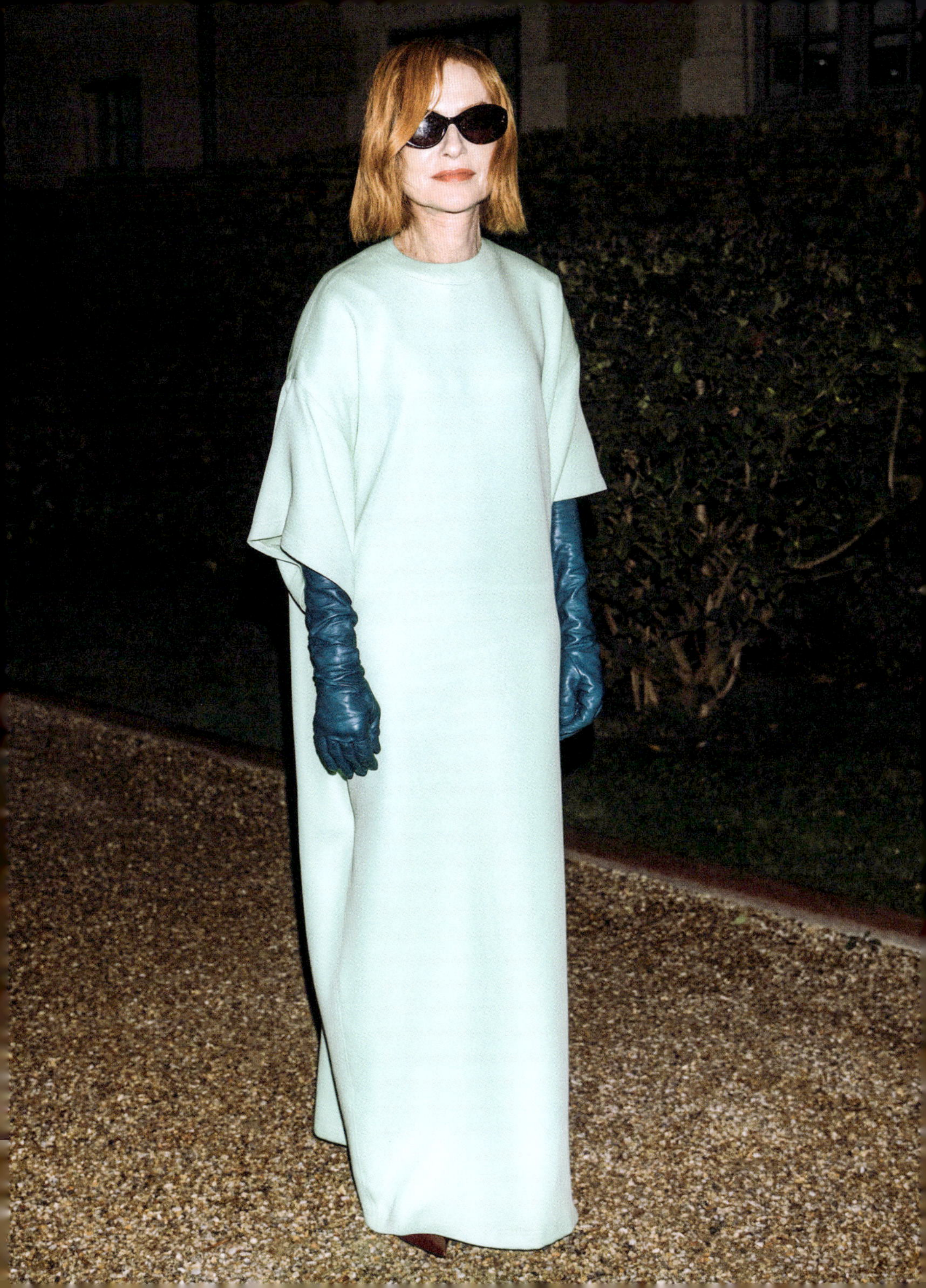

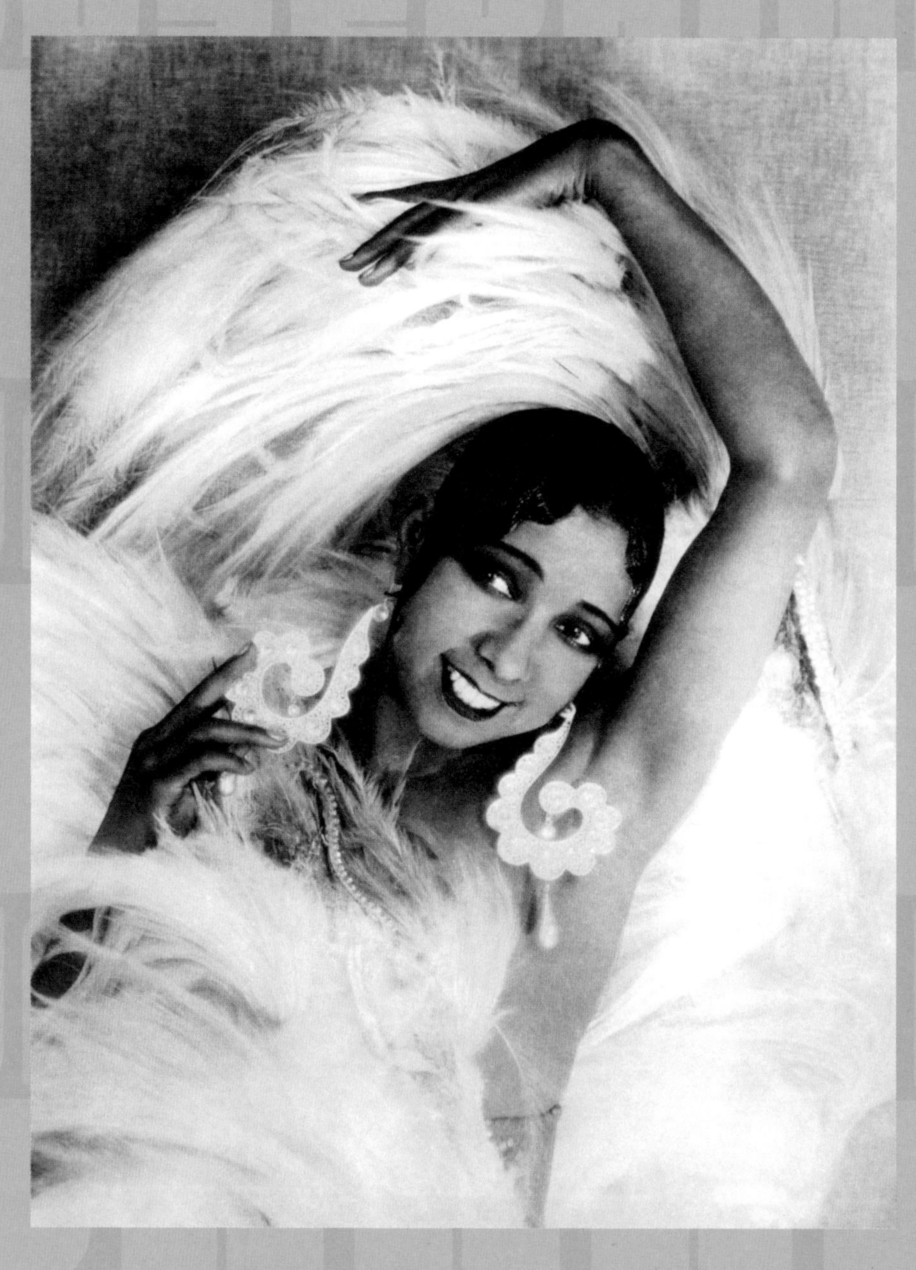

JOSEPHINE BAKER

Josephine Baker arrived in Paris in 1925 as part of the cast of *La Revue Nègre.* Within weeks the city rewrote its own sense of glamour around her. Born in St Louis, Missouri, she had danced in vaudeville shows, but in Paris she found an audience ready for something entirely new. Her performances at the Théâtre des Champs-Élysées, especially the now-mythic banana skirt dance, electrified a post-war capital hungry for speed, rhythm and modernity. She turned jazz into a Parisian language, mixing comedy, eroticism and athleticism in a way the city had never seen. Designers and illustrators sketched her constantly. Posters, postcards and magazine covers carried her image across Europe.

But Baker did more than perform. She lived in Paris, bought property, opened a club and became a fixture at high society events. She shifted the city's beauty standards by introducing a Black, athletic, unapologetically modern body to stages and salons that had long been rigidly white and corseted. Couturiers made costumes for her, jewellers loaned diamonds, photographers developed new techniques to capture her motion. Her presence helped drive Art Deco's streamlined shapes and metallic surfaces, and she became one of the first true global celebrities built in Paris.

Josephine Baker's impact extended beyond style. During the Second World War she worked for the French Resistance, smuggling messages

Opposite: Josephine Baker poses in feathers.

and documents under cover of her touring schedule. After the war she adopted 12 children from around the world, creating what she called her "Rainbow Tribe" and using her fame to argue for civil rights. Paris claimed her as a symbol of freedom and cosmopolitanism. Nearly a century later, she remains shorthand for daring, glamour and activism in one body, proof indeed that the city's fashion image can start on-stage and end by making history.

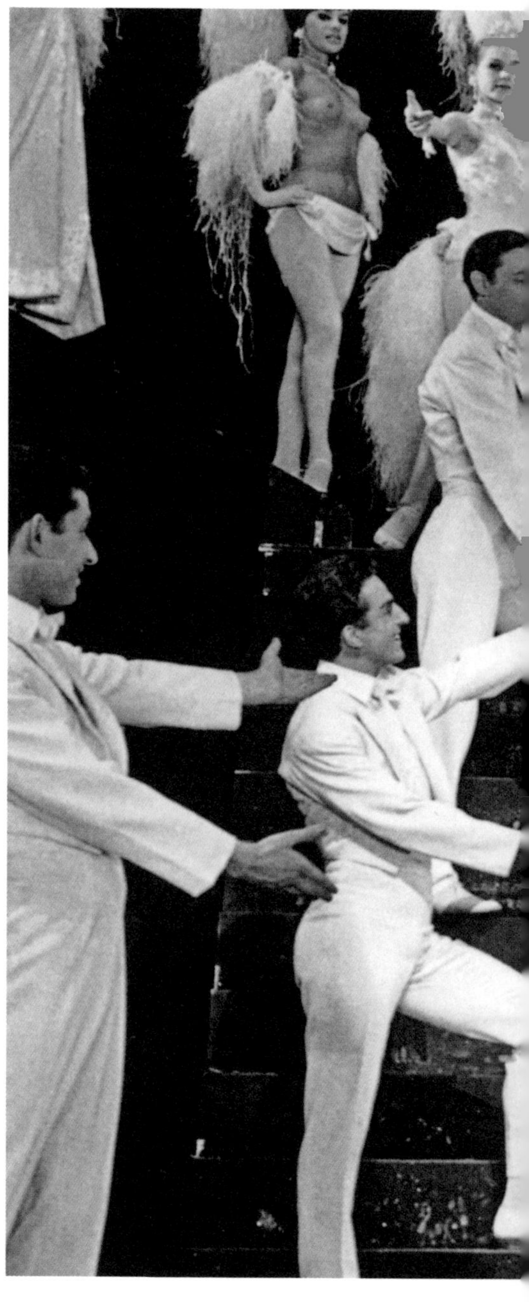

Opposite: Josephine Baker performing on stage in feathers and lace.

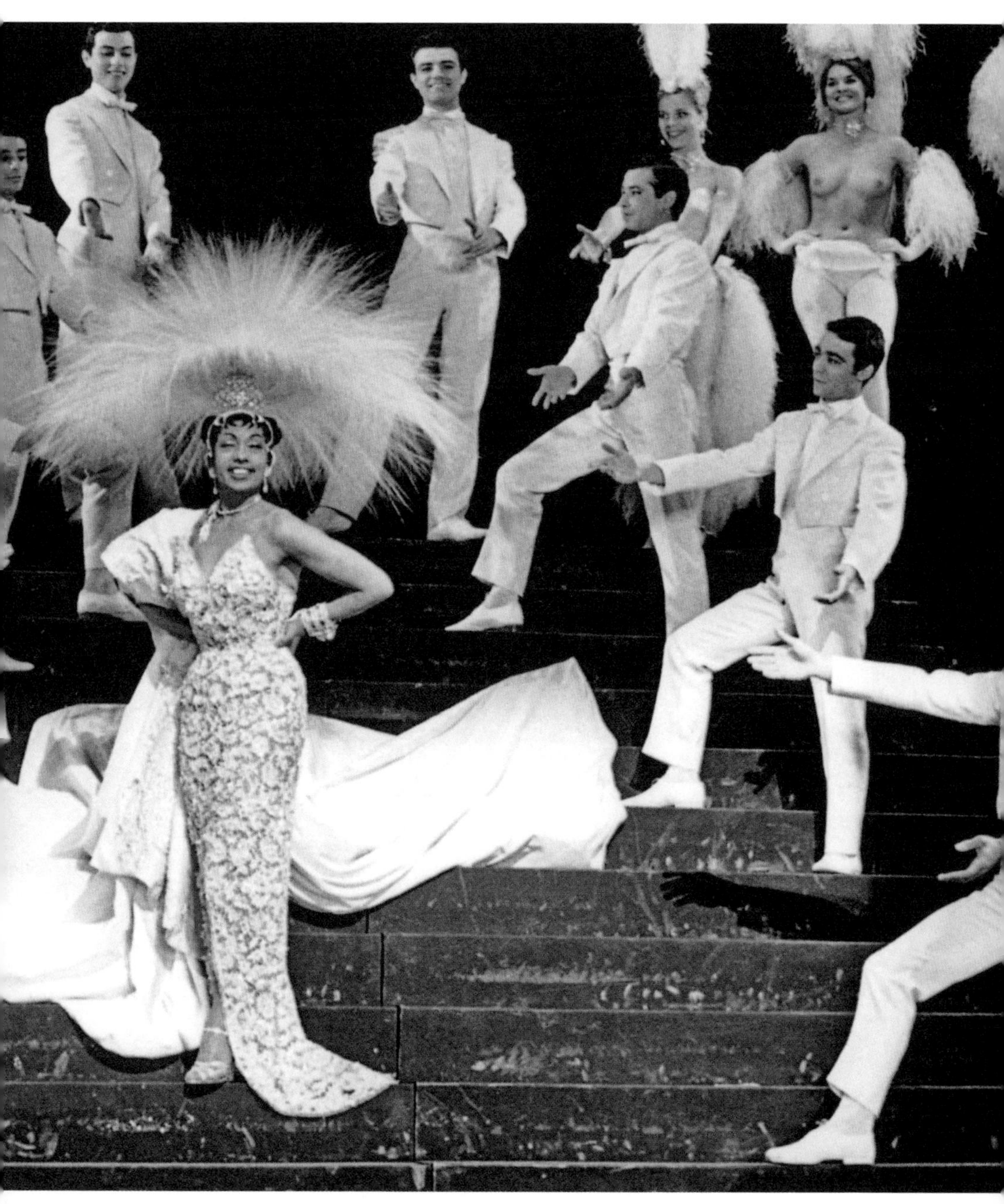

CHAPTER 5:

VOICES, WRITERS & POWER BROKERS

Frames matter. Words, images and gatekeepers decide what survives in the conversation. Essays, interviews, PR strategies, and later blogs and social platforms, filter the work, shape the narrative and place it in front of the right eyes at the right time. They build anticipation before a show and memory after it. They also hold designers accountable, translating a studio's language for buyers, editors and the public.

This chapter looks at the people who cut and shape attention with the same precision ateliers cut cloth. They decide which designers become movements, which moments enter the archive and which silhouettes end up on the mood boards of the next decade. In Paris these voices are not just commentators but collaborators. They supply context, build networks and give experiments a stage. When they work well, a designer's ideas travel further, last longer and become part of a shared culture rather than a single season.

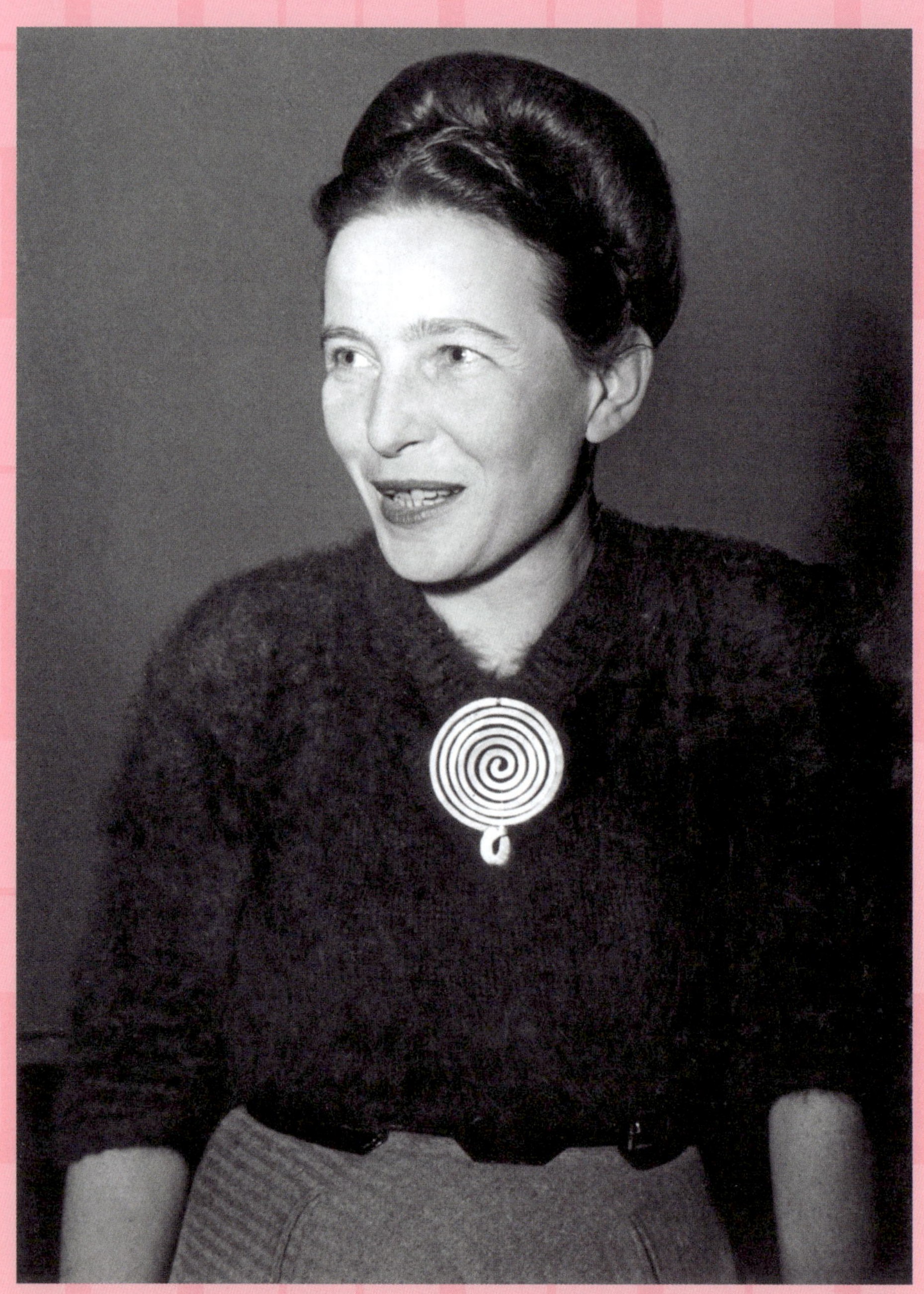

SIMONE DE BEAUVOIR

Simone de Beauvoir walked Saint-Germain before it became a cliché. From the 1940s onwards she turned the cafés of the Left Bank into an office, a salon and a stage. Her uniform was deliberate: men's coats, wool skirts, flat shoes, scarves tied without flourish. She was not dressing down but dressing for freedom of movement, a life spent writing and debating rather than being ornamental. When she published *The Second Sex* in 1949 (one of my absolute favourite books out there), she supplied not only a landmark in feminist philosophy but also a new visual reference: the intellectual woman who claims public space as her own. Designers and photographers noticed. This was not haute couture but it was an aesthetic: no corset, no fixed hair, no hesitation in the stride. Students copied her silhouette in the same way they copied her arguments.

De Beauvoir's impact on Paris fashion was to normalize a cerebral look for women decades before "minimalism" or "androgyny" became trends. She showed that a wardrobe can be a political stance. Magazine editors shot her on the street because she made the Left Bank look like a viable counter to Avenue Montaigne. She did not sell clothes or sit front row, yet her presence reshaped the market. Shops began stocking flat shoes, knits and men's coats for women because that was what young Parisians wanted. Every season a designer referenced her without saying so: a trench coat with no belt, a beret without nostalgia, a shoulder bag meant to carry books. Simone de Beauvoir proved a thinker can be a style code and that Paris can turn an argument into an outline.

Opposite: Simone de Beauvoir wearing a brooch designed by Alexander Calder.

Overleaf: Simone de Beauvoir working at her desk, 1953.

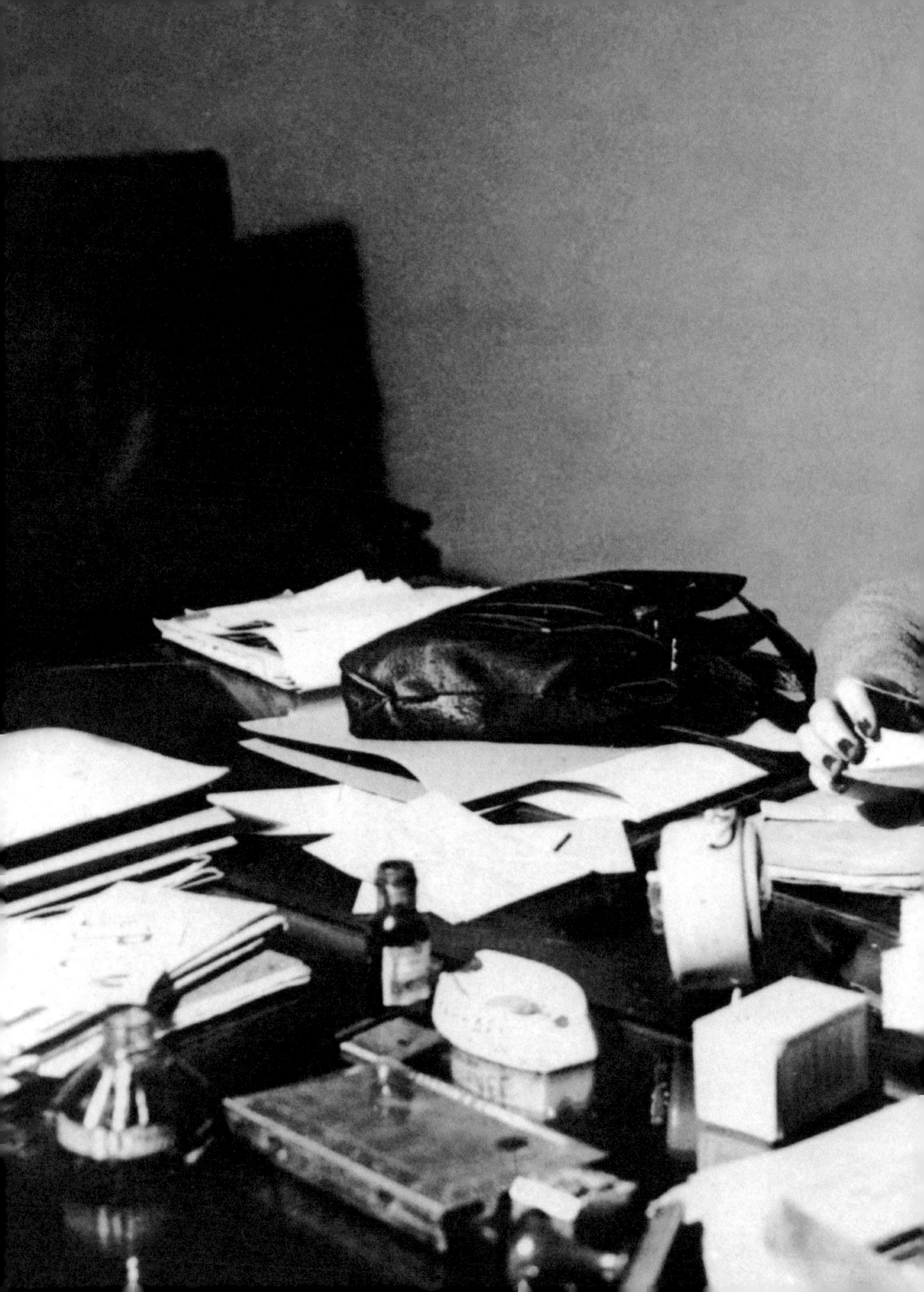

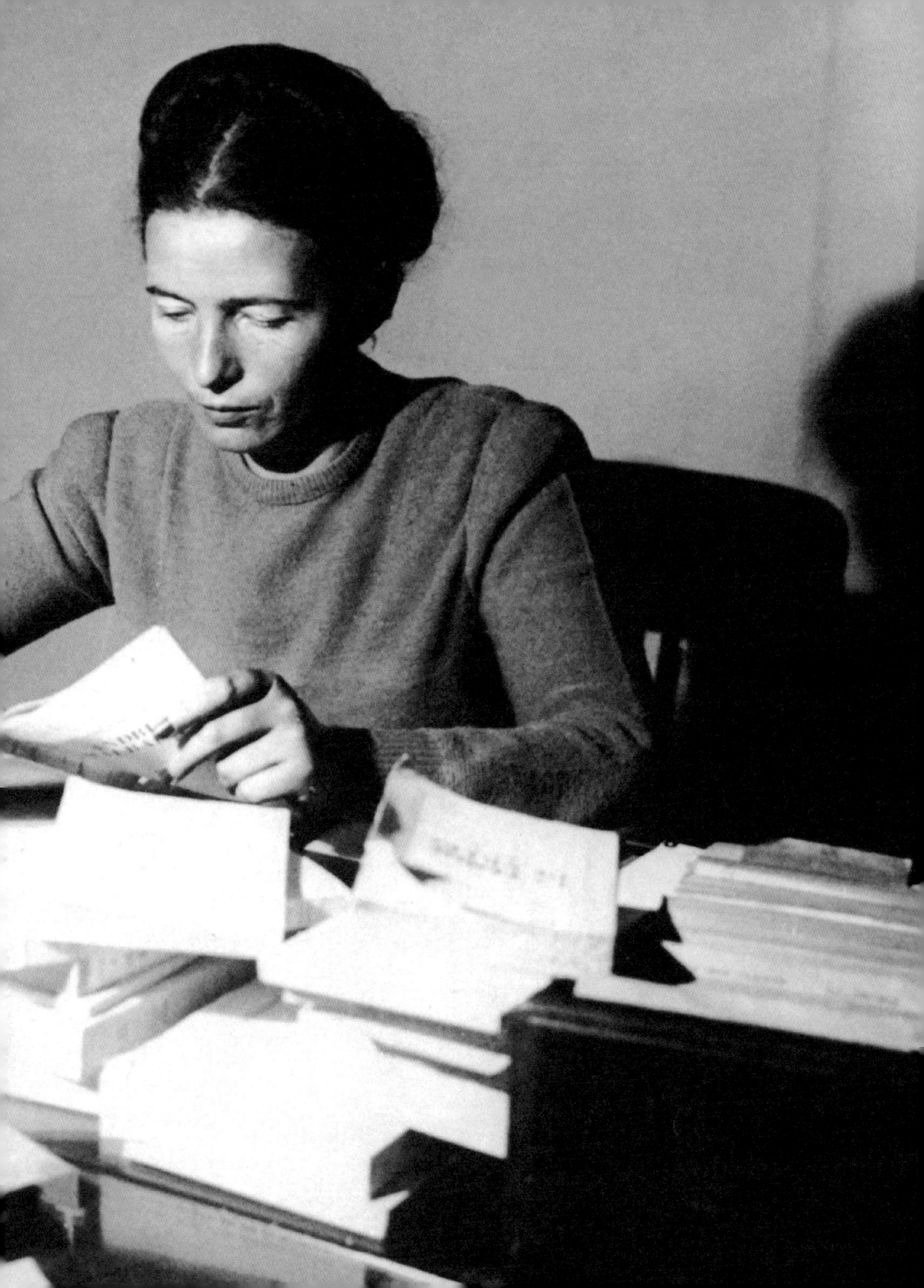

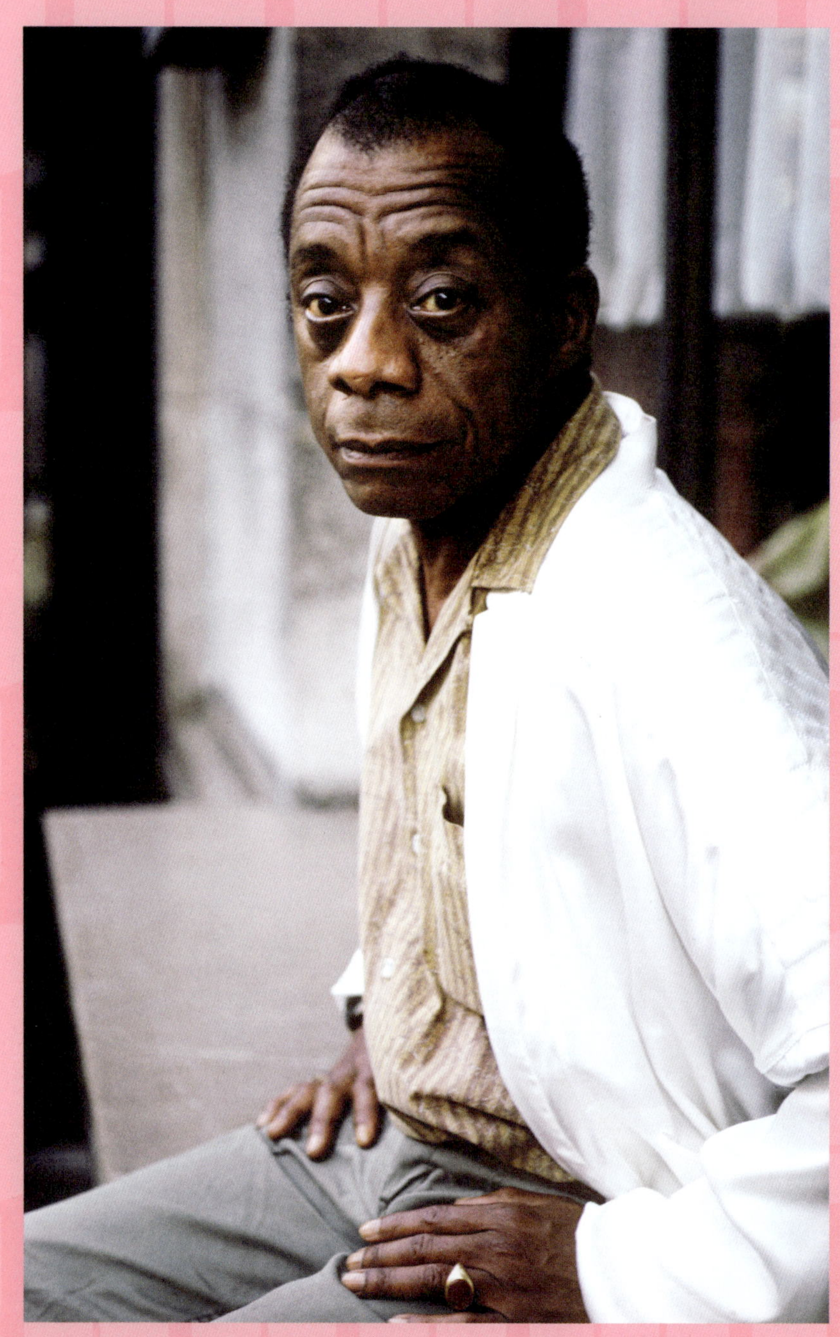

JAMES BALDWIN

James Baldwin arrived in Paris in 1948 as a young writer fleeing American racism, and found a city that let him breathe. He wrote at café tables, finished his semi-autobiographical novel *Go Tell It on the Mountain* (1953), then produced the essays that would define his reputation. He dressed with the same mixture of precision and ease: narrow suits, open shirts, a scarf slung just so, cigarette poised. In a decade when expatriates often played at bohemia, Baldwin carried himself like an intellectual star, turning the Left Bank into an international salon.

Designers and editors caught on. Here was a Black gay writer commanding a room in Saint-Germain when the American establishment would not give him a table. His style was not luxury but authority. The neat tailoring, polished shoes and expressive scarves read as self-possession rather than costume. Photographers shot him because he held light and shadow with the same intensity as his prose. Young Parisians learned that the café uniform can be as sharp as any runway.

James Baldwin's impact on Paris fashion was to widen who belonged in its iconography. He showed that the expatriate could set tone, not just observe it. He made the Left Bank feel like a crossroads of Harlem and Europe, and designers quietly absorbed that hybridity into their cuts and casting. His example still threads through men's fashion: think slim trousers, rolled sleeves, a scarf as punctuation and not a flourish. He proved that intellect and image can travel together and that Paris can be a home for voices and silhouettes outside its old canon.

Opposite: James Baldwin sat posing, Paris 1984.

Overleaf: James Baldwin in sunglasses on the banks of the Seine, with Notre-Dame in the distance.

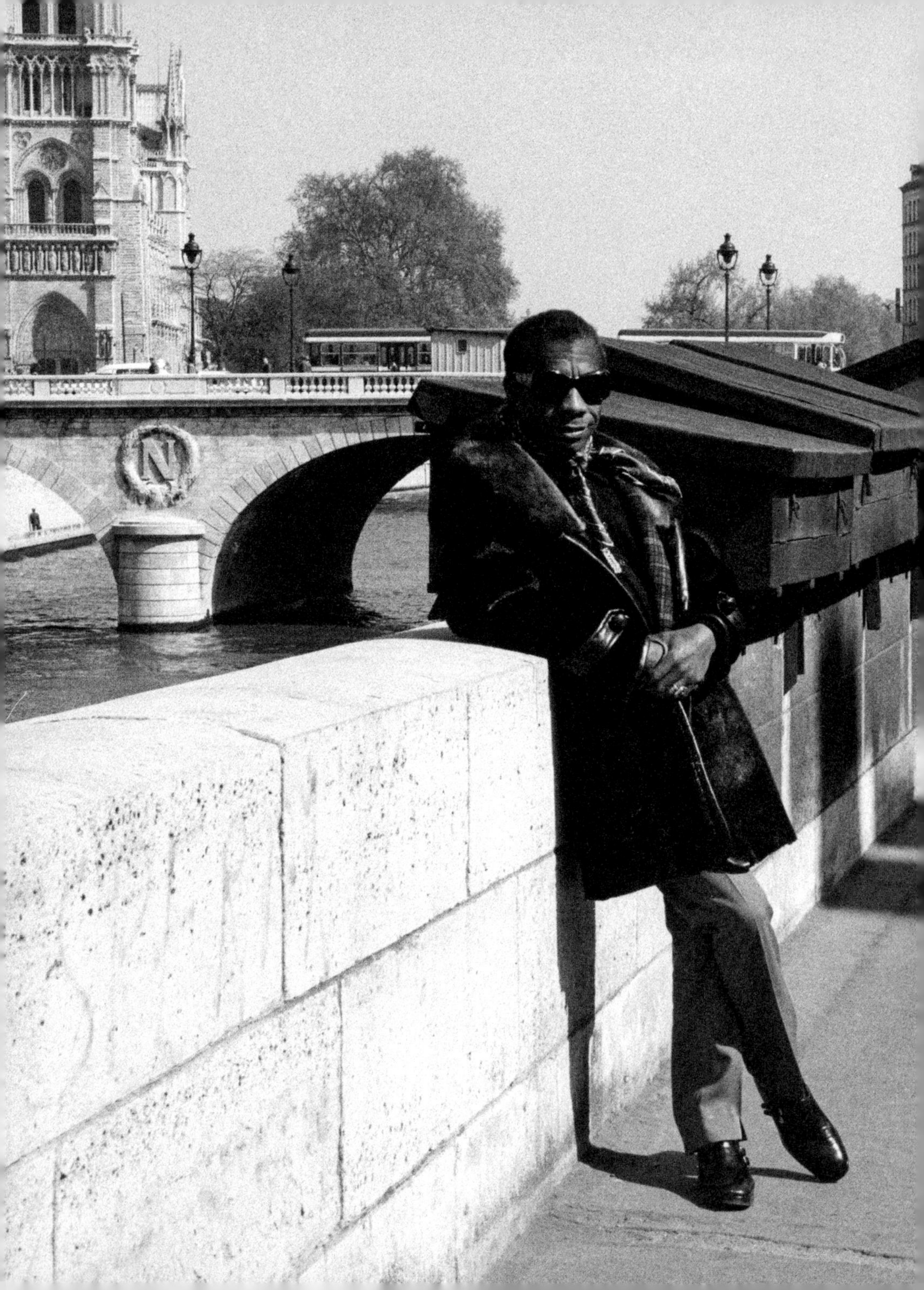

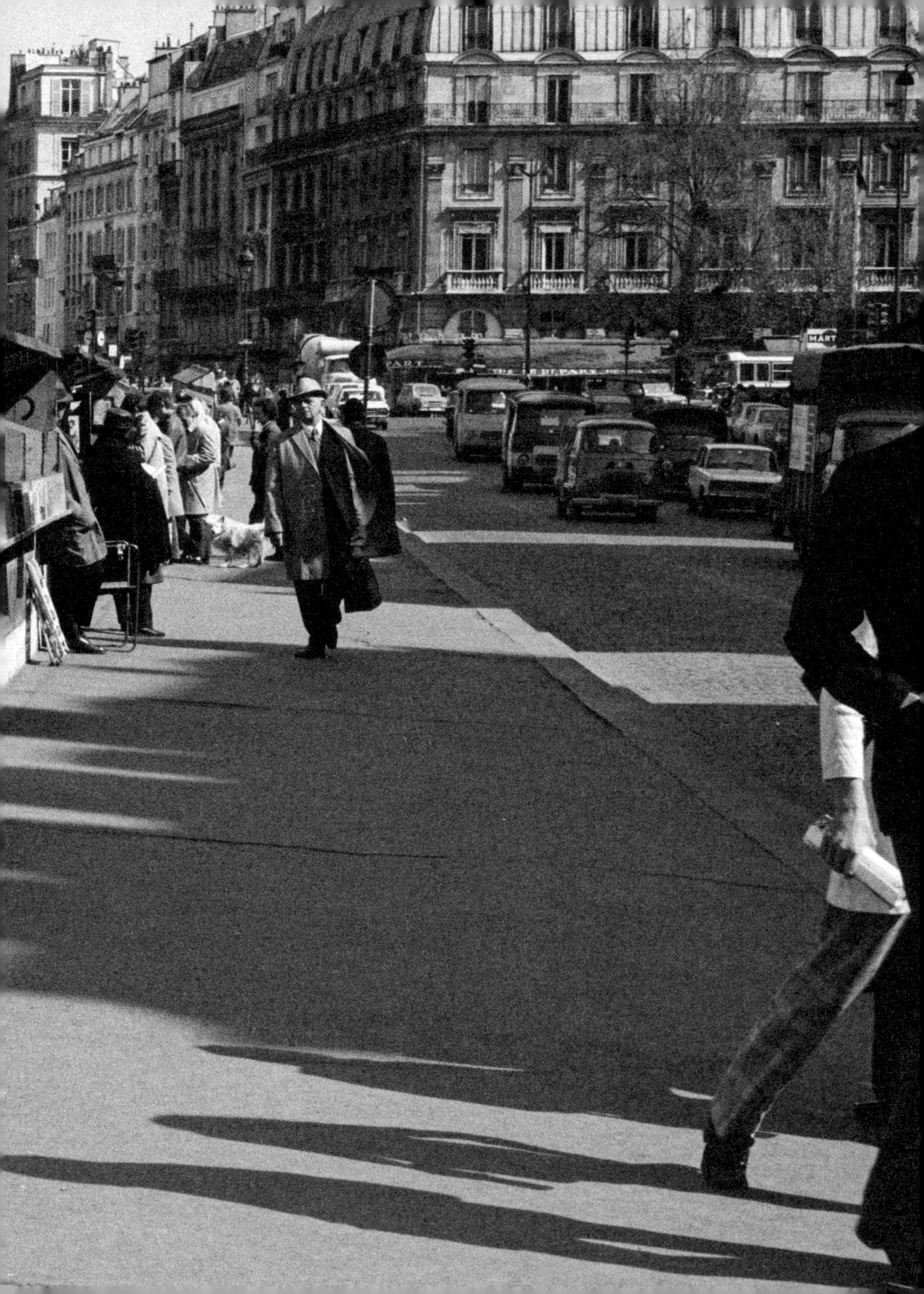

DIANE PERNET

Diane Pernet arrived in Paris in the 1990s after working as a designer in New York. She became one of the first true digital power brokers in fashion, launching A Shaded View on Fashion (ASVOFF) in 2005 when blogs were still marginal. Her appearance is instantly recognizable: black layers, towering hair, dark glasses, a veil. She wears the same look everywhere, from the front row to the street, creating a living logo before "personal branding" became a term.

Pernet's influence moves on two tracks. She uses her site and later her film festival ASVOFF to champion new designers, document shows and archive trends that traditional media ignores. At the same time she makes herself a walking myth in the Paris fashion landscape, proof that you can be an insider without being a publicist or editor at a legacy magazine. Young designers and photographers approach her because they know she will post their work and because her endorsement carries weight.

Pernet's impact on Paris fashion is to shift the information power centre. She shows that digital coverage can run parallel to the big magazines and sometimes outrun them. Her blog becomes a map for editors, buyers and students who cannot attend every show. She treats fashion film as a serious genre, decades before brands turn to video as a main medium. The result is a new kind of gatekeeper: one who archives, filters and promotes all at once, while remaining visually unmistakable. She proves Paris can adapt to the internet without losing its mystery.

Opposite: Diane Pernet photographed by Javier Beto Vargas.

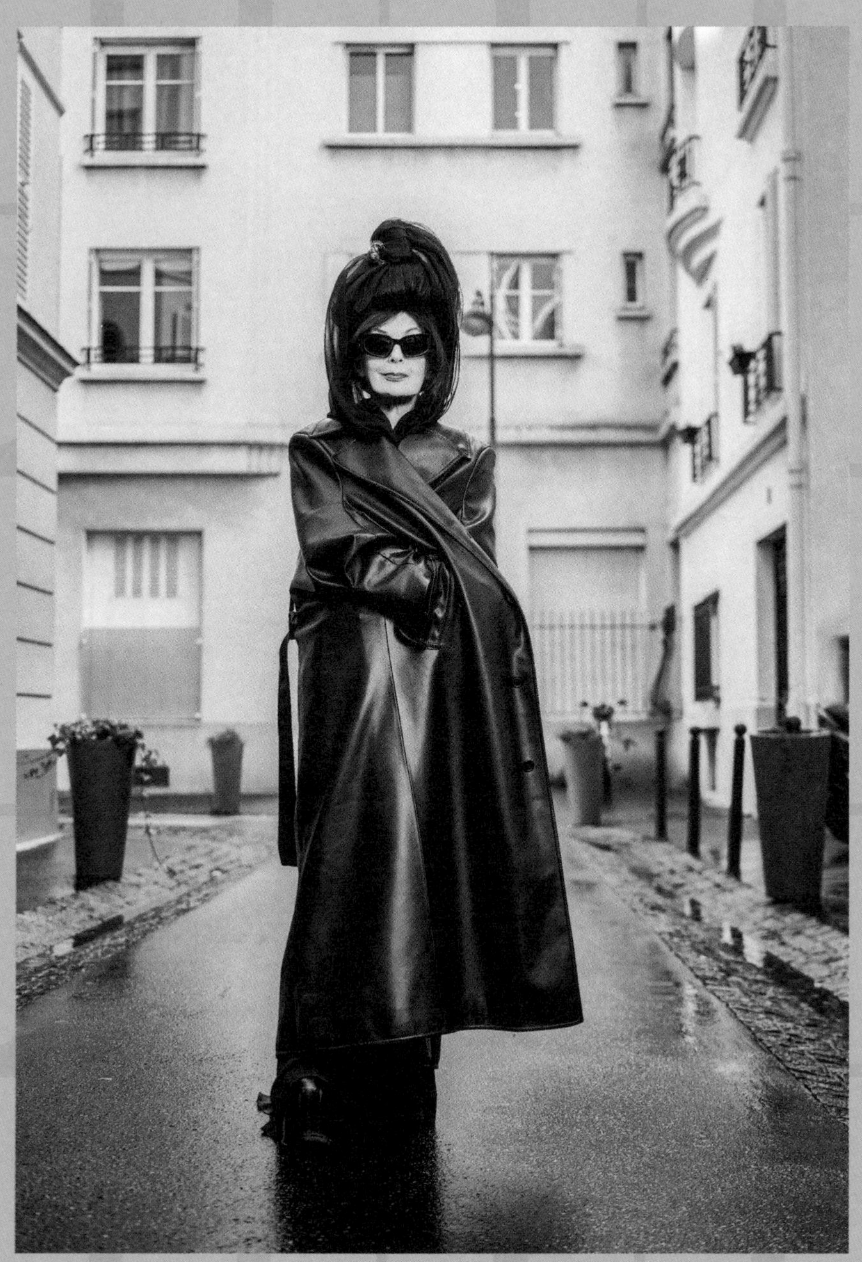

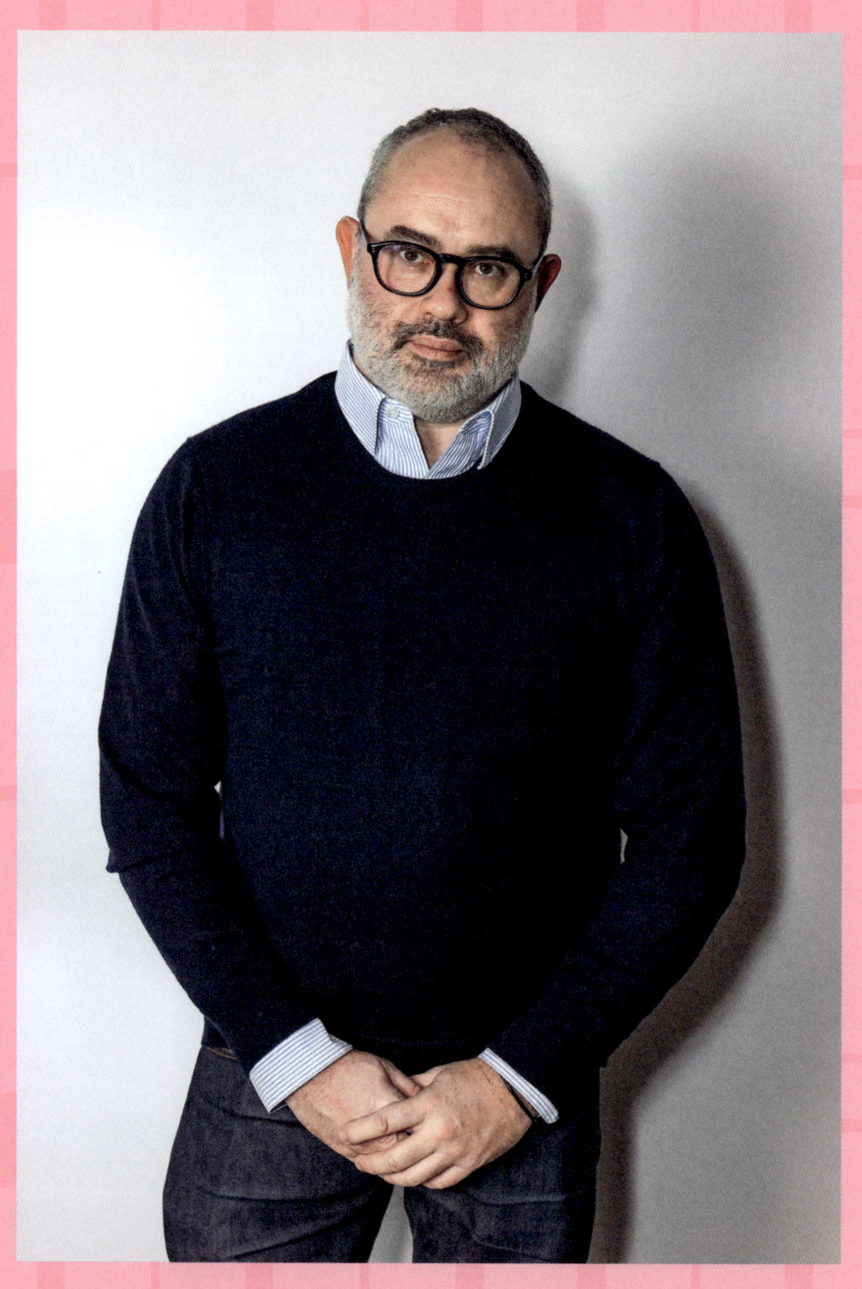

Lucien Pagès

Lucien Pagès grew up in the French press world and built his career not on the runway but on the phone, in showrooms and at dinners. He is the quiet force behind some of the most successful Paris designers of the last 20 years. As a publicist he helps launch or steady names like Jacquemus, Courrèges, Loewe under Jonathan Anderson, and countless others. His office sends invitations but in a way that engineers narrative arcs, calibrates who sits where and decides which images circulate first.

Pagès' skill is to understand both the culture and the commerce. He keeps a boutique roster, picks clients whose values match and builds long arcs instead of hype cycles. He mentors young publicists and grooms talent for press in the way ateliers groom pattern cutters. Designers trust him with sensitive pivots, journalists trust him for access, and the result is a network that only strengthens Paris as a global fashion capital.

Lucien Pagès' impact is visible in how shows now function. Seating charts, backstage photography, controlled leaks and viral moments are not accidents; they are choreographed. Pagès helps turn the old front row into a multi-platform broadcast zone, while maintaining an air of discretion. He ensures the right buyers see the right clothes and the right editors write the right story at the right time. In an era where image can flood the internet in seconds, he proves that a disciplined narrative still wins. His office is the model of a modern Paris press hub: selective, strategic and deeply entwined with the creative process itself.

Opposite: Lucien Pagès attends Suzy Menkes' 80th birthday in London, 2023.

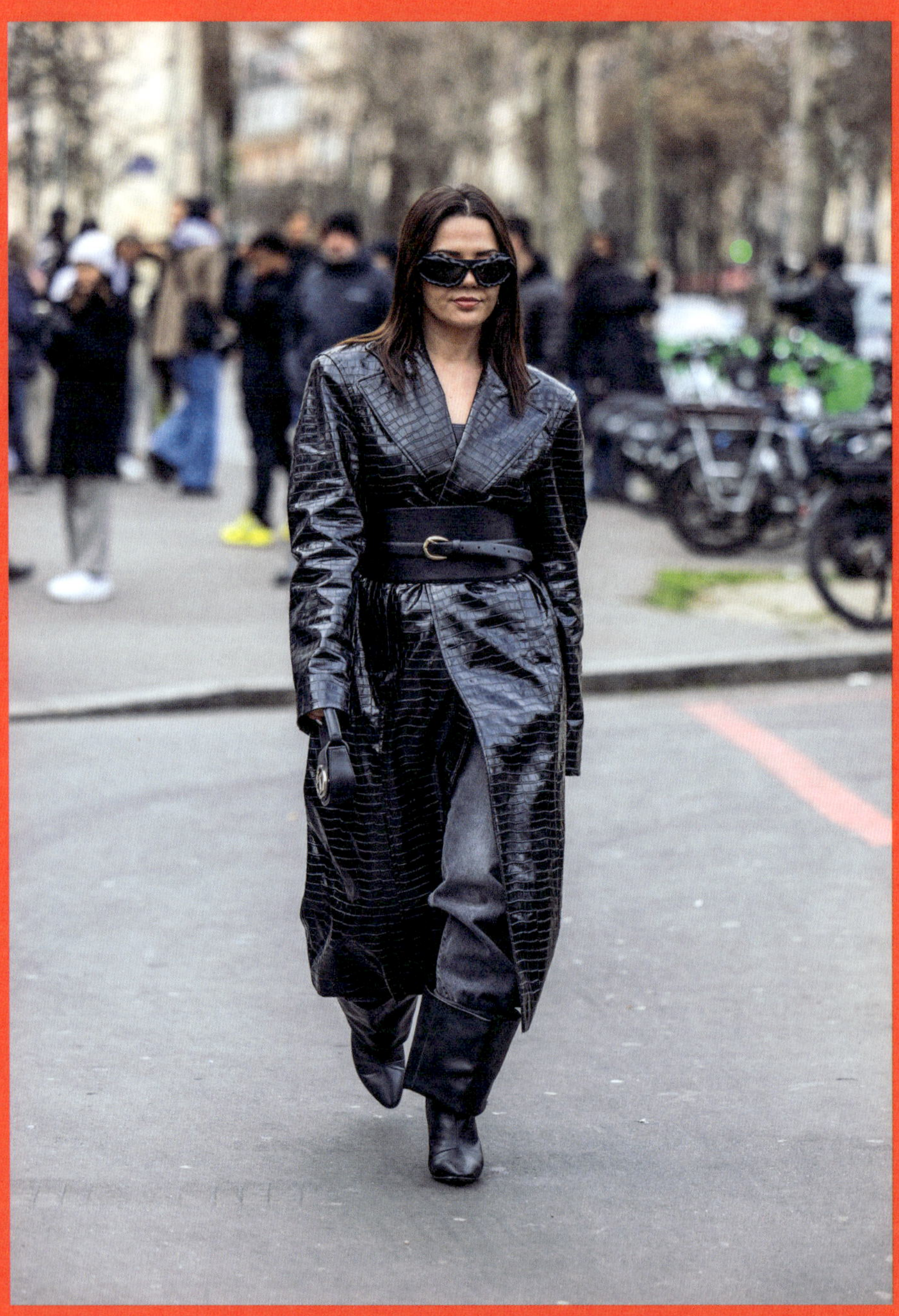

Afterword – Using the Code

If you want to embody the code of a Paris fashion icon, start small. Choose one decision you can defend in any light and repeat it until people can sketch you from memory. If you design, carry a seam across seasons and let it evolve without losing its angle. If you edit, describe what the garment does to the body before you describe how it looks. If you dress for yourself, decide how you want to move through a room, then choose a shoulder, a shoe and a hem that cooperate. The rest will follow.

Paris is a mix of fantasy and daily discipline. Separate surface from structure. Learn to read the cut. When you do, the city's noise quietens and the work becomes legible. That legibility is the real luxury: a line so clear that fewer choices make more looks possible. Keep the foundation steady, let the details rotate and your style will travel without translation.

Opposite: The author in a black corset, high belt and black varnished coat by Diesel during Paris Fashion Week, Autumn/Winter 2023.

Overleaf: Kenzo Takada, Karl Lagerfield and Sonia Rykiel sit in discussion.

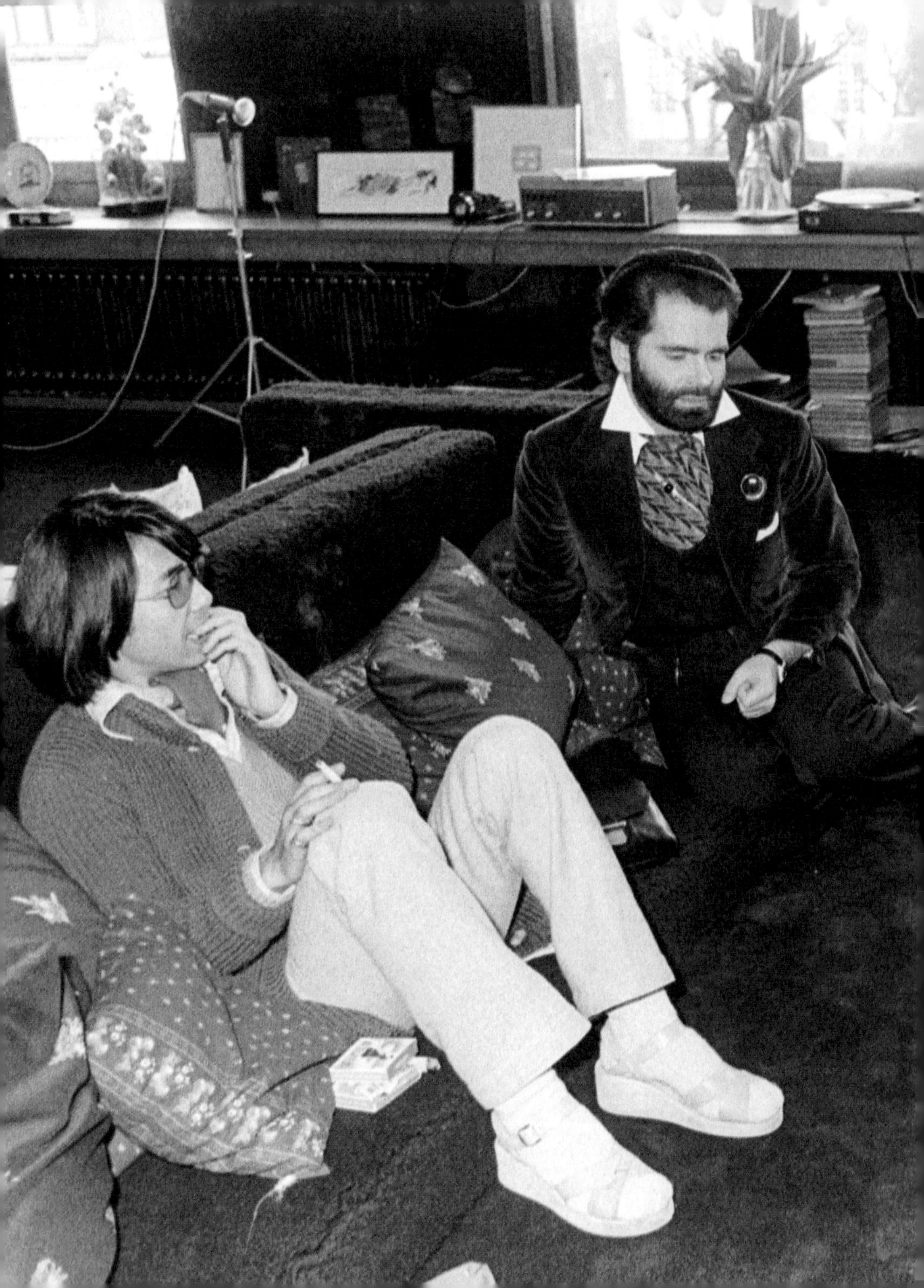

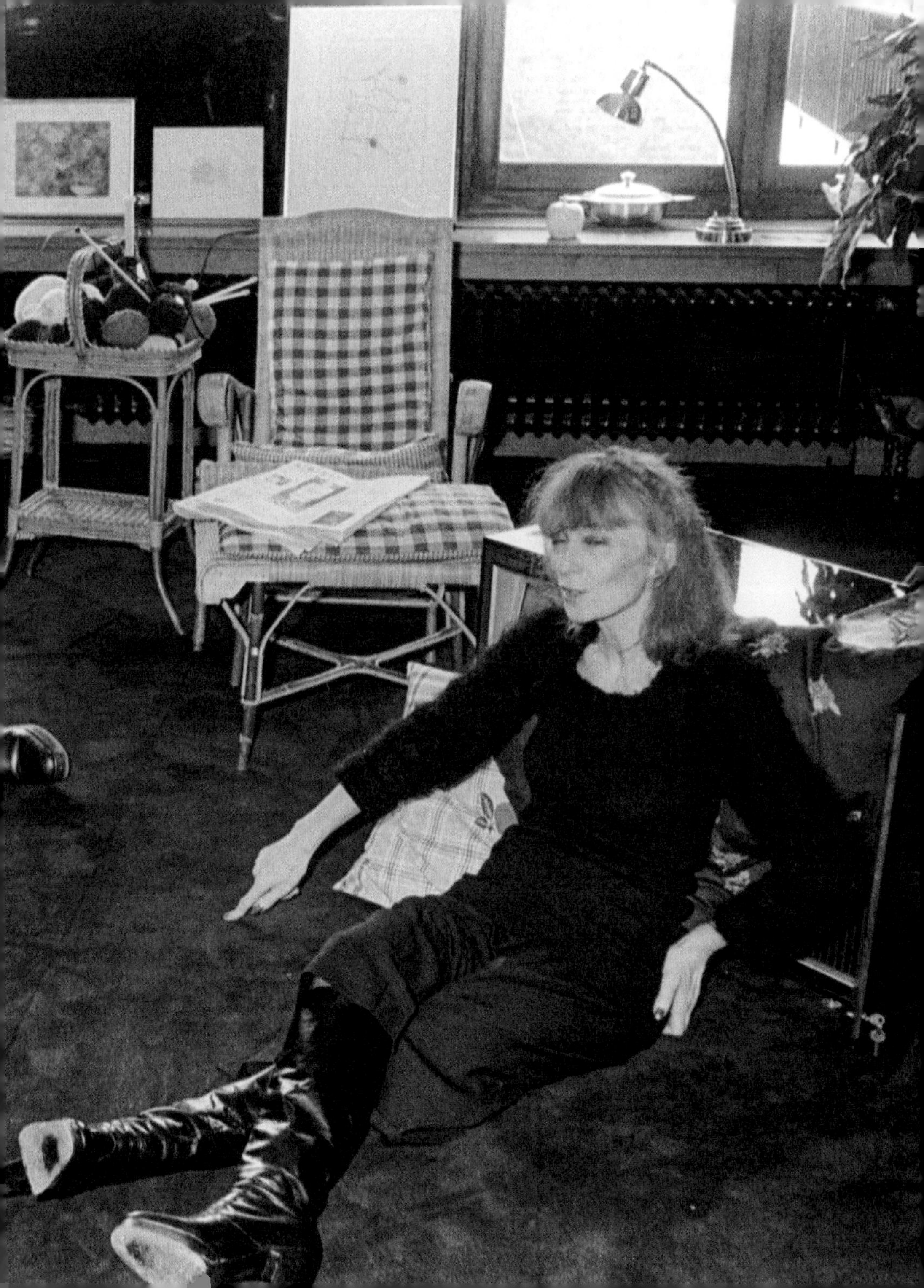

INDEX

Abraham Limited 27
Adichie, Chimamanda Ngozi 127
Aghion, Gaby 65, 66
Alaïa, Azzedine 106, 108, 167
Anderson, Jonathan 19, 199
androgyny 159, 189
anonymity 86
anti-fashion 78, 82
Antwerp 99
Antwerp Six, the 99
Arpège 39
Art Deco 183
avant-garde 78
Avenue Montaigne 19, 23, 189

bags
  "Alma" 121
  "Birkin" 150
  "Chiquito" 140"
  "Motorcycle"/"Lariat" 100
  "Neverfull" 121
  "Paddington" 132
  "Speedy" 121
Baker, Josephine 103, 183
Baldwin, James 193, 194–5
Balenciaga 44, 100, 124, 179
Balenciaga, Cristóbal 20, 27
Balmain 113, 145
Balmain, Pierre 32
banana skirt dance 183
bar jacket 19, 127
Beaux, Ernest 14
Belmore, Edwige 163, 164
Beyoncé 70, 145
"Birkin" (bag) 150
Birkin, Jane 150, 153
Black culture 103, 104
Black designer 103
Black Orpheus 171
Black women 171
Blond Ambition Tour 74
Bourdin, Guy 179

Campbell, Naomi 106
Cardin, Pierre 74
Catroux, Betty 23, 159
Celine 117, 132
Chambre Syndicale 103
Chanel 14, 113, 174
Chanel, Gabrielle "Coco" 14, 17, 20
Chanel No 5 14
chiffon 35
"Chiquito" bag 140
Chiuri, Maria Grazia 19, 127, 128
Chloé 65, 66, 113, 132, 134
chrome armour 73
Cirque d'Hiver 70
Cirque du Soleil 70
club kids 103
Cocteau, Jean 43
Comme des Garçons 78, 81
Copping, Peter 36
corsetry 20, 70
Courrèges 199
  Geometry 44
  "Space Age" 44
  white boot 44
Courrèges, André 44
cut-up jeans 124

Dalí, Salvador 43
Dawn, Marpessa 171

de Beauvoir, Simone 189
de Givenchy, Hubert 28, 32
  See *also* Givenchy
de la Falaise, Loulou 23, 155, 157
Delevingne, Cara 113
Dior 92, 95, 106, 127, 128
  A 19
  Bar Suit 20
  Dior Homme 117
  H 19
  New Look 27
  sculpted silhouettes 20
  silhouettes 19
  Y 19
Dior and I 95
Dior, Christian 19, 95, 96
Ditto, Beth 77
Dover Street Market 78
Duchess of Windsor, the 27

École Nationale Supérieure des Beaux-Arts 28

fashion
  1950s 19
  business 28
  commentators 132
  dark wave 85
  "deconstructed" 86
  empire 35
  film 196
  genius 70
  "high-low" 136
  history 73
  icon 201
  insider 159
  luxury 95
  men's 193
  sci-fication 44
  surrealism 43
Fendi 113
"fashion material" 48
folklore 55
Frederique 106

Gainsbourg, Serge 150, 153
Galliano, John 92
Gaultier, Jean Paul 74, 77, 86, 163, 167
gazar 27
Ghesquière, Nicolas 100, 179
Givenchy 28, 92
Go Tell It on the Mountain 193
Grand Palais 113
Gucci 124
Gvasalia, Demna 124, 179

Hadid, Gigi 140
Hepburn, Audrey 28, 61
Hermès 150
"high-low" 136
history 52, 73, 184, 208
hoodies 124
hôtel particulier 7, 92
Huppert, Isabelle 179

Inez & Vinoodh 179
"intellectual chic" 132
International Wool Secretariat prize 23
"It-dress" 35

Jacobs, Marc 100, 121, 122
Jacquemus 142, 199
Jacquemus, Simon Porte 140
"Joe le Taxi" 174
Jones, Grace 106, 108
Jones, Kim 19

Kardashian, Kim 145
Kawakubo
  "Hiroshima chic" 78
  "Lumps and Bumps" 81
Kawakubo, Rei 78, 81, 82

Kelly, Patrick 103, 104
Kenzo, *See* Takada, Kenzo
Khelfa, Farida 167
knit cardigan 14
knitwear 61
Kusama, Yayoi 121

Lacroix 52
  brides 55
  religious iconography 52
Lacroix, Christian 52
Lagerfeld, Karl 66, 113, 114, 174
Lamy, Michèle 91
Lang, Helmut 95
Lanvin
  Lanvin blue 36
  rue du Faubourg Saint-Honoré 36
Lanvin, Jeanne 36, 39
La Revue Nègre 183
Laroche, Guy 106
Left Bank (*Rive Gauche*) 23, 24, 61, 65, 91, 150, ***155***, 189, 193
Le Palace (club) 163, 167
"Le Smoking" 131, 159
little black dress 14, 131
Loewe 199
Louvre, fashion wing 103
LVMH 127

Madonna 74
Maison Margiela 124
Marant, Isabel 136, 138
Margiela, Martin 86, 89
McCartney, Stella 132
metal-plate mini-dress 51
Michael, George 70
minimalism 189
mini-skirt 44
Moss, Kate 100
Mugler
  chrome armour 73
  chrome trim 70
  insect carapaces 70
  motorcycle bustiers 70
  "wet" latex dress 70
Mugler, Thierry 70, 73, 106, 163, 167
Murakami, Takashi 121
Musée des Arts Décoratifs 55

"New Look" 19, 20, 23, 27
Notebook on Cities and Clothes 82

opera 52, 70, 92
optical tricks 43
organza 19
ornament 14, 39, 55
outerwear 27
Owenscorp 91
Owens, Rick 91

"Paddington" bag 132
Pagès, Lucien 199
Paradis, Vanessa 174
Paris 56
  German Occupation 19
  Fashion Week 20, 131
Patou 113
Patou, Jean 52
Perfume
  Angel (Mugler) 70
  C'est La Vie! (Lacroix) 52
  Chanel No 5 14
  Coco (Chanel) 174
Pernet, Diane 196
Philo, Phoebe 132, 134
pleated gown 10
pleated tulle 127
"Pouf" dress 52
prêt-à-porter 65

Rabanne, Paco 48, 51
"Rainbow Tribe" (Josephine Baker) 184

ready-to-wear 23, ***24***, 44, ***52***, 65, ***85***, 95, 100, 103, 106, 117, 121, 127, 131, 132, 145, 174
Right Bank (*Rive Droite*) 28, 136
Rihanna 145
Rive Gauche 23, 155
robe de style 36, 39
Rousteing, Olivier 145
ruched satin 35
rue Cambon 17
  staircase 14
rue du Faubourg Saint-Honoré 36
Rykiel
  "Poor Boy" knit 61
Rykiel, Sonia 61, 63

Saint-Germain 61, 189, 193
Saint Laurent 23, 24, 117, 131, 155, 159
Saint Laurent, Yves 23, 155, 157, 159, 179
  "Le Smoking" 23
  office 24
  Rive Gauche 23
  "Trapeze" line 23
Schiaparelli, Elsa 43
Second World War 14, 183
Shaded View on Fashion, A (ASVOFF) 196
shocking pink 43
silk 19, 27, ***65***, 136
Simons, Raf 95, 96
skinny jeans 117
Slimane, Hedi 117, 131
Sprouse, Stephen 121
stripes 14, 56, 61, 63
studio rhythm 8
surrealism 43

Takada, Kenzo 56, 58
Talley, André Leon 92
Teller, Juergen 179
terrasse 8
theatre 32, 52, 55, 70
Théâtre des Champs-Élysées 183
The Second Sex 189
Tokyo 56, 136
"Too Funky" 70
trapunto 43
tulle 19, 127
Turner, Tina 106
tuxedo 23, 155
  tuxedo shirt 159
tweed 113

Vaccarello, Anthony 131
Valentino 127
Van Noten, Dries 99
Versus 131
Vetements (brand) 124
Violette Nozière 179
Vionnet
  bias-cut gown 40
Vionnet, Madeleine 40
Vogue 92
Vogue Paris 27
von Bismarck, Mona 27
Vuitton, Louis 100, ***121***, 122
  bags:
  "Alma" 121
  "Neverfull" 121
  "Speedy" 121

Watanabe, Junya 78
Webb, Veronica 106
wedge sneaker 136
Wenders, Wim 82
"We Should All Be Feminists" T-shirt 127
Wintour, Anna 92

Yamamoto, Yohji 82, 85
YSL *See* Saint Laurent, Yves

Zénith 70
Zumsteg, Gustav 27

CREDITS

The publishers would like to thank the following sources for their kind permission to reproduce the pictures in this book.

197 courtesy of the author/Javier Beto Vargas

Alamy: 21 Granger - Historical Picture Archive, 26 booksR, 41 rita Guglielmi, 54 Interfoto, 87 Abaca Press, 94 Thierry Orban/ abacapress.com, 98 Sipa US/Alamy Live News, 117 Wenn Rights Ltd, 119 Nicolas Briquet/abacapress.com, 134-135, 137 dpa picture alliance, 141 dpa picture alliance, 158 Trinity Mirror/Mirrorpix, 168 Abaca Press, 176 adsR, 184-185 Collection Christophel

Getty Images: 6 Keystone-France/Gamma-Rapho, 9 adoc-photos/Corbis, 10-11 Reginald Gray/WWD/ Penske Media, 15 George Hoyningen-Huene/ Condé Nast, 16-17 Keystone-France/Gamma-Keystone, 18 Popperfoto, 22 Keystone-France/ Gamma-Keystone, 24-25 Bertrand Guay/AFP, 29 Reporters Associati & Archivi/Mondadori Portfolio, 30 Keystone-France/Gamma-Rapho, 31 Bettmann, 33 Keystone-France/Gamma-Rapho, 34 Bettmann, 35 Sylvia Salmi/Bettmann, 37 Peter White, 38 Harlingue/Roger Viollet, 39 Edward Steichen/Conde Nast, 42 Bettmann, 45 Ian Cook, 46-47 Jacques Haillot/Apis/Sygma, 49 Stephane Cardinale/Sygma, 50-51 Doreen Spooner/ Mirrorpix, 53 Daniel SIMON/Gamma-Rapho, 54 Pierre Guillard/AFP, 55 Victor Virgile/Gamma-Rapho, 57 Fairchild Archive/WWD/Penske Media, 58-59 Daniel Simon/Gamma-Rapho, 60 Fairchild Archive/WWD/Penske Media, 62 Victor Virgile/ Gamma-Rapho, 62-63 AFP, 66-67 Fairchild Archive/WWD/Penske Media, 71 Daniel Simon/ Gamma-Rapho, 72-73 Michel Arnaud/ Corbis, 75 Daniel Simon/Gamma-Rapho, 76 Dominique Charriau/WireImage, 77 Foc Kan/WireImage, 79 Rose Hartman, 80 Fairchild Archive/Penske Media, 81 Rei Kawakubo. (Photo by Guy Marineau/ Conde Nast), 83 Giovanni Giannoni/Penske Media, 84 Victor VIRGILE/Gamma-Rapho, 85 Fairchild Archive/WWD/Penske Media, 88 Fairchild Archive/Penske Media, 90 Victor Virgile/ Gamma-Rapho, 93 Stephane Cardinale/Corbis, 96-97 Petroff/Dufour, 101 Dominique Charriau/ WireImage, 102, 104-105 Dominique Charriau/ WireImage, 107 Arthur Elgort/Conde Nast, 108-109 Arun Nevader/Getty Images for Art Hearts, 112 Dominique Charriau/WireImage, 114-115 Fairchild Archive/Penske Media, 116, 118 Fairchild Archive/Penske Media, 120 Stephane Cardinale/ Corbis, 122-123 Pierre Verdy/AFP, 125, 126 Estrop, 128-129 Pascal Le Segretain, 130 Victor Boyko, 133 Pascal Le Segretain, 135 Giovanni Giannoni/ WWD/Penske Media, 138-139 Kristy Sparow, 139 Miguel Medina/AFP, 142-143 Francois Durand, 144, 146-147 Victor Virgile/Gamma-Rapho, 151 Daily Mirror/ Mirrorpix, 152-153 Hulton-Deutsch Collection/Corbis, 154 Guy Marineau/WWD/ Penske Media, 156 Guy Marineau/Fairchild Archive, 156-157 Michel Maurou/WWD/Penske Media, 160-161 Henry Clarke/Conde Nast, 162 Foc Kan/WireImage, 164-165 Catherine McGann, 166 Fairchild Archive/WWD/Penske Media, 169 Jean-François Rault/Sygma, 170 Jean Claude Pierdet/ INA, 172 Archive Photo, 173 Daily Express/Archive Photos, 175 Frédéric SOULOY/Gamma-Rapho, 177 Stephane Cardinale/Corbis, 178 Pool Ginfray/ Simon/Gamma-Rapho, 180 Swan Gallet/WWD/ Penske Media, 181 Vanni Bassetti/Getty Images for Balenciaga, 182 Paul Popper/Popperfoto, 188 Hulton Archive, 190-191 Keystone-France/Gamma-Keystone, 192 Ulf Andersen, 194-195 Sophie Bassouls/Sygma, 198 Dave Benett/Getty Images for Mandi's Basement Limited, 200 Christian Vieri, 202-203 Fairchild Archive/Penske Media

AUTHOR BIOGRAPHY

Amelie Stanescu is a fashion commentator and the host of The Fashion Archives podcast, where she talks with designers, image-makers and editors about the business behind clothes. She mixes fashion history with cultural critique, always with a bit of edge. Her work sits between the academic and the underground – personal takes, layered references, runway breakdowns. She treats fashion criticism as a form of cultural work, something meant to inspire the system and respect the audience's intelligence. This book follows the same rules.